FULL CANNON

LOVE, LEADERSHIP
AND
MAKING A DIFFERENCE

by

Carl Cannon

and

Lance Zedric

FULL CANNON

Love, Leadership and
Making a Difference

ISBN 978-0-9838361-5-5
Softcover

Cover photo & design
by Ching Zedric

WAR
Press

Printed in the United States of America

DEDICATION

To my grandparents, Elizabeth & Jess Hazel and Excenia & Granddaddy Williams; thank you for paving the way for our families to achieve our dreams. We Love You!

To Mom, Mamie Pearl; Dad, Charles Henry; siblings, Michael Anthony, William Henry, Alicia Gwen, Anita Janine, Elizabeth Hope, Ramona Joy, Scott, Andrea, and Charles Henry Jr., and to all of my nephews, nieces, and cousins, our bond is eternal.

To my wife, Melinda, the love of my life, thank you for 38 years of bliss and for blessing me with two amazing daughters, Summer Lynn and Danielle Patrice. I see you in their every smile.

And to ours daughters, we love you both, and we expect you to always protect each other and to live life "Full Cannon."

—Dad

ACKNOWLEDGMENTS

There are not enough pages in this book to thank all the people and organizations that have helped me in my life. The following are but a fraction who have impacted, inspired, supported, frustrated, taught, angered and loved me along the way. I appreciate each and every one of you for enriching my life and the lives of those I serve.

Heather Terry, Jay Hardin, Renee Andrews, Sheila Price, Gwen Wilson, Julie Gillis, Demario Boone, Jeff & Jeanette Purham, Dan Wolfe, Tim Reist, Lori Escalante-Allen, Brian Ulenhof, Joe Rogers, Joe & Holly Walker, Dawn Mitchell, Patti Lawless, Lott Pickett, Ernest & Yavonne Starks, Justin Dent, Kenisha Bailey, Corey Scott, Charles Nathan, Gabe Gibbard, Hedy Elliott, Stephanie Churchill, Tim Kruger, Harry Rhodes, Lonnie & Jane Counterman, Natalie Counterman, Amy Stevens, Melody McFadden, Chetea Green, Vatonya Terrell, Derek Brown, Marcus Albert, David Tuttle, Lynn Lane, Marcy Steele, David Williams, Kenny Jackson, Ray Caldwell, Dawnette Jackson, Denzel Sims, Charles Howard, Stan Howard, Jenell Howard, Brian Oates, Shane & Constance Oates, Corey & Ashleh Mozee, Gale Thetford, Todd & Fabian Daniels, Mary Blum, Kalan Blum, Mike & Katie Vancleve, Gayle Johnson, Robin Johnson, Martha Ross, Dan Adler, Lynn Costic, Doug Shaw, Dr. Alexander Ikejiaku, Dr. Sharon Kherat, Mick Willis, Dr. Nicole Woods, Dr. Susan Grzanich, Dr. Jerry Bell, Coach Derek Booth, John Williams, Helen King, Kadar Heffner, Alma Brown, Lori Brown, Eric Turner, Clyde & Lucy Gully, Kim Furness, Sherry Allen, Patience Allen, Rev. Marvin Hightower, Rev. Devoreaux Hubbard & First Lady Christy Hubbard, Drew Hubbard, Dawson Hubbard, Devereaux Hubbard II, Roberta Coatie, Tyarie Coatie, Aaron Adams, Amy Purham, Arrian Purham, Claire Cannon, Malcom Grant, Kord Adams, Taunya Jenkins, Kelly Daniels, Paula Davis, Gale Thetford, Gail Johnson, Gene & Jackie Petty, Joyce Harrant, Michael Everette, Diane Lamb, Dave Mingus, Courtney Privia, Sue Bulitta, Bruce Buddy, Richard Joseph, Jackie Newman, Jason Pierce, Holly Quarles, Rachel Parker, Darrin LaHood, David Koehler, Michael Unes, Andrew Rand, Lynn Scott-Pearson, Jay Pearson, Phillip Salzer, William Watkins Jr., Chief Loren Marian, Tate Chambers, Daniel Hunt, Mark Bronke, Michael Brooks, Tony Ardis, Brad Ware, Brian Fengel, Kamarni (KJ) Gaiter, Doug Huermann, Jason Hunt, Jim Cour, Deborah Johnson, Joyce Jackson, Alma Brown, Warden Krueger, Bryce Stoneburner, Sissy Stoneburner, Mary Peterson, Scott Elger, Lance High, Stacey Crabtree, Vickie Cannon, Greg Cannon, Rickie & Donna Cannon, Roberta Taylor, Garry & Denise Moore, Chris Waible, Roger Potter, Seth Potter, Cal Rychner, Owen Ackerman, Jim Montelongo, Vani Baldwin, Bill Hiederich, Rennie Atterbury, Will Ball, Tom & Cheryl Fligie, Henry Blackwell, James Agbara Bryson, Bruce Budde, Denis Cyr, Elizabeth Jensen, Timothy Riggenbach, Beth Akeson, Zachary Oyler, Rogy Childcare, Ken & Judy Zika, Steve Zika, Sid Ruckriegel, Denise Carter, Ed Maulbach, Governor Foreman, Chuck Grayeb, Glen & Polly Barton, Gary Manier, Angel Morales, Cal Walden, Carmisha Turner, Chris & Diana Russick, Sylvester Bush, Bud Jenkins, Rebecca Moehn, Leticia Richards, Taria Armstrong, Rev. Alphonso Lyons, Jared Lucas, Robert Mosley, Dan Duncan, Jeremy Bieneman, Joe Couri, Chris Buckley, Melvin Timothy, Olivia Blumer, Terrance Bradley, Toussaint Smith, Robyn McCracken, Adam Hermann, John Waltz, Kurt Mankle, Leroy Mack, Liz Blair, Queenie Parks, Rhonda Brown, Tom Blumer, Dr. Rita Ali, Ron Tyler, Sharon Bond, Tre Weathersby, Larry Tinsley, Donald Warfield, Lee Vargas, Chris McAfee, Denise McWhorter, LeeAnn McWhorter, Greg Wilson, Josiah Williams, Lord Mic Williams, Mary Stanbary, Nancy Wright, Rosalind Zanders-Lowry, Stephen Graves, Tom Marchal, Brad Platt, Chris & Sue Duncan, Dr. Sheila Quirk-Bailey, Mark Swanagan, Elizabeth Vilkowski, Daniel Hiles, Cheryl Ellis, Clayton Sanders, Michelle Cruz, and Matt Freeman. A special thanks to Scott Elger for his support in this project and others.

Last, a loving thank you to Uncle Raymond, Cousin Rickie, and to my extended family members, Lance, Ching, Ariel, Ernest, Yvonne, Hedy, Tony, Taunya, Pat, Sally, Rick and others unintentionally omitted. Please know you that you are all in my heart.

—Carl

CONTENTS

GLOSSARY

AAFES	Army-Air Force Exchange Service
AIT	Advanced Individualized Training
ANCOC	Advanced Non-Commissioned Officer Course
APFT	Army Physical Fitness Test
BNCOC	Basic Non-Commissioned Officer Course
BOP	Bureau of Prisons
CHOICES	Can't Have Our Individual Choices Endangering Society Program
CI	Confidential Informant
CID	Criminal Investigations Division
CO	Correctional Officer/Commanding Officer
DA	Department of the Army
DB	Disciplinary Barracks
DHO	Disciplinary Hearing Officer
DI	Drill Instructor
DMZ	Demilitarized Zone (Korea)
DS	Drill Sergeant
ELITE YP	Economic Leaders Integrating Trained Employable Youth Program
EYP	ELITE Youth Program
FCI Pekin	Federal Corrections Institution (at Pekin)
JAG	Judge Advocate General
KATUSA	Korean Augmentation To the U.S. Army
LPU	Licensed Parolee Unit
MEPS	Military Entrance Processing Station
MOS	Military Occupational Specialty
MP	Military Police / Military Policeman
MPI	Military Police Investigation
NCO	Non-Commissioned Officer E5 - E9

NCOIC	Non-Commissioned Officer in Charge
PLC	Primary Leadership Course
PLDC	Primary Leadership Development Course
PX	Post Exchange
PD/PPD	Park District/Peoria Park District
PHS	Peoria High School
PPS	Peoria Public Schools
PVT	Private
ROK	Republic of Korea
SFC	Sergeant First Class (E-7)
SGT	Sergeant (E-5)
SMA	Sergeant Major of the Army
SGM	Sergeant Major (E-8)
SSG	Staff Sergeant (E-6)
SHU	Segregated Housing Unit
SORT	Special Operations Response Team
SRT	Special Response Team
USDB	United States Disciplinary Barracks
WAC	Women's Army Corps

U.S. Army Enlisted Ranks

Private PV2	Private First Class PFC	Specialist SPC	Corporal CPL	Sergeant SGT	Staff Sergeant SSG
E-2	**E-3**	**E-4**	**E-4**	**E-5**	**E-6**

Sergeant First Class SFC	Master Sergeant MSG	First Sergeant 1SG	Sergeant Major SGM	Command Sergeant Major CSM	Sergeant Major of the Army SMA
E-7	**E-8**	**E-8**	**E-9**	**E-9**	**E-9**

PROLOGUE

Then I heard the voice of the Lord saying, "Whom shall I send? And who will go for us?" And I said, "Here am I. Send me!"

Isaiah 6:8

CHAPTER 1
Cell 138

When I entered the United States Disciplinary Barracks (USDB) at Fort Leavenworth, the country's oldest and most secure military prison for the first time after serving a three-year tour in Germany, I wanted to do an about face and leave. As a decorated U.S. Army staff sergeant (SSG) and military policeman with ten years of experience, I had conducted patrols in Korea, worked nuclear and chemical weapons security in Europe and in the Pacific, directed criminal investigations, operated undercover, and been honored by two state governors and the First Lady of the United States, but a month earlier when I got orders assigning me to the prison in Kansas, I tried everything to get them changed.

U.S. Army Photo

Up to this point, I had spent my entire career doing what I considered to be legitimate and valuable police work and by making a difference in the lives of young people. Also, I had just spent three years doing some "real soldiering" in a real-world scenario. How could I view this assignment as anything but a career killer? I struggled to assign value to guarding men who had violated everything I believed in, and who, in many cases, had committed horrific crimes and were beyond rehabilitation. It was a lot to consider.

After returning to my hometown of Peoria, Illinois from Germany in early December 1989, I phoned my Military Police (MP) branch at the Department of the Army (DA) and requested a different assignment, but I got the standard, "We'll see what we can do—try back later" response, which was code for "no." I called in favors from former commanders and enlisted leadership and asked them to pull every military string they had. My former sergeant major even called his gaining counterpart at Fort Leavenworth and implored him to release me, but the man did not know me and vehemently refused.

Then I took a more direct approach and drove to Fort Leavenworth to see what could be done in person. As a large, muscular black man with a little rank and a lot of tact, I was at my best face-to-face, but when I arrived at the in-processing station, a Private Harmon, a low-ranking duty clerk, said that if I signed in on post that day I'd be reporting for immediate duty at the prison. So much for the personal approach. I emphatically declined and instead went Christmas shopping before returning to Peoria to finish my leave. I even took extra time over the holidays hoping that the Army would come to its senses and change my orders before my report date. No such luck.

When I finally reported for duty at Fort Leavenworth, my new sergeant major was already frustrated with me and with my attempts to have my orders changed.

"You've got two options," he began. "One—you take your ass down to that prison—or two—face court martial and become an inmate."

After a quick evaluation of my only good career option, the choice was easy. Suddenly, working in a prison sounded like great duty!

I was assigned to a housing unit and would be trained by SSG Pearce, a jaded, crusty 15-year veteran who was satisfied holding a rank that should have been higher given his time in service. Although we were equal in rank, the similarities stopped there. He was skinny and shorter than average and always seemed to be working an angle, but despite a low-brow con man demeanor, he knew every crack and crevice in the famous but aging prison that had been established in 1875. Although he was only in his early 30s, he seemed as old as the prison.

Life inside the USDB was not what I expected. I thought the inmates would be locked in their cells, but when I entered they were all out and about roaming around. Forty percent of them were serving life sentences for murder, and being ex-soldiers, 100 percent of them were trained killers, so I was a little nervous.

On my first day, Pearce and I entered the guard cage to receive a briefing from the outgoing shift which had been on duty for 12 hours. As we were about to assume responsibility for the cell block and begin our 12-hour shift, Pearce ordered me to check the tiers to ensure that there was not any trouble and that we were not inheriting a mess from the outgoing shift.

"What are tiers?" I asked innocently.

Pearce looked surprised. "Rookie," he said sharply, "the tiers are the floors. There are five floors. There are 50 cells per floor—25 cells on the right—25 cells on the left. You need to go check on all five floors. There is a clipboard on each tier, and you need to sign it proving that you checked each one."

I left the guard cage and strolled through the population like the King of the Jungle watching every move of the lesser animals, but it was they who were watching me. As I moved past the recreation area, inmates aggressively slapped playing cards and dominoes down on the playing tables and leered at me testing my courage and nerve. They were also probing for weakness. In prison, intimidation is the name of the game for everyone, but I didn't play.

After about an hour, I finished my tier checks and returned to the guard cage. Pearce glared at me. "Where you been, Rookie?"

"Checking the tiers like you asked," I said, aware of our equal rank but mindful that he was my superior. "Like you told me to do."

"Look, Rookie," he smirked, "there's a shortcut to all this. Just take the fire escape to each tier, sign the clipboard, and move on to the next floor. You don't physically have to walk each floor. Do it this way and you'll be done in less than 10 minutes while avoiding inmates. Got it?"

I didn't appreciate Pearce's condescending tone, nor did I approve of doing things half-assed, but since I was the new guy on the block and had been in the Army for more than a day, I took it in stride. I knew the time honored maxim, "There's the right way; the wrong way; and the Army way," and I just assumed the latter applied in this case.

Around 10 p.m., Pearce handed me a script and told me to read it over the loudspeaker. "Lock down! Lock down! All inmates, lock down!" I barked.

Then he told me to close the cells in descending order starting with 8 Tier. "Why 8 Tier first?" I asked.

"That's where the rookie inmates are housed," he chuckled. "The new guys—like you."

Rookie inmates were housed on 8 Tier because it was farther for them to walk to get to their cells. Once the inmates were inside their cells, we closed the cell doors one tier at a time—8 Tier—*Boom!* 7 Tier—*Boom!* 6 Tier—*Boom!* And so on until the gates of each tier slammed closed one after another and all were locked down. It was loud and scary like I thought a prison should be.

A short time later, an inmate approached the guard cage wearing only a towel wrapped around his waist and carrying a toothbrush. He had been in the latrine [military restroom] during lock-down and did not get back to his cell in time. I looked at Pearce and he gave me the, *Whatcha gonna do?* look.

I did what I thought he would do—I started cursing. "What the hell are you doing out of your cell!" I barked. "What the hell is the matter with you? You've got to be the dumbest, most ate-up *sonuva-@$#%* on the tier!"

To my surprise, the inmate cursed back, and we went at it full volume for everyone to hear. The problem was, his profanity was better than mine, and I was losing the battle, so I quickly reverted to the training script that Pearce had given me earlier. "Go to *The Bench!*" I ordered. "Do it now!"

Sending an inmate to *The Bench* is like sending him to *The Hole*, which is a jail inside a jail with few amenities and little or no privileges. Truth be told, I could have opened his cell, but I was power-tripping trying to impress Pearce and hoping to earn my reputation among the inmates. I did neither.

A few minutes later, the guard commander arrived and asked me what had happened, but rather than accepting responsibility for my part, I placed all the blame on the inmate for not obeying rules and for becoming verbally abusive to staff. I flat out lied to the guard commander, and he knew it. He then looked to Pearce.

"What happened here?"

"That's exactly what happened, sir," said Pearce, brazenly confirming my story as if it were his own. "Just as SSG Cannon said."

I was shocked that Pearce had lied and had jeopardized his career to cover for me, but that's when I started to understand that in prison it is the guards versus the inmates, and that the inmates were always wrong no matter what the guards did. It was the law of the jungle, and we were the kings of it.

Because I had a little size, it was harder for an inmate to say NO to me, so whenever there was a problem anywhere in the facility, the staff would call me. As a result, I got promoted rapidly and moved up through the system, and within a year, I was placed in charge of the Special Housing Unit (SHU)—aka, *The Hole.*

The SHU consisted of 1 Tier and 2 Tier and contained Disciplinary Segregation, Recreation Segregation, Officer Segregation, Female Segregation, Death Row, and the Death Chamber. Unlike the upstairs tiers where inmates can be out of their cells each day working and enjoying limited free movement, inmates in *The Hole* are locked down 24/7/365 with only a few earning one hour of recreation per day in a cage called the *Bull Pen.* And I was in charge of it all.

One night around nine o'clock, I got a call about a disruption. Inmates had trashed 1 Tier and were stuffing clothes and anything they could find into the toilets. Raw sewage had backed up into the cells and had spilled into the main hall. Feces and urine were everywhere. I went down into *The Hole* to help restore order, and as I was walking toward the end of the tier amidst shouting, cursing, and banging, the inmate in Cell 138 came to the front of the cell.

"Sarge, can I talk to you?"

Typically, I wouldn't stop when an inmate hailed me, especially during a crisis, but something made me stop. "What you got?" I asked.

"Sarge," he began sincerely, "I want you to know that I didn't do this."

"I believe you," I said, sensing that it was important that I believed him. "Don't worry about it. Just clean up your cell as best you can."

About 4:30 that morning, I ordered lights on, and the lone tier guard and I went to unlock the doors so the chow carts could come in and begin delivering breakfast to the inmates. As we walked past Cell 138, something caught my eye. I looked in, and to my horror, I saw the inmate that I had spoken with the night before hanging by the neck from a white bed-sheet draped over a stainless steel grate near the ceiling about ten feet up.

"Open 138!" I yelled into my radio. "Open 138 now!"

Meanwhile, the tier guard called for medical assistance, and we waited for what felt like hours for someone in the guard shack to remotely open the electronic cell door. As it unlocked and slowly inched to the left, I tried to muscle it open the rest of the way, but it wouldn't budge. Finally, I squeezed through and rushed to the inmate followed by the guard. I hoisted the man's body while the guard tried to free the bed-sheet from the grate. My face pressed against the man's lower torso, which was heavy, wet, and soiled, and I strained to hold him up high enough to create ample slack in the sheet for the guard to free it from the grate.

After a few intense minutes, we finally got him down, but there was not enough room in the cell to begin CPR, so we took him out of the cell and laid him in the middle of the tier where the guard performed chest compressions while I administered mouth-to-mouth.

But the inmate was already dead. His body was cold, colorless, and reeked of feces, but that didn't matter, I had to try to save him. Despite whatever crime he had committed, he was still a man and deserved a chance to live. I'll never forget putting my mouth on his and not feeling any breath. It was scarier than anything imaginable, but we kept the CPR going until the medics arrived about ten minutes later.

During that time, the other inmates heard the commotion and came to the front of their cells to see what was happening. As if in a movie, the inmates grew unruly started yelling at us and chanting, "Kil-lers! Kil-lers! Kil-lers!" in angry crescendo.

Were they right? Although exhausted and dripping with sweat, we were alive, but the inmate was dead—cold as stone—and there was not a damn thing I could do about it. I felt sorry for him and sad that somewhere he had a family that would soon learn of his death.

I watched the medics wheel him out and allowed myself a moment of reflection. And then I got mad! Mad at myself and mad that the tier guard had taken the same time-saving shortcuts that night as I once had taken. Hell, we had all been schooled in the thin blue line mentality that less is more and that everyone closes ranks around their own, but this time a man died be-

A tier of cells at the USDB.   *U.S. Army photo.*

cause no one had checked his cell, which should have been done every 30 minutes throughout the night.

The body was so cold that clearly he had been dead for several hours, and the tier guard knew that I knew he had taken a shortcut with the clipboard and was responsible. It's what he had been trained to do—and the result was death. When I left the prison that day, I decided I was never going back.

I got a call from my captain the next day, and I spoke my mind. "You can do what you want to do, sir," I chirped. "Court martial me if you must, but I'm not coming back!"

"Cannon," he said calmly, "I'm not worried about you. You're going to be fine. You're strong. You'll handle this, but I'm worried about your men—the people that work for you—the people that respect you. If you don't come back, what will it do to them?"

I took the next few days off to consider my decision and to ponder my military career. If I did return, I vowed to do things differently. I would not repeat the same mistakes nor would I allow myself to be part of a culture that encouraged silence and rewarded mediocrity. Inmates are people, too, and they deserve the same basic human respect as everyone else. The decision was simple.

When I returned to duty a few days later, I started talking with inmates and listening to them about their lives and their regrets, and I underwent a transformation of sorts when dealing with them. I began using "sir" and "please" and "thank you" in all interactions. Eventually, the language caught on and the inmates and guards alike began using it creating an atmosphere of mutual respect.

After I retired from the military, I returned to my hometown and took a position as a correctional officer at a nearby federal prison. All the while, my thoughts returned to the inmate who had died on my watch. Although I was in charge inside the prison, I was powerless to save this grown man from death. As a military policeman and correctional officer, I was one of the best at putting people in prison and keeping them in, but today, as a retired soldier, former correctional officer, and youth advocate, I'm one of the best at keeping them out.

This is my story.

Full Cannon

CHAPTER 2
Returning the Favor

The St. Paul Baptist Church in Peoria buzzed with excitement. On January 20, 2020, several hundred people filed into the spacious house of worship on a cold Monday evening to attend a watch party for the year's second episode of Mike Rowe's popular internet show, *Returning the Favor*, recognizing me and my four ELITE Youth and ELITE Adult outreach programs. It was a wonderful event that celebrated the hard work of many friends, volunteers, and supporters and brought much-appreciated national recognition to who we are and what we do. But the evening was bittersweet. My beloved mother, Mamie Pearl, the cherished matriarch of our family and the loving glue that held it together, had passed away in Cincinnati, Ohio just two days before, and I was heavyhearted and tired to the bone.

Many concerned people suggested that the family cancel the watch party, while others recommended that we reschedule it for a later date. Given our recent loss, everyone would understand and respect our decision regardless of what it was. But since that tragic day in 1990 when the inmate in Cell 138 took his own life, I promised myself that I would not take shortcuts or choose the easy path to anything even if it were something good.

Inside the church I welcomed guests for several minutes and then sat in a front row pew next to my wife, Melinda, my daughters, Summer and Danielle, and my grandson, Logan. Melinda squeezed my hand and reassured me like she always did. It was time. I stood slowly and took the microphone. My throat was aching and raw, and I took a deep breath.

"What's your name!" I boomed in my best command voice, using a skill I acquired as a senior drill instructor in the Army.

"ELITE, sir!" cheered the some 300 students in attendance from four different ELITE schools.

"Who do you serve?" I shouted louder.

Left: Photo taken during the Returning the Favor Watch Party.

Opposite page: Mom and me.

"My community, sir!" thundered the students, rising to their feet joined by hundreds of adults.

"And where are you going?"

"To college, sir!"

The moment was electric. I raised my left hand. "God is good!" I shouted, initiating a familiar exchange.

"All the time!" the audience responded.

"All the time..." I repeated.

"...God is good!" finished the crowd.

I smiled. "Thank you, everyone, for coming. Please be seated."

Mamie Pearl would have been proud of her son.

PLAYING IN PEORIA

Named after a Native American tribe that thrived in the area into the 19th Century, Peoria is a tough, gritty, industrial city of about 115,000 people nestled along the Illinois River in the center of the state some 160 miles southwest of Chicago. Once known for Vaudeville acts, the Pabst Brewery, the Hiram Walker Distillery, and as the corporate home of Caterpillar and more, it gets a bad rap as one of the poorest, most racially divided and dangerous cities in America with

Peoria, Illinois   *Photo by Ching Zedric.*

a per capita murder rate in the top six nationally. Conversely, it is the site of the first European settlement in Illinois in 1691, home of Bradley University and Illinois Central College and boasts Peoria High School, the first public high school in the state.

Despite its problems—perceived and real, Peoria was wonderful. My six siblings and I were born in the city and grew up living in the old Harrison Homes, Taft Homes, and in the old Warner Homes, which were all low income project areas referred to as "ghetto housing."

MOM

My mother, Mamie Pearl (Daniels) Espy, was born in Hobbs, New Mexico and had her first child at 16. My father, Charles Henry Cannon, was born in Philadelphia, Tennessee and was only 19 when my mother and he married. Both were descended from slaves.

My parents' first child, Charles Anthony Cannon, died shortly after birth. I don't know many details about his death because it was something neither of my parents ever talked about, but it had to be devastating to them both. Ten months later, my mom was pregnant with my brother, Bill (William Henry), and a year after that, I was born. Next came my sisters, Alicia, Elizabeth, Anita, and Ramona. My parents stair-stepped us, and we were close in age, but it felt like my sisters had Bill and me hopelessly outnumbered at every turn.

Some of the Cannon kids. Back row L-R: Tony Daniels, me, Bill, Duane Jordan. Front: Elizabeth, Alicia, and Tony Jordan.

Alicia (Williams) was a year younger than me, but she was the most spirited of us all, and that is saying something. She's as tiny as a minute but as tenacious as a lion, and she never quit at anything. I called her, "Lou," after NY Yankee great, Lou Gehrig, the iron man baseball player, who while we were growing up, still held the record for the most consecutive games played. She had that mentality as a kid, and it even got stronger as an adult. She passed that same trait to her children, Anthony and Melissa.

Then came Elizabeth, or "Liz" as we called her. Her capacity to love was immense, and we were close growing up. Even as a child, she was spiritual and had a strong sense of faith like my mom. She was also practical, easy to please, and always helped me with chores and whatever I needed.

Anita was the smartest of the Cannon litter from Day One and as loving as Alicia was strong. Although I was four years older, she had my number early. She could read something once and retain it, while I had to work at it, which wasn't fair! Today, she is a risk manager at the University of Cincinnati and active in the ministry. She and her husband, Michael, have two children, Ricky and Michael, Jr.

Later, after my parents divorced, Dad had Scott Howard, Andrea Cannon, and Charles Cannon Jr., from other relationships, and we are all blessed to have each other. I became a big brother to Scott, who is close to Anita's age, and Andrea, a talented young woman, is much younger. Charles, Jr., is the baby of the family and a mountain of a man. He is a gentle soul, but today works as a correctional officer at the

Peoria County Jail. It must run in the family.

We were poor, but because of Mom, we didn't know it. She was an eternal optimist and found good in everything even when there wasn't much to find and even fewer places to find it. She raised us all with faith, love, and compassion tempered with consistent discipline. She instilled in each of us a sense of fairness and a strong work ethic. She was a traditional mother where it was important—a strong black woman of great faith who at an early age taught me how to dream and how to see the world bigger than it saw me. Later, when I was a troubled youth, she saw potential in me and refused to let the streets swallow me. She was not blind to the world or naive about the realities of the time, she simply chose hope over despair, and for me, adopting that philosophy has made all the difference.

L-R: Maynell Adams (aunt), Dobie Williams (uncle), Maynard Cannon (uncle w/sunglasses), unknown, Dad (standing), Mom (sunglasses), Bernice (aunt), and Freda Cannon (aunt) and Lamar (seated front). 1968-69.

Before our parents divorced, our household was sometimes idyllic like the Cleavers on *Leave it to Beaver* or the Huxtable's on the *Bill Cosby Show*. Our family often sat at the table and ate dinner and went to church and Sunday school together, and most of us sang in the choir. We attended school and community events and did things that a typical family would do. We all worked hard and did our best to carve out our version of the American Dream—Peoria style.

The first job I remember Dad having was as a piano mover for Byerly Music Company in downtown Peoria. I have an early childhood memory of a time when my family lived in Taft Homes about a half mile away. One night as bedtime approached, my mom left to pick up Dad from work. Since we only had one car, she put us to bed and soon left to get him. In the short time that she was gone and while we were sleeping, a living room window fan sparked and caught a curtain on fire.

When Mom and Dad returned to the house, they saw smoke rolling out the windows. Dad tried to go through the front door to get to us, but the fire was too hot and the smoke too thick, so he ran to the back of the complex, climbed onto the second floor roof behind our apartment, and punched out the window to my sister's bedroom. He then raced into the house and lowered each of us down onto the ground where my mom and the neighbors were waiting. The apartment was burned out so bad that we had to stay with family members for several weeks until our unit was repaired. Dad saved our lives! He was my hero and still is.

As a child, I was known to play with matches and set fires, but I did not set this one. Another time, I unintentionally set a fire by putting a small American flag over a lamp to watch it project the colors onto the ceiling. While doing so, I was called downstairs to eat dinner and forgot about the flag. A short time later, we smelled something burning and discovered that the flag had caught fire and scorched one wall and the ceiling in my room. The impact of it was so strong and serious, and so was my whipping, that it extinguished any further desire for me to play with matches or to set fires. However, I still had some behavior issues to work on.

As a kindergartener at Irving School, I was a terror. My behavior was horrible and I misbehaved at every opportunity. Although I had not been diagnosed with anger problems, which few kids were at that time and at that age, I was out of control. I recall getting mad at my teacher, Ms. Geiger, and chasing her around a large rectangular rug in the center of our classroom while other children laughed. I also remember my first principal, Ms. Potts, choking me when she caught me bullying another child for money. Her method was unconventional but effective, and she probably did more to save me by her actions than anyone else. She and a few other teachers made a believer out of me in a hurry, most times through the business end of a paddle they affectionately referred to as their personal *Board of Education*. God bless them all.

MOVING ON UP

When I was eleven years old, Dad became a city police officer and we moved to the suburbs in Peoria. We were the first black family to move to this part of the city and it was like being in outer space. I had never

been around so many white people!

The adjustment to my new neighborhood and to Von Steuben School was difficult, but I had no one to blame but myself. I was fighting and stealing and had earned a reputation as a troublemaker. My behavior had become so bad that it probably contributed to my parents' marital problems. I recall one occasion when Dad doled out a harsh dose of well-deserved corporal punishment because Mom had reported my behavior to him.

During the beating, I began feeling sorry for myself and started to cry. I looked up at Mom and she was crying, too. I then realized that my pain was hers and that she loved me enough to allow Dad to inflict ample pain to ensure that my lesson was learned. What I did not realize at the time was how often she did not report my bad behavior to him, which reduced the frequency of punishments and preserved the love a son should have for his father. Moreover, she also understood that Dad was trying to teach me how to be a man in the best way he knew how

Top: me.
Right: Bill Cannon.
Opposite: Jess & Elizabeth Hazel

and trying to prevent me from getting into more serious trouble. Regardless, it still hurt her.

Despite my craziness, a handful of people continued to believe in me. My mom and her parents, Jess and Elizabeth Hazel, were my angels on Earth. Elizabeth was the most amazing lady I have ever known outside of my mom, and my older brother, Bill, who often took the blame and suffered the punishment for my transgressions, was my saint. My neighbors, the Centers, an elderly white couple that befriended me, coached me into wanting to be a better person.

With these people and others, including a few key teachers, I began to turn my life around and focus more on school and on improving my behavior. When this happened, I started getting attention for the right reasons.

Mr. Bill Giles was my 7th and 8th grade history teacher, and I loved him. At the time, he was the antithesis of me. He was probably in his 60s, and to me, seemed to be an old man. He wore high-water pants and a thick belt pulled up around his belly, but he was all business. He wore me out, but he taught history in a way that I could see and understand. Because of him

I began liking school, making new friends, enjoying life at home, and getting into less trouble. His consistency and unwavering belief in me allowed me to achieve success, and once I tasted it, he cared enough to make me work even harder and then fed me more. Everyone should have a Bill Giles in their life.

Mr. Bill Giles

At the start of my 8th grade year, I began to focus and was elected class president. I also emceed the school talent show and excelled in baseball, basketball, and track. In a few short months, I transformed myself from the type of kid "most likely to fail" to the "most popular student in school."

At the end-of-year school assembly, I received the *Walter F. Current Citizenship Award*, named after a former principal recognizing the highest performing academic 8th grade student. I was chosen for the award by the faculty and had my name inscribed on a plaque that is permanently displayed at the school. Unbeknown to me, my parents were invited to the awards ceremony, and they were as stunned as I was when I received the award. It was the best moment of my life.

After my 8th grade graduation, Dad asked me what I wanted as a gift. I told him I wanted a new lawn mower and a watch. I wanted the lawn mower so I could start a grass cutting business and the watch so I would not be late for any jobs that I scheduled. I was starting to display a real work ethic and becoming a mature young man.

HIGH SCHOOL

My freshman year at Peoria Central High School was difficult, and I felt like a fish out of water. I had just graduated 8th grade at Von Steuben, which was geographically located in the Woodruff High School feeder area. At that time in the mid-1970s, the area was experiencing bitter, and often violent, civil rights issues, and Dad was assigned to patrol that area. He had dealt with several students from that community who were participating in the almost daily race riots. Because of this, he made a lot of enemies, which meant my brother and I unknowingly inherited them putting our safety at risk. For this reason, Dad, the police department, and the school district decided that we should be allowed to attend Peoria High School, which was out of district. It was a smart move.

But smart is not always easy. In less than three months, I went from being the most popular student at Von Steuben to being invisible in a building with 2000 students. I hated the first semester at Peoria High. Enter wrestling coach Mike Stewart.

Full Cannon

Early in the second semester of my freshman year, Coach Stewart saw me in PE class and asked me to try out for the wrestling team. My brother had wrestled and done well, so I gave it a shot. As it turned out, I was fairly good and wrestled in the 145-pound weight class. Once I started making a name for myself as a standout athlete, I became more comfortable in school. Wrestling gave me a reason to attend school when I needed it most, and had it not been for sports, my future would have been different, and likely not for the better.

Because I had a successful freshman year in wrestling, I tried out for the sophomore football team. I had never played organized football, and everything I knew about the game came from playing sandlot. Since many of my peers had been playing since middle school, I was behind them from the start and had a lot to learn. This slowed me down initially, but I soon caught up. Before the season started, I was named the starting left defensive tackle. I had an all-star year on an outstanding team that only lost one game, and I also enjoyed another stellar wrestling season finishing second in the conference in the 155-pound weight class.

My Pekin rival and me at a wrestling tournament.

My only loss that year was to my rival at Pekin High School. Everything was falling into place, but life is rarely perfect.

Early in my sophomore year, Mom and Dad called a family meeting at our house on Maywood Street and informed us that they were getting a divorce after twenty years of marriage. They had been separated for a while, but before that, their marriage had started to splinter, and although they had shielded us from most of their drama, we had picked up on some of it. The arguments were getting louder and more physical, and Dad was becoming increasingly absent from the house and from our lives. When he did come around, it was either fun or hell. When it was fun, he joked and played with us. When it was hell, he physically and mentally abused Mom and sometimes us. To cope, Mom began self-medicating and drinking heavily. She hid the liquor from Dad, and to add to her shame and embarrassment, she had long known that we had siblings from other mothers.

News of the pending divorce was no surprise to anyone, and the meeting was the most peaceful the family had enjoyed in years. Although our parents assured each of us that the divorce was not our fault, I did not accept it. I believed I was the reason for most of their kid troubles. In my mind, I had taken my behavior too far and was to blame, but I was too young to understand that my behavior was not the only cause.

After the divorce, Mom took my sisters and moved to Cincinnati to start a new life with her brother, Raymond, leaving me in Peoria with my brother, Bill, who, at nineteen, had become my surrogate parent. I was devastated without Mom and my sisters, and it was hard on everyone, but Bill and I remained in our parents' house while Dad moved in with his new girlfriend. Few people knew how dysfunctional our lives were or how little we had, and because of this, I had to get a job to help make ends meet.

My junior year at Peoria High was difficult. Bill was having trouble maintaining employment, so the household was very unstable. Eventually, I moved in with Dad and his girlfriend, Hatti-May Howard. Hatti is the mother of my younger brother, Scott, and she treated me like her own. Although my bedroom was a roll up cot on the floor of a TV room in the back of the house, it was a mansion to me. I was happy just to be part of a family again.

Some might think that Bill and I should have been

Bill and me in the 1970s.

angry at our mother for leaving us home alone, but we were not. We knew that if we needed anything, Grandmother and Dad were nearby and would provide for us, and we understood that the only way for Mom to be free from Dad was to move far away out of his reach. Although they were divorced, Dad would not leave her alone, and her life became unbearable. Leaving was her only option.

Mom has always been there for us, and to her credit, she raised six children to adulthood when the prison population went from less than one million inmates 20 years ago, to the current population of 2.3 million while navigating through poverty, geography, family dysfunction, and other challenges. None of her kids have ever been locked up, and all have finished high school and completed some level of higher education. Some have earned doctorate, master's, bachelor's, and associate degrees, while others have achieved distinction in the United States military. One even was selected as a national humanitarian and inducted into the *National Hall of Fame for Caring Americans*. None of this would have been possible, from the first child to the last, and including their children, without the guidance, support, and nourishing love of a mother deeply rooted in the love of Christ who, above all else, passed that love on to her children. Mom was amazing.

With my parents' divorce behind me, it was time to focus on my senior year at Peoria High School. Going into the football season, I expected great things from the team and from myself. With a little luck and a lot of hard work, nothing could stop me.

WORK

I have never been afraid of hard work because effort was the one thing that I could control. Whether it was mopping floors, working out with weights, or studying for a test, I never failed at anything for lack of trying. My family life growing up was far from ideal, but despite my parents' differences, they instilled a tenacious work ethic in me and in my siblings that all but ensured success at whatever we did.

The first job I ever had was selling Kool-Aid from a makeshift stand in our neighborhood with my younger sisters when I was only six years old. After business got slow, we moved to other neighborhoods with more promising traffic. We learned early that people will cough up spare change for kids.

Fresh off my summer success as a Kool-Aid salesman, the entrepreneurial bug bit me, and I soon graduated to shoveling snow in the winters. Peoria used to get significant snowfalls, and when I was eight or nine years old, I learned that I could earn money by shoveling the sidewalks and driveways of the neighbors at the Taft Homes and of our new neighbors on the East Bluff.

We were too poor to afford a snow shovel or gloves, but I didn't let that stop me. Like a lot of other poor kids, I wore white tube socks over my hands to protect them from the cold. I often used the neighbors' shovels to complete the job, and then I used the money I earned to buy my own shovel and gloves. I always arrived at my customers' houses as early in the morning or as late in the evening as needed to make them happy, and I was proud that I kept them loyal to me.

My work philosophy continued after middle school when Dad bought me the lawn mower and watch he had promised. Soon, I had a thriving grass-cutting business with residential and commercial customers, including the Thompson Food Basket grocery store near Bradley University. I made seven dollars for the job and placed it all in an open account at the store that I used to buy groceries for my family. It was the thing I was proudest of in my early life, but I needed to do more.

I got my first real job at McDonald's as an under-age cook when I was 14 years old. The minimum age to legally work there was 16, but I lied about my age on the application. I worked this job for approximately six months and was one of the hardest workers that McDonald's had. I ran the grill, mopped and cleaned the facility, stocked the shelves, cut the grass, ran the cash register, and helped keep peace between employees and customers, which was sometimes difficult in my part of town. Although management knew I was in school, they always requested that I stay and close the facility. Six months into the job, the district manager forced all employees to produce IDs verifying our ages. Local management wanted to keep me, but I was just too young, so that put a quick end to my McDonald's career.

During the summer of my sophomore year in high school, I got a full-time job as a dishwasher in the cafeteria at Methodist Hospital. Again, I was the best dishwasher there, but had to quit at the beginning of football season my junior year.

At the end of my junior year I got a job as a custodian at the Peoria Park District swimming pool at Peoria

High School and kept it until I graduated. The job put money in my pocket and taught me to balance school, sports, and work. I never dreamed that 25 years later I would return to work for the park district and help give students like me an opportunity at a better life.

After graduation, I got a job at Pittsburgh Paints in Peoria. I enjoyed the job because of the people I worked with and even considered a career with the company. At one point, the company flew me to Milwaukee, Wisconsin for a three-day training. It was the first time that I had ever been on an airplane, and it was a memorable experience. I kept the job the entire summer and even had my position transferred to the Pittsburgh Paints store in Galesburg, Illinois where I planned to attend Knox College in the fall of 1978. Although I loved the job, I disliked the Galesburg store manager because he was a racist redneck and treated me like a houseboy. Even his friends noticed how poorly he treated me, but I let it go. I was moving on.

That summer, I also worked as a custodian at the Pabst Brewery in Peoria Heights on weekends. I went in on Saturday at noon and worked a 16-hour double shift (excluding one hour for lunch) until Sunday morning at 5 a.m. It was one of the dirtiest jobs I ever had, and I spent most of the shift sweeping and mopping the floor and came home smelling like cheap, stale beer, but because of that job, I learned that I wanted to be a professional and not an unskilled laborer for the rest of my life. But first, I had a lot of growing up to do.

CHAPTER 3
Trial by Fire

In July 1979, I sat in my tiny apartment in Galesburg, a town of about 35,000 some 45 miles west of Peoria, crying my eyes out. I had gone there a year earlier to attend Knox, a prestigious liberal arts college, to play football and to get a good education, but I did neither.

Knox had recruited me during my senior year of high school, but my test scores were not high enough to get in, so the Knox football coach offered to help. After graduation, he arranged for me to move to Galesburg to be tutored for the summer in hopes of being accepted in time to begin fall football practice. He also helped get me transferred to the Pittsburgh Paints store there so I had an income. My parents, despite their divorce, together helped move me to Galesburg and anticipated my attending college and playing football at the next level. They were so proud.

But I was depressed. For the first time in my life, I was out of my league. Many of the students at Knox had attended elite public or private high schools and were already prepared for the academic rigors of such an institution. I was just trying to get accepted to play football, but regardless of how much I studied, I failed to get in. I simply did not have the academic foundation and skills to perform at that level, and had I gotten accepted, I probably would not have been there for long. I simply was not smart enough—or so I told myself.

For over a year, I had deceived my family and friends into believing that I was attending college, and the emotional weight of sustaining the lie was crushing me. I told my parents that I was on scholarship, and since Dad was doing his own thing and had not attended a single one of my high school football games or wrestling matches, he never asked how my fictitious college football season was going. Mom had moved to Ohio and was out of the loop and given that I worked a lot of hours at the paint store, I seldom returned to Peoria. But like all lies, mine began to unravel.

Because of my overwhelming guilt, the rest of my life began to suffer. I was not getting along with my boss and my relationship with my girlfriend was strained by distance. I was homesick and had little money for gas or time to go home. Also, I was still dealing with our family's ongoing turmoil. In short, I couldn't find my ass with both hands. Thank God, the U.S. Army found me.

While at my lowest point, I had returned for a quick visit and found myself at the recruiting station in downtown Peoria. I went seeking an alternative to going home and telling Dad that I had deceived him. Sensing my desperation, I must have looked like red meat to the recruiter. Also, I was a ripped 200 pounds and an athletic specimen for that time. I had been named *Mid-State 9 All-Conference* and *Honorable Mention All-State* my senior year and had continued to work out after graduation in anticipation of still playing football. I looked every bit a soldier, but inside I was still a boy.

The recruiter asked me what I wanted to do with my life, and I responded, "I want to be a businessman."

"I can do that for you," he beamed, making his confidence my own. "Whatever you want, I will make it happen."

Before I knew what was happening, the recruiter had me take a practice aptitude test. The next day, I was at the old Peoria Armory taking the real test. A day after that, I was on a bus to Chicago to the Military Entrance Processing Station (MEPS) to take a physical and to get talked into enlisting before I had time to think about it. I was so gullible!

When I arrived in Chicago, the Army put me and scores of other potential recruits up in a nasty, rat trap motel where I bunked with a guy from northern Illinois. We did not sleep well that night, as the motel was dirty and roach-infested, but it was close enough to the MEPS station to walk.

The recruiters woke us at 6 o'clock the next morning and fed us the worst eggs I have ever eaten, and then they then marched us down Michigan Avenue to the MEPS, where we stripped down and were given a thorough mass physical in a room with 30 other men. A short time later, Army counselors pulled us into a room one-by-one and we selected our career fields. While I was waiting my turn, a guy I knew from Peoria was just leaving a counselor's office. He looked dejected, and I asked him what was wrong. He stated that the Army denied the MOS (Military Occupational Specialty) he wanted because his aptitude score was not high enough. I asked what job he was applying for, and he said, "The Military Police Corps."

His answer intrigued me. It was the first time that I had considered becoming an MP (military policeman). Dad was a civilian policeman and that seemed interesting and exciting enough at times. Maybe it would be even better in the Army. When it was my turn to speak with the counselor, I asked if my score qualified me to become a military policeman. He left the room to go check and returned a short time later.

"I have good news and bad news," he said.

"What's the good news?" I asked.

The counselor baited the hook. "You scored high enough to become a military policeman. Congratulations!"

"So," I began, "what's the bad news?"

The counselor didn't blink. "If you want to be an MP in the next six months, you have to leave today for training."

I stood frozen in disbelief and immediately began spouting excuses why that was not possible. "But I have a job," I stammered, "and I have to give them notice."

The counselor had heard that excuse before and was locked and loaded with an answer. "Not a problem," he began, "When you join the military, federal law requires your employer to hold your job until you complete your tour in the military."

"I have to talk to my girlfriend," I countered.

"I got you covered," he replied with well-rehearsed concern. "Just call her and explain what's happening. She'll understand. You can use my phone here in the office."

I was trapped. The counselor had a comeback for

every excuse, but I had an ace in the hole.

"I have to get clearance from my dad," I mumbled. "I can't do anything without his okay."

I knew Dad would cover for me and demand that I come home, so I gave the counselor his telephone number and he called him right in front of me and handed me the phone.

"Dad, it's me," I began nervously. "I'm in Chicago at the Military Entrancing Processing Station..."

My dad had no idea that I was in Chicago. The last he knew, I was still in Galesburg attending college or visiting my brother in Peoria, so the call was a shock to him on several levels.

"Boy...!" He snarled, "If you don't bring your black ass home, I will..."

I hung up right then. I had two choices; either return home with my tail between my legs and face the music from Dad, or to enlist in the Army. After about three seconds of deliberation, I determined that enlisting in the military was the safer choice.

Dad had served in the Army during the Korean War and was not keen about me enlisting. The country was still stinging from the divisiveness of Vietnam, and the reputation and quality of the military had suffered. He had seen the horrible effects of war, and no man wants to see his child experience it. Moreover, he had entered the Army a few years after desegregation, and the service was still rife with inequality and prejudice, which still affected his view.

Dad had also been an MP, but despite desegregation, the MP Corps of the time was effectively still segregated. In most cases, black MPs handled issues concerning black soldiers and white MPs did the same with whites to avoid trouble.

Later that afternoon, six other guys and I were transported to the Amtrak station in downtown Chicago and placed on a train for an overnight 11-hour ride to Birmingham, Alabama to begin Basic Training. Sensing that this might be our last night of freedom for a

An African-American military policeman on a motorcycle in front of the "colored" MP entrance, Columbus, Georgia, in 1942. National Archives Photo.

while, we all got ripped, totally drunk. I only got 90 minutes of fitful sleep because I cried most of the time. My buddies were unaware, but I was having deep regrets about my decision to enlist. I had joined the Army by accident, and unknown to me at the time, my own road to Damascus and manhood had begun in Galesburg.

All I knew about Birmingham was that it was in the deep South and had a reputation as a dangerous place. I had watched television and seen film clips of the city taken in the 1950s and 1960s during the height of the Civil Rights Movement when homes were being burned, fire hoses were being unleashed on humans, and vicious dogs were biting hunks of meat out of protesters that looked like me. I was scared to death.

When we arrived in Birmingham, a bus was waiting for us with soldiers already on board. We were the last stop on the way to Fort McClellan, Alabama, named in honor of Major General (MG) George McClellan, General-in-Chief of the U.S. Army from 1861 to 1862. The base was situated adjacent to Anniston, a city of about 20,000 people and home of the U.S. Army Military Police School, the Chemical School, and formerly, the Women's Army Corps (WAC) Center and School, which had been disbanded in 1978. Major General Mary Clarke, the last Director of the Women's Army Corps and the first woman to attain the rank of major general, was our base commander—and affectionately known as "Mother Mary."

MG Mary Clarke, 1981.
US. Army Photo

MG George McClellan, 1862.
Library of Congress Photo

53

KENNY to CARL

We arrived at the fort in the late hours of the night and were in-processed at the reception center. A drill sergeant (DS) or drill instructor (DI) gave a brief building orientation and we were issued two green itchy wool blankets, a pillow, and two sheets. The drill sergeants separated us by gender, and we bedded down. I made one phone call to my girlfriend from a pay phone before I went to sleep. We had not spoken since I decided to join the Army. My family had told her that I had enlisted, and she was relieved to know that I was all right, but we would not see each other again for five months until after my graduation from basic training and MP School. It did not end well.

The next morning, we were awakened at 5 o'clock and taken to the chow hall and fed a delicious breakfast. The DIs allowed us to eat and drink whatever we wanted and gave us time to enjoy our meal without being hassled. Little did we realize that life at the reception station was a friendly three-day fattening up process like the evil witch pulled on Hansel and Gretel. Afterward, we returned to the barracks and were given 30 minutes to make our beds, which was about 29 minutes more than we would soon receive. We then went to the personnel and finance departments and filled out paperwork and opened accounts for our pay, which took most of the morning.

After lunch, we were issued uniforms, other clothing items, and combat gear, and were instructed on how to pack all of it into a nice, green duffel bag without an inch of room to spare. This was followed by a military favorite—getting shots—during which my life would be forever changed.

I was born Kenneth Carl Cannon, and had gone by "Kenny" most of my life, but as I stood in my underwear in a long line preparing to get shots in each arm, I noticed that my paperwork read, "Carl Kenneth Cannon." I told my drill sergeant, and he screamed, "Your name is, '*Private...*' and I don't give a f@#k!"

Since my paycheck had "Carl" on it, and because I did not want to get yelled at again by my drill sergeant, the transition was easy. From then on, I have gone by "Carl." Who was I to argue with the United States Army?

Kenny Cannon
Central

A photo that appeared in the Peoria Journal Star naming the 1977-78 all-conference football team. Note my name.

The next morning after breakfast DIs gave us lessons on the "Army Way." We learned how to use the Army 24-hour clock and the Army alphabet system. We received classes on enlisted and officer ranks, when to salute, Army traditions, and other information.

Much of the instruction was boring, and it was hard to stay awake, especially when the drill sergeants closed the windows, lowered the lights, and sat us shoulder-to-shoulder on tiny folding chairs. But a recruit did not dare fall asleep or get caught nodding off. If that happened, the drill sergeants converged on that person like a pack of hungry wolves on a pork chop—snapping, snarling, and spitting at the recruit like they had dishonored everyone in the room and the entire U.S. Army for nodding off for five seconds!

Afterwards, the DIs assigned us to work details in the building, which included vital tasks like sweeping, mopping, and scouring toilets with toothbrushes. After each job was complete, we'd move to chow and then lights out, which was the best part of the day.

BASIC TRAINING

I was just starting to get used to life at the reception center when I got assigned to my basic training unit, Company A, 10th Military Police Training Battalion. We were then herded onto a "cattle car," an appropriate term for an Army bus used to move troops to their training sites and taken to our new AO (Area of Operations).

It was a short ride to the basic training area. The bus rolled to a stop, and we all sat nervously with our gear resting in our laps. Suddenly, an angry-looking soldier in a round brown Smokey the Bear hat exploded onto the bus and started yelling.

"Scum-bags! You've got two minutes to get off my bus and 90 seconds are gone! Now get off! Move your ass-es!"

Imagine 60 scared men trying to get off a bus at

 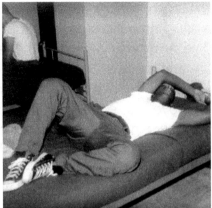

Doing what every basic training soldier does when they have a spare minute!

the same time. We were stepping and climbing all over each other, and time was running out. While we were trying to get to the company area, other drill sergeants appeared and began screaming at us making hurtful and unkind references about our mothers and intellectual capacity. They even disrespected our soon-to-be former girlfriends and their connection with some guy called "Jodie." To add to the fun, the DIs had watered down the sidewalk and we were all slipping and falling. We were like fattened chickens in a coop being chased by hungry foxes; trapped and panicky and not knowing what to do. It was controlled chaos, but I loved it!

Basic Military Training is a million-dollar experience that most people would not give a dime to repeat. Normally, basic training lasts about eight weeks, but MP training at Fort McClellan included MOS training that extended the experience to about 16 weeks.

The time-honored premise of training was simple; break a recruit down, strip his/her civilian identity, instill military discipline and self-confidence, teach soldiering skills, and build them back up again as part of a team. The Army has almost 250 years of experience doing it—and it works.

Once a recruit understands that they can never move fast enough or are always too slow, the rest is easy. Once the individual learns that success only comes through teamwork or that no one succeeds if only the individual completes the task, they become more than themselves and become part of something greater. For me, having been part of football, track, and wrestling teams gave me an advantage. That, and I could do 100 push-ups in a minute!

It wasn't long before I gained the attention of the DIs and was made a student platoon sergeant. One of the other platoons in our company was all female and we were the first mixed-gender company at the fort, which made for an interesting and memorable experience.

Upon graduation from basic and AIT (Advanced Individualized Training), I had become the longest serving student platoon sergeant and was named *Trainee of the Cycle*—my first military recognition. It

*Previous page:
Standing tall as the
student platoon ser-
geant during basic
training.*

*Right:
AIT Graduation Photo.
1979*

was the most rewarding experience of my life to that time, and I believed that I had found my home.

KOREA CALLING

On November 12, 1979 I boarded a plane to Bupy-eong, South Korea (ROK) for a one-year tour with the 55th Military Police Company at Camp Market halfway between the U.S. Army Garrison at Yongsan in Seoul, the capitol city, and the Port of Inchon, 30 miles to the west.

My arrival in Korea was memorable. Most of us stayed a few days at Camp Coiner, a small in-process-ing station on Yongsan, and were then transported to our permanent duty stations. A buddy and I were taken by jeep to our camp where we reported to a small ad-min building and waited for the first sergeant to arrive. When he did, we sprang to parade rest.

"Relax," he said. He then reached into his lower

right desk drawer and pulled out two fifths of Scotch whiskey—*Johnnie Walker Red* and *Johnnie Walker Black*. My buddy and I looked at each other and surely wondered, *Is this really happening? What kind of MP unit is this?*

We both took the *Red* since more had been drunk from it. For me, it made sense to go along with what everyone else was doing. That was the Army I went into. Many of the men were Vietnam War veterans who were tired and needed to relax. Although there were very few blacks in the MP Corps, the white soldiers taught me a lot and befriended me. My buddies and most of my leaders did not look like me, but they treated me like one of them. NCOs went to the club at noon, got drunk, and returned to work. It was a different Army and a different culture then.

At that time, Korea was not as developed as it is now, and it was downright primitive in places, but what an experience. The people, the food, the different customs, and the sense of purpose and camaraderie with my fellow soldiers contributed to making it one of the best years of my life.

Besides raising the flag for reveille and lowering it

My MP ID issued to me the day I arrived in Korea. My name and my birthday are wrong!

for retreat each day, our MP unit had two basic missions. Our primary mission was conducting 24-hour security for the Army-Air Force Exchange Service (AAFES) depot. Everything that came into the country that went to the military Post Exchanges (PXs) went through our depot. One GI and one KATUSA (Korean

On patrol with two U.S. soldiers and a KATUSA soldier (far right). Republic of Korea, 1980.

Augmentation to the U.S. Army) would ride along on depot trucks and guard AAFES shipments from Pusan in the south up to the DMZ. At each stop we would remove the security seal from the truck, unload the cargo, and reattach a new seal. Security was needed because the black market was thriving in Korea, and American goods were in high demand and quite valuable.

Our second mission was patrolling all areas of our post including living quarters and all business establishments, which included occasional interaction with ROK Army personnel.

Truce City, Panmunjom, DMZ. The small buildings are in South Korea and the far building is in North Korea.

One night I got a call about a disturbance at the KATUSA snack bar on post. The snack bar served food and alcohol, including *soju*, a strong liquor enjoyed by many Koreans. When I arrived, a drunk ROK sergeant had about 10 KATUSAs in a single line formation chewing them out, probably for being drunk, too. He slapped the crap out of the first soldier, so I radioed my desk sergeant. "What do I do?" I asked.

"Nothing. Not a damn thing," he said flatly. "That's their way of justice. Stay away from them."

I held my radio and watched the sergeant go down the line slapping each man out of the position of attention and almost knocking him down. KATUSAs were mostly college educated and bilingual, and ROK soldiers did not like them because they had a sweet job serving with the U.S. military and often enjoyed the same perks and good treatment as American troops. After that incident, I had a new appreciation for our system of military justice.

Right:
 Doing my part to maintain good international relations with our hosts.

Bottom:
 Specialist-4 Carl Cannon.

At that time, tensions with North Korea were still high due to the August 1976 killing of two U.S. officers at the Joint Security Area of the DMZ by North Korean soldiers during a tree-trimming detail. In October 1978, the South Koreans detected a massive tunnel dug by the North Koreans extending over 1,400 feet into the South Korea side of the DMZ. It was the third tunnel discovered within four years and could accommodate more than 2000 invasion troops and equipment per hour. With the possibility of war always on our minds, "pucker factor" was high.

But great danger some-times brings great opportu-nity. During my tour in Korea, I was promoted three times and received my last promotion to specialist (E-4)—one rank below a non-commissioned officer—on November 11, my final day in country. Earlier that day, my first sergeant had made a special trip to Seoul and

picked up my promotion orders and hand delivered them to me at installation headquarters, where he and my commander and platoon sergeant promoted me in a private ceremony. I rushed off post to a local shop and proudly had my favorite Korean tailor sew my new rank on every travel uniform.

I left Korea on November 12. After a few weeks leave, I reported to Fort Rucker to serve with the 141st MP Company of the 1st Aviation Brigade.

There's no place like home.

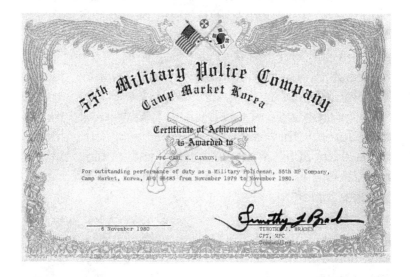

55th Military Police Company
Camp Market Korea

Certificate of Achievement
is Awarded to

PFC CARL K. CANNON,

For outstanding performance of duty as a Military Policeman, 55th MP Company, Camp Market, Korea, APO 96483 from November 1979 to November 1980.

6 November 1980

TIMOTHY J. BRADEN
CPT, MPC
Commanding

CHAPTER 4
A Close Call

Years before cell phones, email, and personal computers were available to U.S. soldiers serving in Korea, mail call was the primary means of communicating with family and friends back home. In mid-August 1980, I received an unexpected letter from Hattie, Dad's fiancée. I quickly opened it and scanned the contents, which included a brief note and a clipping from my hometown newspaper, the Peoria *Journal Star*, dated August 3rd. The headline read, "3 Shot, Including Policeman." My heart skipped a beat.

The article that Hattie sent to me in Korea showing a photo of my dad. Courtesy of the Peoria Journal Star.

The article was almost two weeks old, and from it, I learned that Dad, now a 44-year-old detective and 10-year veteran with the Peoria Police Department, had been shot in the face and was lying in St. Francis Hospital in serious condition. But the toughest man I knew was a fighter, and if anyone could pull through, it was my dad.

Shortly after 6:30 p.m. on August 1, 1980, he responded to a dispute over a card game at a local tavern where gun shots had been reported. Although details of the incident were sketchy, the suspect and a 65-year-old bouncer were on the lawn in front of the tavern when the suspect shot the bouncer in the abdomen and in the leg. A few moments earlier, a woman standing in a nearby alley had flagged Dad down in his squad car, and when he got out of his car to talk with the woman, he received a radio call. While he was on the radio, the suspect who had shot the man, ran around the corner straight into him. Dad had no time to

Dad and me preparing to go for a ride in his police car.

draw his weapon, and the suspect fired a single shot into his face with a .38-caliber revolver and fled, only to be wounded and apprehended in a shootout with police a short time later.

The high-caliber slug entered Dad's mouth and lodged in his neck close to his spine. Immediately after the surgery, the surgeon, who had attended to President John F. Kennedy at Parkland Hospital after he was shot in Dallas in November 1963, said that Dad was "very, very lucky," and that they decided to leave the bullet in his neck rather than risk further damage by attempting to remove it.

According to the clipping, "The suspect had been previously convicted for the armed robbery of a taxi driver in Peoria in 1974 and sentenced to 10 to 50 years in prison. But he was released for good time after serving less than six years."

Eight months after his release, he shot my dad. After reading the article, I immediately called home and was told that Dad was fine. He did not want anyone to tell me about the incident because I was so close to coming home, but when I pushed the issue, my family convinced me that he would be fine and that an emergency trip home was unnecessary.

Although Dad stayed in the hospital for over a month and spent six more months at home convalescing, he returned to duty and continued to serve the Peoria Police Department and the City of Peoria. He retired as a police sergeant after 31 years of exemplary service, and after retirement, worked as a bailiff in Peoria County courts until 2017.

Despite a life of outstanding public service, I was

most proud of the work Dad and I did together. He worked side-by-side with me for 20 years in the creation of the ELITE Youth and other outreach programs, and I valued his courage, experience, and counsel.

DAD

The relationship between a father and son is not always easy, and ours was no exception. The dynamic between my father and me taught me a lot about how to be a father figure, a mentor, and man—and sometimes how not to be. Over time, I learned that some of his attitudes and behaviors, good and bad, had profoundly affected the entire family, and thus, impacted how each of us raised our own children.

What I had not considered, was how poorly his father, Samuel Cannon, had treated him. By all accounts, Sam was the meanest man who ever walked and died in his sleep of natural causes at age 44, although some in the family attributed his death to alcoholism. On the other hand, had he not been so cruel and chased my grandmother out of Philadelphia, Tennessee, my father would never have come to Illinois.

The more time I spent with other people's children, the more I learned about the impact that a good and loving father has as provider, protector, and role model. I began to see the value of a positive relationship between father and child, and to understand why so many fatherless children, or children with absentee or horrible fathers, gravitate toward gangs with a strong leader and a rigid male hierarchy that provides the discipline and acceptance they may have lacked and crave.

My dad was a role model for many people in our

community, but at times, he was not a good one at home. My senior year of high school he did not attend my football All-Conference/All-State Recognition Banquet in the ballroom of the famous Pere Marquette Hotel in Peoria. It broke my heart, and since my mother had to work, my grandmother and my sister, Anita, attended the banquet. It was the same story with my siblings, but looking back, I was more fortunate than some teammates who did not have anyone attend.

My brother, Charles Cannon, Jr., Dad, and me in 2007.

Although Dad had a mixed history as a husband and father, he shined when I needed him most. He was better than his father in every way, and he learned from his mistakes and tried to be a better man. He was disappointed when he learned that I had not made it into college and angry that I had enlisted without his consent, but he understood that I needed to be my own man.

When I returned home for two weeks after AIT, he chewed my ass the first night back. But I spit back at him, and he saw who I was and that I was different. And he was okay with it. He even took me to St. Louis to catch a plane to Travis Air Force Base bound for Korea.

Dad was proud that I had made such an important decision on my own, and because of that, he acknowledged that I was growing into manhood, which is all a young man ever wants from his dad.

My father died of cancer on May 2, 2018, at age 82, and was buried with full military and police honors. I believe that he became a better man each day since the day he was shot, and I was blessed to have seen him evolve into a loving husband of 1, father of 9, grandfather to 26, and great-grandfather to 28 children with more on the way. It was his time to rest.

Charles Cannon, Sr.
1935-2018

CHAPTER 5
Down South

Fort Rucker was not my first choice of duty stations, but the delicious southern fried chicken in southeastern Alabama made the cultural transition from Korea easier. While I did not relish the thought of returning to a post in the deep South, which was a four-hour drive further south than Fort McClellan where I had completed basic training and AIT, I was still close enough to my dad and brothers in Illinois, and to my mom and sisters in Ohio, to be there in an emergency.

On December 29, 1980, I reported to the 141st MP Company attached to the 1st Aviation Brigade. The unit was part of Aviation Center, home of the Army Aviation School, which trained warrant officer helicopter pilots. It was also the place where the seeds of my life's work took root and reached for the sky.

	FORT RUCKER
0025 AUDIT NO.	MILITARY POLICE
	Crime Prev Insp — POSITION / T1702 — BADGE NO.
	Carl K. Cannon — NAME / SP4 — RANK
	THIS IS TO VERIFY THAT THE ABOVE NAMED INDIVIDUAL HAS BEEN APPOINTED MILITARY POLICE FOR FT. RUCKER, ALABAMA

Carl K. Cannon
SIGNATURE

PROVOST MARSHAL SIGNATURE

NCO MATERIAL

I spent most of my first year at Fort Rucker learning the ropes and attending military schools. I hadn't been on post long when I attended the Special Weapons Assault Tactics (SWAT) course in Selma hosted by the Alabama State Trooper Academy and supported by the U.S. Army Special Forces. I then attended the Primary Leadership Course (PLC) at Fort Benning near Columbus, Georgia. Benning is home of the Infantry School, Ranger School, and the Airborne School, and is one of the most intense bases in the Army.

The PLC, later renamed the Primary Leadership Development Course (PLDC), is the first step in the NCO school system and is required for promotion to sergeant (E-5). Over the four-week course, we learned the basics of junior leadership and sharpened our soldiering skills in the classroom and in the field. We conducted organized physical training, ran obstacle courses, practiced drill and ceremony, and negotiated challenging land navigation courses. It was great training, but the red clay at Benning was cold, wet, and infested with Infantry types that we affectionately called, "grunts." I was happy to leave.

After PLC, I appeared before the E-5 promotion board and received the maximum score. Although I did not get into Knox College, I could do some soldiering. Two months later, I returned to Fort McClellan and completed the eight-week Military Police Investigator Course. Finally, by the end of May 1981, I settled back in at Rucker and spent the next six months conducting criminal investigations and physical security inspections, writing citations, and doing routine police work.

OFFICER FRIENDLY

In early December 1981, under the direction of the MP Command, I incorporated a police community relations program known as, "Officer Friendly," into the southern Alabama school system of Dale and Coffee counties in the Fort Rucker area. The genesis of the Officer Friendly concept began with a popular kids' television show, "Officer Friendly and Jimmy Duck," starring comedian and singer Dean Allen, that aired in 1955 and ran into the mid-1960s. Allen had worked for Walt Disney and was the original voice of Donald Duck.

In 1966, the Chicago Police Department launched the first organized Officer Friendly program in urban public elementary schools to instill trust between the public and the police. Other police departments and school districts quickly followed suit. The program caught fire when the Sears Roebuck Foundation got behind it with money for classroom kits that included coloring books, videos, board games, and other items that were distributed to scores of school districts across the country. Military posts then rolled out their own Officer Friendly programs based on the original model, and these were popular throughout the 1980s.

I was selected among the MPs at Rucker, and I went into classrooms wearing my semi-formal Class B uniform with a military name tag reading "Officer Friendly." I spoke to children about what it was like to be a police officer, how to be careful around strangers, and how to settle conflicts without hitting or using physical violence. I also taught the children the importance of safety, responsibility, respect for the law, and most important, how they could assist their community by reporting crime.

The program was an immediate success. Normally, my Officer Friendly duties were in addition to my assigned police work, but when the commanding general read several glowing reports about the program and received positive publicity from the local media, he went to the provost marshal, head of the post police force, and wanted to know more. My commander, COL Tom Regal, also wanted brought up to speed, and after I briefed him, he appointed me as the full-time Officer Friendly and tasked me with expanding the program into our community relations model.

As the new Officer Friendly, one of my duties was to serve as a crossing guard at two local military elementary schools. Most of the children were polite and respectful as they passed by me in the intersection and crossed the street. For whatever reason, one blonde five-year-old boy did not like police and took it out on me. One morning as I waved him and a few of his friends into the intersection to cross the street, he stopped and kicked me in the shin as hard as he could.

"Pig!" he screamed.

He defiantly jutted out his chin, glared at me, and then walked on. He had no fear.

Memories of how my dad would have handled the situation gushed over me. I wanted to grab that little guy and light him up in front of all his friends, but that was not my place. Despite my frustration and surprise, I saw this as an opportunity to change his negative view of police and to address his disdain for authority.

Opposite: COL Regal swears me in as Officer Friendly. Above: Directing foot traffic through the intersection before school. U.S. Army photos.

Soon after the incident, I met Mrs. Dianah Oates, a pre-school teacher at one of the schools, and shared what had happened. She sympathized and suggested that I come and talk to her class about what it's like being a police officer. I did not know it yet, but that class visit would play a role in my life like no other.

It wasn't too long until I spotted that little guy again. He was a military dependent, and I made it a point to

get his name and the name of his parents, which led to a meeting and my retelling them about my encounter with their son. I also met his beautiful seven-year-old sister, Summer Day. I have since forgotten the boy's name and the name of his parents, but her name is unforgettable.

Although the boy and I shared a couple high-fives and settled our differences like men, his belief system was already in place. He had developed a negative attitude toward authority and a disrespect for adults from his parents, and that was a shame. I have never forgotten that interaction, and how it impressed upon me the impact that good or bad parenting can have on a child and how it reinforced the value of human interaction based on kindness and respect.

CADET PROGRAM

Due to the success of the Officer Friendly program at Fort Rucker, my role over the next two years increased. My area of operations expanded into the Northern Alabama School System, where the program reached 13,000 children and youth ages 10-17 of all ethnic groups and economic and social backgrounds. This involved several thousand classroom and community hours, but it was worth it.

The program was met with so much enthusiasm that it was incorporated into seven additional schools in the surrounding areas. Two offshoots of this program were the "School Crosswalk Guards" and the "Junior Police Cadet" programs.

Opposite: Talking bicycle safety with kids. Above: Playing a game of foosball at the Youth Recreation Center. U.S. Army photos

The Cadet program was for youth 10-17 years of age. The original concept was to provide youth with constructive activity during the summer months only, but it was so successful that it was expanded as a permanent activity. Through the Junior Police Cadet Program, I organized a free Christmas party for over 3,000 youth in the Alabama Wiregrass area. We also sponsored a Mother/Daughter Banquet for over 500 peo-

ple to honor mothers of the community. Other annual events included the Halloween Haunted Fun House and the creation of the annual *Chief of Police Citizenship Awards*. While not on duty, I coached youth football, baseball, and basketball.

I had accomplished a lot in three short years at Fort Rucker, and I was hungry to do more. Increasingly, my work with the Officer Friendly program was paying off.

In August 1982, I traveled to Montgomery and was recognized by both houses of the Alabama Legislature and by Governor Fob James. Following a promotion

Opposite page: SGT Rick Grant and me refereeing youth soccer.
    U.S. Army photo

Right: The post general presents me with a proclamation.
    U.S. Army photo

Bottom: Proclamation from Governor Fob James of Alabama.

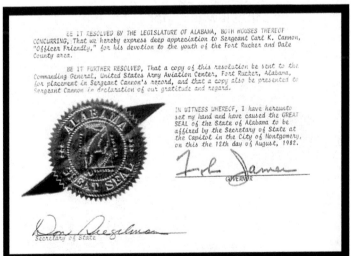

BE IT RESOLVED BY THE LEGISLATURE OF ALABAMA, BOTH HOUSES THEREOF CONCURRING, That we hereby express deep appreciation to Sergeant Carl K. Cannon, "Officer Friendly," for his devotion to the youth of the Fort Rucker and Dale County area.

BE IT FURTHER RESOLVED, That a copy of this resolution be sent to the Commanding General, United States Army Aviation Center, Fort Rucker, Alabama, for placement in Sergeant Cannon's record, and that a copy also be presented to Sergeant Cannon in declaration of our gratitude and regard.

IN WITNESS WHEREOF, I have hereunto set my hand and have caused the GREAT SEAL of the State of Alabama to be affixed by the Secretary of State at the Capitol in the City of Montgomery, on this the 12th day of August, 1982.

GOVERNOR

Secretary of State

to sergeant and a substantial raise, I was named the *Fort Rucker NCO of the Month* and subsequently decorated. At the conclusion of my tour, the Army awarded me the first of my three Meritorious Service Medals in recognition of my work. But just when a soldier thinks they've got a good thing going, the Army steps in and messes things up. In February 1984, I found out how bad that could be.

NEW ORDERS

Receiving orders to a remote Army base in Turkey during the height of the Cold War was not my idea of fun, so I called my DA branch representative and asked if anything else was available.

"I have something off the coast of Hawaii," he said benignly.

All I heard was "Hawaii," and I was hooked. Apparently, I was not listening when he mentioned that Johnston Island was about 720 nautical miles off the coast of Hawaii, and that it was so far out in the middle of the Pacific Ocean that fish had to pack their lunch to get there.

Aerial view of Johnston Island   *U.S. Army photo*

Johnston is the largest of four islands that make up the Johnston Atoll, but only it and Sand Island are natural. The two smaller islands are man-made. While Johnston Island may sound like paradise, the most interesting part of it is its history. An American ship accidentally discovered it in 1796, but the U.S. formally did not take it over until 1898 when "nearby" Hawaii became a U.S. territory.

The Navy built an air station there during World War II, and a few years later, turned it over to the Air Force which conducted secret high altitude nuclear tests there until the early 1960s. Then it came under the command of the Defense Nuclear Agency from 1974 to 1999, and later became a weapons destruction site. Today, the atoll is a bird sanctuary, like Sand Island was when I was there. Thousands of birds would fly over and crap on us and on everything else. It was like a bombing raid, and we could not get under cover quick enough. The daily raids added insult to injury, but at least they broke up the boredom a little.

Although a commercial flight arrived once a week, I flew in on a C-141 military transport with a few other guys and a load of supplies out of Hickam Air Base in Honolulu. When I got off the plane, I was immediately issued a gas mask, and it was tested to ensure that it effectively sealed and did not leak. Everyone on the island always carried a mask regardless if they were on duty or not. At that point, I wondered what the hell I had gotten myself into.

I was assigned to a small MP platoon under the U.S. Army Chemical Activity (Pacific), which was part of the Pacific Command, and guarded the facility where the

Army stored its chemical munitions. This included rockets, projectiles, mines, mortars, and huge containers of Sarin and VX nerve agent, mustard agent, and other deadly weapons. Pretty nasty stuff.

As MPs, our job was to safeguard the Johnston Atoll Chemical Disposal System, which was a contract civilian group charged with destroying outdated, expired, or unwanted munitions. Our platoon consisted of about 30 men, and as a sergeant, E-5, I was second in command. The Army also had a company of engineers that we referred to as, "bullet heads." They had the primary responsibility of caretaker for all munitions. They hated the MPs, and we didn't care much for them either. The base commander was an Air Force major, but only a handful of Air Force personnel were stationed there. The rest were civilians.

The south end of the island contained several acres of bunkers where the munitions were stored. Since the wind blew continuously from north to south, the bunkers were strategically placed so that if any of the con-

Munitions bunker on Johnston Island.   *U.S. Army photo*

tainers of chemical agent leaked, the wind would blow the vapors out to sea. The bullet heads would rotate the bombs, and if there was no wind, they would shut that bunker area down for the day and discontinue work.

We were 24/7 security for entry into the bunker area known as the "red hat area," but we did not handle munitions or do anything in the bunkers other than check access. Only authorized personnel were allowed in the bunker areas, and everyone had to carry a mask. No exceptions.

Each bunker also contained a caged rabbit whose sole purpose was to detect chemical leaks. The rabbits were extremely sensitive to chemical agents and were used as early-warning systems much like canaries were in coal mines. Each rabbit had a rank, such as a private, corporal, sergeant, and so on, and the higher the rank, the longer that rabbit had survived. The bullet heads checked each cage daily and if the rabbit appeared sick or dead, they knew we had a leak. Masks were donned immediately, and the island-wide alert system activated.

WORTH THE WEIGHT

Despite the remoteness of the base, life on Johnston Island was not all bad. I even got a part-time job at the PX (Post Exchange) to help pass the time, and the barracks were the best I ever had in the Army. They were more like apartments or college dorms than the open bay setup like we had in basic training. Each apartment housed three men, and each man had his own bedroom and bath and a shared living room with a television. We even had satellite HBO.

The civilian mess hall served the best food available, and I took advantage of it. Every Wednesday was prime rib day, and the cooks prepared it however we wanted it. The staff also allowed us to take food back to our apartment. I would buy a quart bottle of milk at the PX and fill it in the mess hall each day. With so much free food and extra time on my hands, I got serious about eating right and working out with weights. I had some great workout partners and was soon bench pressing over 400 pounds and putting on the physical size that later defined me.

The island had other perks, too. It sported the Tiki Club and the private NCO Club, and there were plenty of opportunities to swim, fish, and scuba dive. We played a lot of softball, too, and we even had announcers calling play-by-play of the games. It was a big deal trying to stave off boredom and find normalcy.

The base also had an extensive collection of old record albums and a cassette recording studio where we recorded music and messages on tape and mailed them home.

*Opposite page: the base walk-in outdoor movie theater.
Above: Rick Grant (to my right) on the plane moments before
being strapped down and evacuated to avoid the hurricane.*

Being isolated in such a remote location at a time when communication was difficult and expensive, it was important to maintain morale. Each service member was given one free pre-scheduled 15-minute phone call home each week. Mine was every Friday night. That call was my lifeline to the world and my weekly escape.

For the mostly male population, the lack of a social life was the greatest drawback to living in a tropical paradise. Except for a few married Samoan women who worked on base, and the monthly arrival of *Ms. January*, *Ms. February*, and other bunnies courtesy of Hugh Hefner, there was not an eligible woman for hundreds of miles, which was sad because the setting was beautiful, and the weather was always 70 degrees or better. Although the outdoor theater only played classic movies, it was still nice watching an old favorite under the moon and stars.

Weather-wise, the only drawbacks were the wind and an occasional storm—like *Hurricane Kelly*, which got everyone evacuated from the island. The Air Force flew in a C-141 and strapped us down like cargo and flew us back to Honolulu. We had received word that the hurricane was heading directly toward us, and we left minutes before it hit. We stayed in Schofield Barracks near Honolulu for a week waiting until it was safe to return.

I got off the island one other time when I had to be evacuated to Tripler Medical Center in Honolulu for the removal of a brain tumor that had been discovered after I was found unconscious on the sidewalk between the barracks and the medical dispensary. After the procedure to remove the tumor, the Army let me recuperate in my hometown for two months doing light recruiting duty. In February 1985, I returned to the island and completed the final month of my tour before returning to Alabama.

The one-year tour on Johnston Island was an inconvenient and lonely stop in my military career. But it taught me a lesson. My own carelessness, lack of attention to detail, and failure to do my homework, had created my mess, not the Army. I deserved what I got and vowed to never let that happen again. But more important, the tour made me slow down, refocus, and rededicate myself to the most important people in my life.

CHAPTER 6
Melinda

In early September 1982, Billy Adkins, the youth services director at Fort Rucker, asked if I would chaperon a dance at the Youth Center. I arrived at the dance dressed in my Class B khaki uniform wearing my "Officer Friendly" name tag. I must admit I looked good, but I had no idea that ten minutes later my life would change forever.

Mrs. Oates, the preschool teacher who had invited me to speak to her class after the boy kicked me, arrived at the dance to drop off her two sons. I greeted her warmly, "Good evening, Mrs. Oates, how are you?"

"I'm great," she said. "It's nice to see you again."

We spoke briefly, and then she dropped the bomb.

"I would like for you to meet my daughter," she said coyly, motioning toward the parking lot. "She is waiting for me in the car."

I was a deer caught in her headlights, but I played it off. "Yes, ma'am," I replied like a good soldier, not reading too much into her offer nor wanting to sound too eager. "I'd like that."

I then headed toward the parking lot, but before I reached the exit, Melinda walked in and we came face to face. She was stunning, and her eyes were the most beautiful I had ever seen. I think I fell in love right there.

SHE SAID

I was a freshman attending Enterprise State Junior College in the town of Enterprise outside Fort Rucker. I was taking general courses because I had no idea what I wanted to be. I was still living at home and had to take the college bus to and from school because I didn't have a driver's license or a car of my own. When I first saw Carl, he was working as a crossing guard at the intersection of the school. He wasn't just any old crossing guard though. He was wearing his military policeman uniform and was as sharp as a tack! He would tip his hat to all the ladies that drove by and flash that big bright smile of his

Melinda

at all the children. The intersection was close to my house, so I would see him often, but never spoke to him until that night at the dance. I had been impatiently waiting in the car for my mother to drop off my younger brothers because I had a date later on, and I didn't want to be late, so I went inside to hurry her along. I no sooner walked in the door and looked up and there was Carl. I was scared to death of him! He was so mature and awesomely built that I was intimidated by him. He asked if I was Melinda, and I said yes. He then told me who he was and asked if he could call me.

Being a military brat, I was tired of the military. I said I would never marry anyone in the military because I was mad at my dad for moving so many times. We had been to Fort Hood, Fort Bliss, Fort Rucker, and Korea, and I knew what military life was about and how hard it could be. But Carl stole my heart, and the rest is history.

HE SAID

About a month after Melinda and I met, I got promoted to sergeant, which included a pay raise, so I bought an engagement ring. Melinda's dad, Foster Oates, Jr., was in the Army stationed in Germany, and Melinda and her mother and brothers were getting ready to join him after Thanksgiving. The night I learned this, I drove her to MP Lake and proposed in hopes of keeping her in Alabama with me. She said, "Yes," and we drove back to her house and broke the news. We showed her mom the engagement

Carl

ring, and I asked her for permission to allow Melinda to spend Christmas with me in Peoria with my family with the understanding that she would join her family in Germany after the Christmas holidays. After Melinda's mom saw that we were engaged and spoke with Melinda's dad, she was elated and gave us her blessing and permission.

I took Melinda to Peoria and my family fell in love

with her, too. When we returned, she could not find her plane ticket to Germany, so she stayed with my best friend and his family for a few weeks while we looked for the ticket. I was still living in the barracks, and we were getting impatient, so we just decided to see the justice of the peace. To this day, each of us claim that the other intentionally lost the plane ticket!

On March 24, 1983, we got married at the Daleville Courthouse by Winston T. Snellgrove, a man with an unforgettable name and a personality to match.

"Boy," he said, in a slow southern drawl. "You take this here woman to be your wife?"

"I do," I said.

"I hereby pronounce you man and wife."

On the way home we stopped and bought a bucket of Kentucky Fried Chicken for our wedding meal. It's still my favorite.

As newlyweds our top priority was getting a place of our own. A couple days before we got married, Billy Atkins helped find us an old two-bedroom trailer in a secluded spot in Daleville with only a couple neighbors. Billy was a godsend who ensured that Melinda and I got started in our new life in the right way. On the surface we were polar opposites. He was an elderly tobacco-chewing southern redneck and I was not. But he loved me like a son, and I loved him back.

Once we moved in, Melinda and I scrubbed that trailer from top to bottom, and it looked good by the time we were through. Friends and fellow NCOs gave us pots, pans, and other household goods to help set us up. We even had a big red rooster that came into our yard and crowed at the crack of dawn. As a soldier, I was up early anyway, but he worked weekends, too, and seemed to enjoy waking Melinda up. We hated that rooster, and we often joked about having rooster salad for dinner.

For the next eleven months, we settled in and enjoyed our new lives together. During that time, we were selected to represent the Army Aviation Center in the Second Annual Great American Family Awards Program for 1984, for which we were blessed to receive the prestigious *Nancy Reagan Family of the Year Award* presented by the post commanding general.

A month before we got married, I had received a letter from the First Lady commending the Officer Friendly program, and it was nice to that we were still on her radar. But the best was yet to come.

On September 9, 1984, our daughter, Summer Lynn Cannon, was born in Dale County Hospital in Ozark,

Alabama and became the new love of our lives. But her arrival came with a twist.

Melinda was nine months pregnant, and we had just returned from a pee wee football game that I was coaching, and as I was getting ready to lie down for the night, I heard a knock on the bedroom door—it was Melinda's girlfriends. She had called them saying that her water had broken and that she did not want to panic me. I sprang up, and we all rushed to the hospital narrowly getting smashed by a semi-truck on the way.

When we arrived, I was not allowed in the delivery

Left & Below:

Melinda & Summer.

Opposite page:

BG Teeth presents us with the Nancy Reagan Family of the Year Award. U.S. Army photo.

room and had to sit in the waiting room. The doctors had told us that we were going to have a son, but when they came out of the delivery room they said, "Congratulations! You have a beautiful baby girl!"

"Excuse me," I said, "Are you talking about the Cannon baby?"

The doctor con-firmed, and I was elated. I am faith based to start with, but when I saw this little angel, it was scary, because I was now responsi-ble for her and life had forever shifted. I will never forget the first time she looked at me, and I saw the trust in her eyes. I do not know how someone can experience this

and not make it a battle cry for life. We had already decided on a name for a boy, but shortly after the birth, I remembered "Summer Day," the sister of the little boy who had kicked me in the street near Melinda's house, and I shared it with Melinda. She loved it. Every time I hear Summer's name it holds special meaning.

It was a wonderful year, but as a military family, we knew that separation was inevitable and that our mettle would be tested. All this occurred before I was sent to Johnston Island for the unaccompanied tour previously described. Anyone who has endured family separation in the military knows how lonely, painful, and challeng-ing it can be. Had it not been for those weekly Friday night phone calls to Melinda from Johnston Island, and my taped messages home, our separation would have

Melinda's parents. Foster & Dianah Oates.

been even more miserable.

However, after my surgery in Hawaii, I took a military flight to Frankfurt, Germany, where Melinda and Summer had joined Melinda's parents. They were all waiting at the air base and picked me up. It was the first time I had met Melinda's father, and we got along wonderfully. He was a senior warrant officer and a helicopter pilot, and I proudly saluted him. I also saw future NBA Hall of Famer, Shaquille O'Neal, who was the son of an enlisted man and then attended middle school with my brother-in-law, Brian Oates. As a pre-teen, Shaq was already man-size and delighted in playfully teasing Brian. However, the story cannot be verified because neither Shaq nor Brian will return my call.

My trip to Germany was a godsend, and the best part was seeing my wife and daughter. It was a joyous reunion, and as any father and husband will attest after being away from his family, a time of love and hope for the future.

FRIENDLY AGAIN

I reported for duty to the 291st MP Company at the Redstone Arsenal in Huntsville, Alabama on April 4, 1985. It was a different world than Johnston Island with essentially the same job of chemical security and routine police supervisory patrol duties, but I wanted no part of that.

Fortunately, COL Regal, my former provost marshal at Fort Rucker, was good friends with COL Adderley, my new provost marshal at Redstone, and he had spoken highly of me and my work with the Officer Friendly program. Adderley asked if I would like to do the Officer Friendly program at Redstone, and I did not hesitate. It was a blessing to go right back into police community relations where I could make a difference.

I was more focused at Redstone than at Rucker,

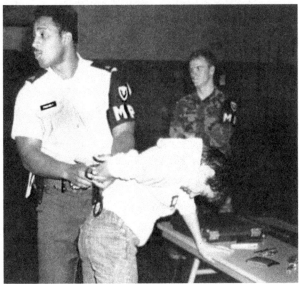

Demonstrating how to apply handcuffs to teenagers. U.S. Army photo.

and I had the advantage of experience. I also had a department with people working for me. I asked my best friend, Rick Grant, to help. He and I had been partners in the Officer Friendly program at Rucker, and he had also served on Johnston Island before I got there. He gave me the lay of the land, and soon I was up and running just like old times. I spent hundreds of hours visiting local middle schools and high schools reaching out to vulnerable youth. The 13 and 14-year-olds were my

Left: Weapons safety class

U.S. Army photo.

Opposite page: Rick Grant, Santa, and me helping kids.

U.S. Army photo.

biggest challenge. They were beginning to form their own opinions about police, and some of them were not positive, but at the end of most of my visits, kids got over being too cool and were eager to ask questions.

In November and December 1985, I taught security and safety techniques to over 2,000 school children and helped promote a positive image for police officers, military police, and the military community. I even took an M-16 into the schools and demonstrated weapon safety—something that would never be allowed today.

I was most proud of my work organizing one of the largest free Christmas parties in Alabama by collecting over 2,500 toys, which we presented to the disadvantaged children attending schools that served the Redstone Arsenal.

Before I became Officer Friendly, I was doing routine police work, which sometimes was anything but routine. When I made patrol supervisor I received a brand new squad car, and as I was giving it the once over, I heard a gunshot and see two of my MPs running toward my car with another MP who had accidentally shot himself in the foot with his own .45 pistol. The MPs put him in the back seat of my car, and I rushed him to the hospital Code 3 with lights flashing and sirens

Parade duty in my patrol car.

blaring. Unfortunately, he bled all over the back seat of my new sedan because he was too stupid to clear his weapon.

Another time, I got on duty and got dispatched to the hospital where about 10 medics had a patient holding an infant surrounded on the helipad. He was holding a razor sharp 6-point Ninja throwing star, and his wife was pleading for him to let the baby go. The medics looked at me, so I start talking to him about how it's going to be okay and asking him why they are messing with him. I told the medics to get back, and I convinced the patient that I was not one of the bad guys. Then I persuaded him to give the baby to his wife, and when he did, I got behind him and put him in a full nelson and slammed him on the ground. All the medics jumped on and whisked him away. He had lost his mind.

In addition to running the Officer Friendly program and performing the duties of a military policeman, I competed in several soldier boards, including the *Redstone Arsenal Non-Commissioned Officer of the Year* competition, which I won. Afterwards, I was runner-up for the *Army Material Command Non-Commissioned Officer of the Year* award and was selected as the *Alabama Enlisted Soldier of the Year*. But two of my favorite honors were being named an *Honorary Member of the Huntsville, Alabama City School Board* and receiving the *Huntsville Alabama Chamber of Commerce Policeman of the Year Award*.

In the spring of 1986, I was named as the *Governor's Alabama Enlisted Representative of the Year*, and on May 16 of that year, Alabama Governor George Wallace presented the award to me on the floor of the Alabama House of Representatives in Montgomery. I knew of his reputation as a bitter segregationist governor during the Civil Rights Movement who had tried to block the Reverend Dr. Martin Luther King's famous march from Selma to Montgomery in 1965 and who had defied President Lyndon Johnson's order to use the National Guard to protect the marchers.

I was nervous going in, but to my surprise, Wallace was everything opposite of what I thought he would be. He had been paralyzed from the waist down from an assassination attempt in 1972 while running for the Democratic presidential nomination and had been confined to a wheelchair since then. He smiled and shook my hand and seemed sincere. He congratulated me and thanked me for my contribution. Although I had

Governor George Wallace presents me with the Alabama Enlisted Representative of the Year Award. Photo courtesy of Alabama Department of Archives & History.

heard that he was a changed man, far removed as the face of southern racism of the 1950s and 1960s, I did not believe it until I met him.

The encounter with Governor Wallace affected me profoundly. It proved that even someone who had been full of hate and anger for so long could change, and it was a lesson that I have carried ever since and have tried to pass on to others through my actions.

Shortly after meeting Wallace, I attended BNCOC or Basic Non-Commissioned Officers Course for six weeks and graduated in July. It was my second leadership school and focused on the upper levels of command on the law enforcement side of the Military Police and on the upper levels of operations on the field MP side. It was another separation from my family, but it was a good challenge, and like everything in the military, I stepped up for it.

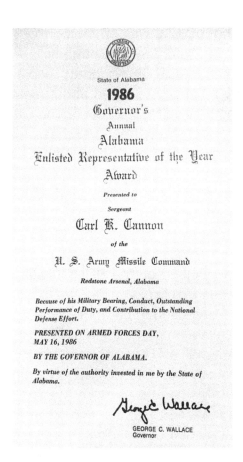

State of Alabama

1986

Governor's

Annual

Alabama

Enlisted Representative of the Year

Award

Presented to

Sergeant

Carl R. Cannon

of the

U. S. Army Missile Command

Redstone Arsenal, Alabama

Because of his Military Bearing, Conduct, Outstanding Performance of Duty, and Contribution to the National Defense Effort.

PRESENTED ON ARMED FORCES DAY, MAY 16, 1986

BY THE GOVERNOR OF ALABAMA.

By virtue of the authority invested in me by the State of Alabama.

GEORGE C. WALLACE
Governor

Sometime in the fall, the E-6 promotion score came out and I was two points shy of making it. I was dejected and could not understand how I had not made the list, so I went to see the post sergeant major, who called the MILPO (Military Personnel Office) sergeant major and asked him to review my records to see if anything had been missed or not recorded. Ten minutes later, the MILPO sergeant major called back and said that he had found 78 points that I had earned, but the Department of the Army had not credited to me.

With that phone call, I was promoted to staff sergeant and soon received orders to Germany.

My commander, COL Adderley, wanted me to go to Germany because he cared about me and wanted me to be competitive for promotion. The Officer Friendly program was a tremendous success, but Adderley knew that without field time in a combat unit, my military career would hit a dead end. I was going to work every day in a Class B uniform and effectively made my own schedule. It was easy duty, but the more I did it, the less I felt like a soldier. The MP motto is *"Of the Troops for the Troops,"* but with each passing day, I felt less like one. Putting on the BDUs (Battle Dress Uniform) made me feel like a soldier not like a cop. It was where I was supposed to be at that time in my career.

Upon completion of my tours at Fort Rucker and at Redstone Arsenal, and based largely on my work in the nationally recognized Officer Friendly program, I was awarded two Meritorious Service Medals, two impact Army Commendation Medals, two Army Achievement Medals, and numerous certificates and official Letters of Achievement. Moreover, my work had gained the attention of statewide civilian leadership and the Department of the Army. I was interviewed by several newspapers and appeared on various Huntsville television and radio shows. Near the end of my tour at Redstone, my work was featured in the November 1986 edition of *Soldier* magazine that was read by soldiers all over the world.

CHAPTER 7
Nukes

My new 1986 maroon Chrysler LeBaron was slick. It was my first new car and had all the bells and whistles that a new staff sergeant and his family would want. I bought it before leaving Redstone because I needed reliable transportation and because my family deserved it. I also wanted to show it off!

En route to Germany, we opted to enjoy a large family Christmas in Peoria, so we drove up from Alabama and celebrated together before embarking on a three-year accompanied tour of duty. Unaccompanied tours were normally one year for soldiers, but if the family came along, the tour was extended to three years, which Melinda and I welcomed as a chance to homestead for a while. We left the car with my dad and he generously made the payments while we were away. He took us to the airport in that car, and I remember watching everything below get smaller from the airplane window as we climbed toward our next adventure. Soon, all I saw were clouds.

Several hours later, we landed at Frankfurt Am Main Airport and were met by the unit clerk and taken to *Siegerland kaserne* (barracks) in Burbach in southwestern Germany. Initially, we stayed in a small apartment above a local German civilian's house for about a month and were treated wonderfully. The Army then moved us into a spacious apartment on the 7th floor of a large apartment building. When we got our apartment, we had the beer guy deliver beer in the same way a milkman delivers milk, and we also loved the food there. Our favorite was *henchen*, or German roasted chicken. It was so good that one night Melinda and I brought two home, and we ate one and set the other aside. Later that night, we found three-year-old Summer sitting in a chair devouring the chicken. She had already eaten most of it and had grease all over her face. She was so happy and content. And so were we.

NATO

I was assigned to the 52nd U.S. Army Artillery Detachment, and our mission was simple in theory; guard the Nike nuclear missile site and keep it operational. The unit, an element of an isolated Strategic Air Defense Detachment, was so small that we only had one building. There was one company of MPs, one company of bullet heads, and one headquarters company, for which I served as a platoon sergeant. I was responsible for classified communications security (COMSEC), maintaining the orderly room and supply room, and for managing the administrative workings of the company. I answered to the first sergeant, while the command supported the down range elements. I directly supervised six subordinate section chiefs with 70 subordinate security and administrative personnel and was responsible for the security of top-secret documents, communications equipment, and classified weapons. I also oversaw the operational budget and controlled and monitored the security of $3.5 million of weapons and equipment. It was a lot of responsibility, but I was up to it.

Like most NCOs, I had duties outside of my primary job. I was selected as the unit Equal Opportunity (EO) advisor, and I conducted training sessions dealing with discrimination and fair employment opportunities for

Opposite: Siegerland Kaserne.   *Above: Nike missile*

soldiers regardless of race, gender, creed, or social economic status. The title did not mean much, but the job went to my head a little. If something happened to me or to someone of color that I did not think was legitimate or seemed unfair, I saw it as racially motivated, which was not necessarily the case.

Having the EO title and a staff that was mostly African-American created some friction within the company. Some of the other platoon sergeants were white, and they pushed back when I squawked too loud or strong about something. In turn, I pushed back even harder, but I later learned that I was part of the problem. A good friend once told me that "to a man with a hammer, everything looks like a nail."

I put down my hammer.

After a month, the unit sent me to Bad Tolz in southern Bavaria for two weeks, where I completed Sig 34 training and learned advanced procedures for handling classified material. For the first time, I experienced the stark reality of the separation between communist East Germany and democratic West Germany. Although I had sent troops to East Berlin on pass to see life behind the Iron Curtain, I regret not going or taking my family. Soon after we left Germany, the Berlin Wall came down, and we missed a once-in-a-lifetime opportunity.

While serving in Korea, I had toured the Joint Security Area (JSA) at the DMZ in Panmunjom, and felt similar tension among divided countries, but the atmosphere at Bad Tolz was more warlike than any place I ever served. Located south of Munich, it had been the home of the 10th Special Forces Group since 1953, and the soldiering was serious. I rediscovered the swagger of a warrior there, and every minute spent training had a Cold War feel to it. Everything we did was predicated on preparing for war with the Soviet Union and its allies. Each day when I put on my uniform, I worked liked I was trying to save the world. And maybe I was.

Back in the day.

When I returned to Burbach after Sig 34 school, I worked out every day with the same warrior mentality. Although we had few training facilities, we had some weights in the cramped, unheated attic of our administrative building. I spent so much time working out and sweating in the frigid air that I contracted double pneumonia and spent two weeks in a military hospital in Frankfurt. One night before bed, the departing shift nurse gave me an IV, but she unknowingly missed the vein, and when I woke during the night, my arm was three times its normal size because the IV fluid had accumulated in my muscles. After that, I had a strong dislike for military hospitals and for nurses who were in a hurry to go home.

ON THE MOVE

In mid-1988, I was transferred to Fischbach, Germany, where I served as an assistant platoon sergeant with the 165th MP Company. It was a real MP field company, and I supervised four subordinate squad leaders and seven different sections. This included coordinating administrative and logistical support and training security personnel responsible for controlling strict entry control into a billion-dollar restricted "red hat" area containing nuclear weapons. I worked for SFC Julius Reitthoffer, and he taught me more about being a combat MP than anyone to date. He was an old Fort Hood Cavalry NCO and made a lasting impact on my professional life.

My family and I were housed in Pirmasens, close to the German-French border on the other side of Kaiserslautern, known to GIs as K-Town. The base was one of the largest in the world, and we lived in a huge apartment on the second floor. Melinda worked at the Post Exchange down the street. The only drawback was that I had to commute to work in a dark blue 1978 French-made Peugeot. You heard it here first.

The U.S. nuke site at Fischbach was a 45-minute drive straight down a mountain from where we lived. It was a two-lane road but there was barely room for my car. That beast was louder than loud and held together by rust. It was so bad that it did not pass German vehicle inspection, but since I was a GI and a policeman, I got by without it. Fortunately, I sold the car to another GI, and about 15 months before my tour ended, we took a military flight home and brought my LeBaron back. We drove from Peoria to Baltimore Port and

Street view in Pirmasens   *Gerd Eichman Photo*

put it on a ship. We then went to Dover, Delaware and caught a military flight back to Germany. It was worth the extra time and effort to bring the car over and made the journey down a snow-covered mountain less perilous. More important, I looked good doing it!

It was also at that time that Melinda and I toured the former World War II Nazi concentration camp at Dachau outside of Munich. It was the first camp opened in Germany in 1933, and some of the buildings and structures were still standing and had been turned into a working museum. I will never forget the human suffering we witnessed on the film clips and in the photos. Seeing that gave me another purpose. Patriotic pride and duty were the reasons I was serving in the military, but touring Dachau took it to a new level. If anyone doubts that evil exists and that people are incapable of such inhumanity, they need to visit the camp.

Seeing Dachau also boosted my pride in the Army and in my commander-in-chief, President Ronald Rea-

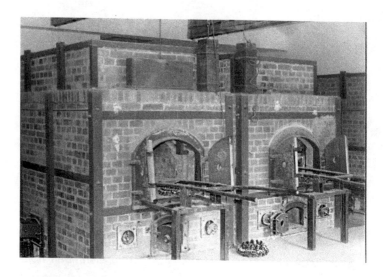

gan. Within a couple years of taking office, he and his new Army chief of staff began strengthening the military and restoring pride to the services. When I entered the Army in 1979, it was not uncommon to see a specialist (E-4) with 18 or 20 years in, and it was common to serve with troops who were out of shape, unmotivated, and just hanging on until retirement.

Reagan changed that. He increased military pay and implemented sweeping changes. Fitness standards increased, and we began doing PT (physical training) every day. A soldier had to obtain rank within a specified time or they were put out of the service, and tolerance for alcohol and drugs was abolished. In late 1981, the duty uniform was also changed from the solid OD (olive drab) green to woodland camouflage and renamed the Battle Dress Uniform or BDU. The uniform was more functional because we did not have to blouse the trousers nor tuck in the tunic, which was cheered by paunchy soldiers everywhere.

The summer khaki uniform also was phased out by 1985, and we upgraded from driving simple jeeps to operating more sophisticated and durable Humvees, which was a tremendous change. There were other changes, too, and after Reagan left office, President George H.W. Bush continued to support the military during the invasion of Panama and in Operation Desert Shield/Desert Storm, the largest military deployment since Vietnam. The leadership had done their part, and I had done mine. It was good to be a soldier.

In October 1989, I received orders that I was coming home. On one hand, the tour had gone quickly. I had learned a lot about leadership and teamwork and service in a foreign land where the threat to peace was constant and real. I learned that I was a good soldier and proud that my family and I had played a meaningful role in our nation's defense. On the other hand, three years was a long time to be away from home.

Opposite page: human crematorium at Dachau.
Above: Dachau Memorial sculpture.

Full Cannon

CHAPTER 8
A Hard Cell

Every time I walked past Cell 138 at the United States Military Disciplinary Barracks at Fort Leavenworth, I felt a little something. A few months had passed since the inmate had hung himself and life had returned to normal—or as normal as it could be in a maximum security military prison. Life inside the 30-foot walls at Fort Leavenworth was not easy for anyone; not for the prisoners because they had no freedom; not for the guards because they denied it to them; and not for the families of each because they lived with the choices of both.

I had completed 10 years of military service and was halfway to retirement. My family was strong and had supported me in my career. Together, we were in it for the long haul.

THE SECOND HALF

When I reported for duty at the prison, I stayed in a military apartment until I found a house in the city of Leavenworth. Melinda and Summer soon joined me, and we enrolled Summer into school. Melinda got a part-time job at the PX, and my hours were steady enough that I took a part-time job at the local movie theater to supplement our income. I finally embraced my new assignment at the prison despite my initial resistance. After all, I was a soldier. And good soldiers follow good orders.

By mid-summer of 1990, I was a guard commander responsible for 1400 inmates in the domicile wings and supervised a staff of 14-50 correctional officers. Regarding the inmates, I supervised work details, ensured cell security, monitored movement, conducted head counts each shift, and oversaw feeding and counseling. I also performed daily cell shakedowns, strip searches, and forced cell moves as part of a specialized reaction team

Inmate cell.

U.S. Army photo

(SRT). We conducted shakedowns to find contraband or unauthorized amounts of items, such as soap or any common item that could be traded. The staff broadly defined contraband to inmates as, "anything I didn't give you," since an inmate controlling something that the prison population needed or wanted was the same as him having money. Shakedowns also reduced the potential for serious injury to staff and prisoners and reinforced the message to the inmates that we were in charge. We found shanks and some of the most unique and creative handmade weapons, some of which were used to stab other inmates and unarmed guards, who carried only a radio, a body alarm, and a whistle.

One night when I was supporting the guard cage in *The Hole*, a guard reported that a prisoner kept verbally harassing him, so the guard and I went to the cell to move the inmate to Disciplinary Segregation (DS) and to shake down his cell. Initially, the inmate refused to go with the guard, but when he saw me outside his cell, he agreed. First, he asked if he could retrieve his shirt hanging from a bedpost, but instead of grabbing the shirt, he grabbed a coffee cup full of old urine, feces, and shaving cream, and threw it over his shoulder directly into my face and down the front of my shirt.

Before I realized what had happened, the other guard was on the radio yelling for the guard cage to close the cell. I backed up and about went crazy! I radioed the commander and requested immediate authorization to use the high pressure fire hose on the tier. I returned to that cell and tore that inmate up. I shot water into his mouth and everywhere else. Then we sent in a five-man SRT and forcibly removed him to

DS. I went down there later that night and several of the inmates were chattering. The inmate who attacked me had disrespected me in the worst way and the other inmates wanted to avenge the act.

"You want me to get that motherf@#$er?" asked one. "Just let me know."

"We'll take care of him for ya, Sarge!" said another.

Most were in agreement, but I declined their offers. "I don't need you to exact revenge," I told them. "That's part of the reason why some of you are in here in the first place."

The next day, I walked down the tier and passed the cell of the inmate who had attacked me.

"I wasn't trying to get you," he said with regret. "I was trying to get the guard who had been messing with me all day."

The act was considered assault and given the biological threat of HIV and the possible transmission of disease, I was treated as a victim. Official statements were taken, and I was photographed as evidence of the assault. Danger could come from anywhere.

We also found some bizarre items during shakedowns. One time I was shaking down a cell and found a beautiful handmade box containing an ornate, inlaid book with hundreds of blank pages. As I thumbed through it, the inmate returned to the cell.

"You can't read that, can you?" he asked knowingly.

I just looked at him, and then I got an eerie feeling. The inmate knew that his comment bothered me, and that was his intent. I found out later that he was a Wiccan, a practicing witch, and that he found great meaning in the book. That shook me to the core for a little while, and since the U.S. Supreme Court had recognized the Church of Wicca as a religion in 1985, he was free to worship like he wanted.

Unlike some constitutional rights, religious freedom was guaranteed and extended into the prison. Witches, Native Americans, and followers of alternative faiths had the same access to their religions as Protestants, Catholics, Jews, Muslims, Buddhists, and others if they did not violate prison rules or hurt anyone when practicing their religion or philosophy. Some inmates tried to use religion to their advantage and antagonized the guards with it, but inside a prison there is a higher level of control than in society.

One time shortly before the Super Bowl, I was shaking down a housing unit that had a drop ceiling. Some of the inmates acted nervous, and then I noticed that one of the ceiling tiles was sagging. I had a sixth sense about such things, so I got a chair and broom and began pushing up on the ceiling tile with the handle of the broom. When I felt some resistance, I pushed harder, and the next thing I know, *Whoosh!* I get drenched by a 40-gallon trash bag of homemade hooch that dropped through the ceiling. I had to go home and shower. I was a hero among the guards but not among the inmates. They were heartbroken. They had their Super Bowl party all planned out, but they paid little attention to the game because afterward they knew they had a lot of cleaning and mopping to do, and that I had a lot of legal paperwork to fill out. But I did mine during the game.

The mental state of inmates was always a concern. Mental illness was prevalent in that environment, as in any prison. Most inmates were there because of a mental illness that contributed to them committing whatever offense that got them incarcerated. These guys were not living a life of crime in the military. They were either mentally unfit when they entered the military or developed a mental illness resulting from their military experience. Many were prescribed anti-psychotic drugs that controlled behavior, but without them, behaviors would recur and escalate. In many cases, PTSD, isolation, depression, anger, violence, family issues, and other pressures were too much to handle and inmates had full mental breakdowns. Once during a heavy rainstorm, an inmate preparing to go into *The Hole* sat on the disciplinary bench outside the Control Center chanting, "In the name of Jesus, open the gate! In the name of Jesus, open the gate!"

We wound up tackling him. Spooky stuff.

Rape was another issue. Most rapes and sexual assaults in the prison were brutal acts of violence and intimidation and went unreported. If a victim reported an attack, they were known as a "snitch," which was the most unwanted and dangerous label an inmate could have because other inmates would distrust them and target them for retribution. If a victim did not report the assault, either out of fear or shame, the attacker and others might interpret that as an invitation to wage additional attacks or as proof of their fear or weakness. Many inmates suffered horrible injuries during the assaults and were hospitalized or segregated for their own protection. We had several inmates with HIV, and some tried to rape other inmates as a way of killing them slowly. There was no easy way out.

Inmates were not the only victims of sexual assault.

At one point because of serious staff shortages at the USDB, the prison began allowing inexperienced 19 and 20-year-old privates and junior enlisted ranks to guard inmates. Normally, in the evening after all work details had been completed, some inmates removed their white t-shirts and tied them around their heads like a dew rag. Unfortunately, an inexperienced white guard snatched the shirt off a black inmate's head starting a riot in one wing of a housing unit consisting of some 250 inmates guarded by only three men. Several inmates barricaded and trashed the unit and set fires. Others grabbed the guard and held him down while another inmate brutally violated him with a toilet plunger for several minutes. Two others stood watch.

After we put down the riot, we carried the seriously injured guard out on a stretcher and later caught and court-martialed the men responsible. Two other guards were also injured, which reminded everyone how dangerous prison was and how quickly the worm could turn.

Former rank meant nothing inside the prison. Every inmate was a former military man and had been distinguished from others by the insignia, badges, and decorations he wore on his uniform. In Leavenworth, every inmate wore a plain khaki work uniform and no rank. They had lost that honor.

One former Army major who was a prick for an inmate, thought that since he was a West Point Academy graduate and an officer, that he could carry that rank in the prison, but he got a rude awakening when the lowest-ranking privates on duty routinely told him what to do, which they often did just to prove the point.

The former major had twice tried to murder his wife —the last time while attending the Army Command and General Staff College at Ft. Leavenworth while working toward promotion. He was planning to kill her on their anniversary and had taken her to an Embassy Suites in Kansas City to celebrate. Pretending to carry her over the threshold and into their room on the 7th floor, he dropped her over the balcony onto a grand piano. Months before that, he had tried to beat her to death with a toilet seat. Fortunately, she lived despite suffering horrible injuries. He was stripped of all rank and sentenced to 23 years.

THE GULF WAR

When Saddam Hussein and his Iraqi forces invaded Kuwait in early August 1990, we were already preparing for war. Immediately, I requested for deployment in Operation Desert Shield but was denied because I was already serving in a war-time environment by working in a prison. While I did not agree with the decision, I understood it. I have always felt that I could have done more as a soldier had I deployed to Kuwait or Iraq. However, my friend Joseph Harmon, the enlisted clerk at the in-processing station who told me I had to sign in when I first reported to Fort Leavenworth, came down on orders to deploy. He and I were avid weightlifters and worked out regularly at Gruber Gym on post. One evening when I was working at the theater, my sister, Ramona, who had been visiting us from Ohio, shows up and says that she has a date, and that he is parking the car. That date was Joe—and he and my sister have been married for 32 years.

Ramona is the baby of our family and everyone spoiled her. We all had a part in helping to raise her, and today she is one of the strongest people I know. She and Joe have an international household consisting of three biological children, Greg, Jasper, and Tyler, and two adopted children, Amia and Natalie. Amia is Caucasian and Natalie is Filipino. These beautiful souls exemplify what is best about the spirit of America and they have woven themselves in the fabric of our family. They are loved as our own and are Full Cannon.

Soon after the Gulf War ended, some soldiers that had committed crimes during the war began arriving at the prison. War can bring out the best and worst in some soldiers, and many of the worst were sent to the USDB at Fort Leavenworth, including several that had committed serious crimes during the Vietnam War.

Although no U.S. soldier had been hanged at the prison since 1961, and that being for murder, some older inmates recalled knowing inmates from the World War II and Korean War eras. The most infamous hanging occurred in 1945 when 14 German POWs were hung for murdering three fellow prisoners. They were buried in the prison cemetery with their headstones facing away from the rise of the sun as a mark of dishonor.

The playing of reveille was another daily reminder of the dishonor associated with being incarcerated in a military prison. If an inmate was walking across the large open yard when it sounded, they had to stop and stand at the position of attention, but they did not have the privilege of rendering a military salute. Prison could be a cruel place.

Prisoner cemetery at USDB. *U.S. Army photo.*

LET THE GAMES BEGIN

Working at a prison could be fun, too. While at Fort Leavenworth, I was the NCOIC (NCO in charge) of the post honor guard, and we had the privilege of posting the colors at the birthday celebration of former president, Harry Truman, at the Truman Memorial in Independence, Missouri, a suburb of Kansas City. It was there that Sergeant Major of the Army (SMA) Richard A. Kidd "coined" me for my attention to detail.

The presenting of a unit coin is a leader's way of giving immediate recognition to someone for an outstanding service or act without going through official channels. As an NCO, receiving a coin from the SMA was a great personal honor and earned me an automatic outstanding rating on my annual evaluation. It was the second coin I had received. In 1986, SMA Glen E. Morrell, had coined me for earning runner-up in the *Army Material Command NCO of the Year* competition.

One of the most enjoyable duties at Fort Leavenworth was serving for three years as the NCOIC at the International Corrections Competition. Each year, the fort hosted 32 elite military corrections teams from around the world that competed for the coveted title. Each team consisted of 6-8 men and squared off in general knowledge, precision, land navigation, and physical fitness competitions. The quality of soldiering was outstanding and was a huge morale boost for corrections soldiers who rarely got to recognize the quality of fellow soldiers who do what they do.

It was rare when inmates and staff got together to have fun, but it did happen. Well, not necessarily all fun. The staff and the Licensed Parolee Unit (LPU) inmates at Leavenworth each had a flag football team, and the biggest brawls occurred when we played each other. They hated us, and we hated them. Flag football was anything but flag. We usually won because we were more disciplined, but the biased refs often allowed the final score to be closer than it should have been. Maybe they were partial to men in stripes—I don't know! Despite the fun, the games were brutal and could have been right out of the Hollywood movie, *The Longest Yard*. Our team was aptly named, *War Pigs*.

ANOTHER ANGEL

On May 15, 1991, my second angel, Danielle Patrice Cannon, joined our family. She was born at St. John's Hospital in Leavenworth, and unlike when Summer was born, I got to participate in her birth. Melinda delivered her without pain drugs, and I was reminded how strong she was when I held her little hand, and she squeezed so hard that she almost dropped me to my knees a few times. Having another girl was a blessing. When Danielle was born I was on a cloud, and I still am.

Melinda, Summer, and I were excited to welcome Danielle home, and the differences between Danielle and Summer were evident early on. Summer was reserved and quiet like her mom, but Danielle was every bit her father's daughter. As a toddler, she hated to stay with the post childcare people while Melinda was working. She would cry until Melinda came and got her, and then she just wanted to play. No sitting and watching cartoons for her. Just like her dad!

Above: Danielle Cannon.
Opposite page: Official DA
photo.

BACK TO SCHOOL

In early 1992, I attended the Military Police Advanced Non-Commissioned Officers Course (ANCOC) [pronounced A-NOK] at Fort McClellan. The 12-week course was the gateway to upper NCO leadership and had over 60 candidates. The course was challenging, but we were treated like upper level NCOs and not like recruits. Each man had a private room with a shower and bath, and most weekends were free, which was a godsend since my in-laws lived at Fort Rucker, and I visited them often. Spending weekends with them was my refuge and allowed me to get breaks from the rigors of the class and to eat a good meal.

About 30 percent of the course involved formal administrative training in the classroom, and we spent the rest of the time in the field practicing combat leadership skills and military police operations. The course included conducting drill and ceremony and learning advanced leadership techniques. Also, each candidate was required to teach a class in a tactical skill, and mine was

CANNON CARL K
90 09 19
990 95830

map reading.

With help from my father-in-law, I created a dramatic Power Point presentation that related map reading to life and death on the battlefield. That presentation changed everything for me at Leavenworth. Peers and other NCOs gave such strong reviews that I gained a lot of credibility. It turned out to be a game changer for me in my career progression.

During the latter part of the course, I got promoted. Prior to attending ANCOC, I had earned an associate degree and had made the E-7 promotion list but had not yet pinned on the rank. My best friend did the honors. Melinda drove down from Kansas and surprised me at the school. On March 1, 1992, she and the brigade commander pinned on my new rank—sergeant first class. My life would never be the same.

CHAPTER 9
My Show

When I finished ANCOC, I replaced a commissioned officer and became the first enlisted soldier and the first African American to become Chief of Military Police Investigations (MPI) in the history of the USDB. My investigative unit consisted of a joint service team of Army, Air Force, and Marine NCOs and serving in that capacity was the most fascinating and productive time of my career in law enforcement. I had earned it, but not everyone was happy.

My new position ran the gamut of police work and the pressure to succeed was enormous. Not only because of the great professional responsibility associated with the job, but because of the extra weight of being black. A lot of people counted on me not to be the last person that looked like me to hold that position. I was only accountable to the DOC commander, LTC Terry Bartlett, and to COL William Hart, commandant of the prison, and I had to be on my game. I expected near perfection from myself and from my staff, and I did not want reports going out with misspellings, incorrect grammar, and poor punctuation. This kind of strict attention to detail was good but also led to problems.

The Disciplinary Barracks security sergeant major was an old redneck who did not like me because I was black and because he did not get to pick the person for my job. He had placed his good ol' boys in my department before I started, and when I took over, I personally reviewed every report that came out of my office. This included redlining his favorite staff sergeant's reports and having him make corrections. The sergeant had not had that level of scrutiny before, so he went to the sergeant major complaining that I was excessive and out of control.

One morning after my number two, SSG Michael Rath, and I, had just returned from a meeting, the DOC sergeant major called me into his office and chewed me out. I stood at parade rest, which is the enlisted soldier's version of standing stiffly with one's arms behind their back, feet spread apart, and eyes looking forward, and took it. Although I wanted to bark back, I maintained my military bearing.

The sergeant major wanted me to react so he would have a reason to get rid of me, but I knew what he was trying to do and held my emotions. I did not like it, but I took that dressing-down like a man. Now it was my turn, but my immediate commander, LTC Bartlett, the DOC commander for the prison and one of the finest men I have ever met, was not available, so I immediately called LTC Will Stovall, the chief of staff for COL Hart. I went to his office and shared what had happened. The next morning when I got to work, the DOC sergeant major called me to his office, and there were boxes everywhere. He had gotten fired and reassigned to another battalion. That's when I knew that the Army I loved was about justice, and in my new position, I was determined to uphold it.

I worked out of 1 Base (of 7) in the bowels of the prison, aka *The Hole*. From this office we conducted investigations and interrogations, monitored listening and visual devices, and administered drug tests to the prison population and staff if necessary. We were federal investigators, and depending on the level of the crime, we supported the FBI, U.S. Marshals Service, the Criminal Investigation Division (CID), and the U.S. Postal Inspection Service. I had 15 subordinate investigators and two clerks, and our uniformed and civilian people worked in the prison and often in the community. Since most of the staff and prison population knew us, we also used confidential informants (CIs), and my office processed an average of over 1500 cases a year. My first case was almost too good to be true.

HIGH TIMES

Soon after I took over as chief of MPI, I got credit for discovering $20 million of marijuana growing on the installation near the prison farm. The unfenced farm was worked by trusted minimum security inmates that had been in long enough to earn lower security levels and more privileges. These inmates had progressed from the main facility, known as the *Castle*, down to Building 466, then to Building 465, and finally, to the minimum security Licensed Parolee Unit (LPU). Many of these inmates worked on the farm with little supervision, but over time, increasingly more of them were coming up hot on a drug test, and when we shook down their cells, we found nothing. We knew the drugs were coming in from somewhere, so I sent one of my new agents to investigate. On the way to the prison farm, he passed a large hemp field that had been created in WWII to produce hemp for large mooring ropes.

The inmates knew the untended field was out there growing wild, but we did not. No one had ever paid attention, and we were just lucky to find it. We immediately secured the field and later employed a battalion of MPs to go out and cut it down. The Engineers built a burn pit and threw the marijuana into it. We kept security overnight, and for two days my MP investigation team burned the pot. Everyone wore Scott air packs and was excluded from drug tests for six months. The find made me look like a genius, and I was awarded an impact Army Commendation Medal because of it. However, several inmates received additional sentences, and others inside were not so happy that their drug supply went up in smoke.

Every drug known to man was inside the walls of the USDB, and it was my job to find them. At one point,

The Castle   *U.S. Army photo*

we had a bad LSD problem because the drug was being placed on incoming postage stamps which made it difficult to detect. Staff was muling in some of the drugs, and others came in through the mail system. To combat this, we opened every piece of mail looking for drugs, and we used water pens to seal the letters back up. We usually did this on the midnight shift to have mail ready for the mail room to distribute each morning.

Other drugs were smuggled in by girlfriends, wives, and family members. They would seal the drugs in some type of container, and often the visitor would pass them to the inmate by mouth. The inmate would swallow the drugs and later defecate and recover them. Often, we would be watching and intervene. We even had drugs passed in infant's diapers. All cases resulted in additional charges in federal court.

Steroids were also a problem. We had an inmate powerlifting team that was incredible. These guys were beasts and we allowed them to get protein and vitamin supplements to increase muscle size and strength, but some smuggled in various illegal anabolic steroids to gain an advantage in competition.

The team competed regionally and had a weight room in the prison. In my position, I sometimes worked out with the inmates to get intel, and although I suspected some were using steroids, I did not push the issue unless we found them in a shakedown. The powerlifters were some of the nicest and most helpful inmates, and I had fewer problems with them because they did not want to lose lifting privileges. My problem was with the guys who robbed the lifters' cells while they were at the gym. There was no honor among thieves.

UNDERCOVER

Most of the intelligence gathering work in the USDB was done by cultivating confidential informants that traded information for favorable treatment, reduction of sentence, or other incentives. MPI work also reached outside of the prison and included investigations into active duty soldiers that were suspected of committing violations or crimes either on their own, or for, or with, inmates. I worked dozens of staff misconduct cases—many of them criminal. It was important because ensuring the integrity of the staff was the highest priority for the effective functioning of a prison.

Inmates have nothing but time on their hands, and their mission is to gain "wins" in their minds and to elevate their status in prison society. An inmate who can get sex from a female or male staff member is a hero because they undermine prison authority, referred to as "the man." Once this happens, the inmate uses the illegal contact to coerce the staff into giving them preferential treatment or getting them something they want, including drugs or other contraband.

Some inmates are predators and study the moods of staff to find and exploit their vulnerabilities. If a person is having trouble in their marriage, has low self-esteem, or is lonely, these inmates seize on this and begin grooming them. I once caught a female staff member who was sleeping with inmates, and that behavior made every female a target. I even had inmates that had sex with female staff in our prison church, and some of these inmates were serving life sentences for murder. These inmates had no sense of shame or moral conviction and were experts at convincing staff that they were victims. Some of the naive and gullible staff even developed Stockholm Syndrome and began feeling sorry for the inmates and believing that the prison was a place of refuge and comfort for them. Not so.

Another CI came to me and reported that a female staff member was having sex with a former inmate who she met while working in the prison. This type of relationship was strictly prohibited by prison staff, and based on that tip, we conducted a night surveillance outside the soldier's off-post residence that resulted in an arrest. We watched her come out with the former inmate and get into her car. We then followed and watched as he drove her to the prison and dropped her off at work. And that is when we went to work. Later, I questioned her, and when she lied, I confronted her with the facts. I was good at getting staff to confess, and sadly, her military career was ruined.

Work details were another opportunity for inmates to manipulate staff or civilians. We had a Disciplinary Barracks car wash located outside the prison, and we caught several inmates and active duty soldiers having sex with civilians. The inmates often groomed the staff inside the prison and coordinated a brief encounter inside a car, in a restroom, or wherever they could steal a few minutes. Most soldiers that we caught were court-martialed and dishonorably discharged, and the inmates, although punished, climbed another dirty rung up the prison ladder.

WHAT A RIOT
In the early spring of 1992, the prison administration, in all its wisdom, implemented stricter rules on

smoking, banned the wearing of colored headbands, prohibited the speaking of a non-English language, and eliminated inmate worker pay. This infuriated the inmates. To make matters worse, the Rodney King beating had occurred a year earlier, and racial tension and anger were boiling.

I learned through CIs that the inmates were planning a peaceful sit down in opposition to the new policies. 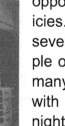 They had planned it several times over a couple of months, and I spent many nights working intel with no results. But one night around 11 o'clock, I received a call from my duty investigator asking me to come to the prison. When I arrived, I learned that the entire guard force had been mobilized to report to battalion. The minimum custody inmates housed in Buildings 465 and 466 were outside talking smack, pissing on the steps, and daring us to do something about it. Because of the volatile environment, prison staff is unarmed, always outnumbered, and must pick their battles wisely, so the guards had vacated their posts, but I walked through that courtyard with about 20 angry inmates milling around me. I was mad, too, but I didn't say much and went on to the *Castle*. When I arrived, two of the housing wings were in chaos. Inmates had set fires in one and were trashing the other, so I got an overview and we devised a plan of action. Guard Commander Sergeant First Class (SFC) Mendez and I went straight into the 7 Wing housing unit and got on the PA. "Lock down!" I yelled. "Lock down!"

I heard voices. "Boss Cannon—is that you?"

"It's me," I replied with authority. "What the hell is going on?"

"We're going to quit."

And they did. This was supposed to be the honor unit of medium security with more privileges, and the inmates' next step would have been to Building 466 and even more freedoms, but these knuckleheads had thrown pool balls through the windows, smashed televisions, and had busted in and taken over the guard cage where the controlled medicines were kept. They broke into the counselors' offices and burned most of the case files, too. It was crazy! And then we had to

Opposite page and above; the guard cage. U.S. Army photos.

devise another plan for the other wing since the media was there filming down from the hill overlooking the prison. The inmates had barricaded the entrance and destroyed the unit causing about $50,000 damage. They had also spray-painted pornographic images and the Rodney King battle cry, "No Justice No Peace" everywhere, and had tormented the weaker prisoners. We knew who did what because we used CIs, and it was no secret that wrath would come to that unit. But we waited to avoid injury to staff and to innocent inmates.

The next day, the inmates laid down because we waited them out instead of taking them by force. We shut off the power and the water and made it miserable and as primitive as we could. The toilets were overflowing in the dark, and the smell was horrible. Moreover, the inmates had not eaten and had little to drink, so it did not take long for them to quit.

At Leavenworth, no inmate had access to the outside world because they were confined inside the yard

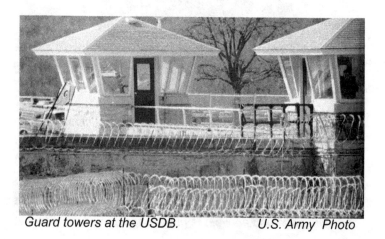

Guard towers at the USDB.   *U.S. Army Photo*

within the prison walls. Inside those walls we had towers, and inside those towers, we had M-16s. And behind those M-16s, we had experts in their use. There was never a threat to the outside world, but the world didn't know that.

Eventually, all culpable inmates were charged and convicted, and the Disciplinary Hearing Officer (DHO)—the judge inside the prison—meted out internal punishment. Most were court-martialed, but some were sent to *The Hole*, and others were placed on restriction. Anyone that had a negative interaction was punished to the fullest extent of the law. We could not let anyone get away with anything or more riots would have occurred. We prosecuted over 500 cases associated with the uprising.

NO ESCAPE
The highlight of my service at the USDB was foiling two escape attempts. The first occurred on January 22, 1992 shortly before I attended ANCOC. I was already serving as the MPI chief as a promotable staff sergeant when a confidential source relayed information to one of my new investigators through his CI that several inmates serving life sentences for murder were planning an escape. The CI happened to be going to his cell one evening when he met three inmates returning after preparing for the attempt. Although the inmates confided in the CI and told him of their plan, they advanced the escape date just in case he talked.

We brought the CI in and he explained everything. I immediately briefed my superiors and consulted with the Judge Advocate General (JAG) officer. Everyone agreed that we had to allow the inmates to initiate the plan and to catch them in the act to prove intent and to charge them with attempted escape.

Acting on timely information, SSG Rath and I reconnoitered the catwalk on 8 Tier where the escape was supposed to occur and where we planned to catch the inmates trying to escape. First, we went to 4 Wing into the catwalks and sneaked to the 8 Tier roof, where we found clothing with no dust, which indicated that the inmates had recently hidden them there to use during the escape. We also found that the duct work had been manipulated to allow access, so we entered it and secretly crawled down to 1 Tier to where the inmates would come out. We then found tools and other evidence that they would take the civilian boiler room operator hostage, steal his pickup truck, and leave with him through the west gate. Once outside the prison, the inmates planned to kill him.

After we reconnoitered each location in the escape plan, we set the trap. We assembled a squad of men, including the USDB command sergeant major, and moved to a capture spot and waited. As planned, we confronted the inmates in the tunnel under the 1 Tier catwalk, and although they tried to run back to their cells, we pulled them back out on 3 Tier and arrested them. The look on their faces was priceless.

Following the arrest, we feared for the CI's safety, so another investigator and I put him on a plane and escorted him across country to a detention facility at Fort Lewis, Washington. We each carried a snub nose .38 pistol onto the plane, and we were seated in the last row away from most civilians. When we arrived in

Cell tiers at the USDB.

U.S. Army photo

nearby Tacoma, a rental car was waiting for us. On the way to Fort Lewis, the inmate asked to stop at a gas station to wash his face, and when we pulled in, we spotted a local police officer fighting with a suspect at a Burger King across the street. We told the inmate to stand down while we rushed to help the officer. When we arrived, I flashed my credentials and shouted, "Do you want help?"

"Yes!" Blurted the officer.

We then helped tackle the suspect, but unexpectedly, the inmate also jumped on him while we were trying to cuff him. The officer was grateful, but he never knew that federal inmate had aided in the arrest. Had he known, the inmate could have faced additional charges and it would have been embarrassing for us, but the officer assumed that we were all MPs from Fort Lewis. The investigator and I chewed the inmate out good, but we did appreciate that he had helped with the arrest and with the capture of three murderers.

We delivered the inmate to Fort Lewis to hide him, but a few months later, we returned to Washington and flew him back to testify against the inmates who had tried to escape. The informant got released early, and the inmates got life—plus a little extra. Mission accomplished.

Several months later, we foiled another escape attempt when we caught two men trying to get on top of the commandant's house through the roof of the vocational center attached to the house. They had cut a hole in the roof of the vocational center and were going to lower themselves onto the commandant's house and slip away. Thanks to information supplied by a reliable CI, we stopped that attempt, too. After that, escape attempts reduced dramatically.

MARRY GO AROUND

Working inside a prison was dangerous, loud, and dirty, but my life outside the walls was beautiful. On March 24, 1993, Melinda and I renewed our marriage vows at the Post Chapel, the oldest chapel west of the Mississippi River. My lovely bride and I said, "I do" again 10 years to the day that we were married in an Alabama courthouse by a simple justice of the peace. It was a grand affair. Our parents and dozens of family and friends came in, and we went through the whole wedding process like it was our first time. Melinda wore a white wedding dress, and I wore my Army dress blue uniform, and the bridesmaids and groomsmen were decked out in full attire. Every detail was perfect, and if it wasn't, we didn't notice. We were blessed to have the people we loved come from near and far to celebrate, and even more blessed to reaffirm our commitment to each other in a house of God filled with joy and laughter, and to leave His sanctuary under an arch of sabers more in love than the first day we met.

Melinda and me leaving the chapel under an arch of sabers.

ABOUT FACE

During my tenure as Chief of Investigations, I devised a criminal information network and an escape profile that contributed to my staff being the first in five consecutive administrations without a successful escape despite numerous attempts. I was good at keeping people locked up, but by late May 1994, I was ready for a change and a new chapter in my career.

I'd had enough prison life and was getting burned out. For an enlisted soldier, I had tremendous power, but also enormous responsibility. I was at the prison more than I was at home—and when I was at home, my thoughts were at the prison. I had worked so hard and long to get to the top that I was having trouble finding balance. Deep down, I knew just where to look. I had requested Drill Instructor (DI) School because it was a wise career move. I was 34 years old and already an E-7 when I applied. It was rare for a soldier of my age and rank because of the difficulty of the course and because of the rigors of the job. Being a DI was a younger man's game, but it was the fastest way to achieve my goal of becoming a command sergeant major (E-9), the highest enlisted rank in the United States Army.

CHAPTER 10
Back to Basic

FORT LEONARD WOOD

"Front leaning rest position—move!" shouted the drill instructor, clearly delineating the preparatory command from the command of execution.

The motivated candidates of our class dropped into the familiar "push up" position ready to knock them out while the DI glared into the early morning sun.

"Ready—exercise!" He began to count. "One-two-three-ONE! One-two-three-TWO!" And so on, until everyone reached muscle failure. We were exhausted, but he was just getting started.

"On your backs! Ready—move!"

Ten minutes into Day 1 of Drill Sergeant School, I wondered why in hell anyone would want to endure basic training a second time—especially in the sweltering summer heat of western Missouri. I chuckled to myself and squeezed out another sit-up, my hip flexor and abdominal muscles burning with each rep. In my position at the prison, I had to train harder, work out harder, drill harder, and have my guys be better than everyone else. I loved to work, I loved to compete, and even more, I loved a challenge. The tougher, the better. Over the next nine weeks, I would not be disappointed.

I weighed about 250 pounds going in and scored 297 out 300 on my qualifying Army Physical Fitness Test (APFT), but the course smoked me from the start. It was designed to replicate the basic training process that recruits experience and to teach potential drill instructors (DIs) how to better train them in the Army Way. The physical aspect of DI School was relatively easy for me. I started a routine at DI school called the "10-minute rule." Every hour when we were given a break between classes, I made my squad drop and do as many push-ups as they could do in 10 minutes, and at graduation we had one of the highest APFT scores in DI School history.

The course was the most academically challenging environment I had ever experienced. We had to know the Army Regulation (AR) manuals by heart, and we had to memorize and perform 147 drills while enduring the same harassment that recruits did. The space between the hangers in our wall lockers had to be so many inches apart, and a hanging thread on our uniform was criminal in the eyes of the instructors. Each infraction, regardless of how small, was egregious and punished in some diabolical way, such as cleaning a latrine with a toothbrush. I was used to being in charge, and although the younger and less experienced E-5 and E-6 instructors had treated me just like a private, I relished the stress they put me through because it made me a better leader.

I survived DI School, but it pushed me like no other. I dropped 30 pounds and was in the best shape of my life. I scored 364 on the extended physical fitness scale and received the *Leadership Award* given by my peers.

But the greatest honor came a week before graduation after I had passed my last drill and academic phase of the course and fitted for the coveted "Round Brown" drill instructor's campaign hat known as a *Smokey Bear* hat. That meant that I would graduate and that I had completed one of the most difficult schools in the Army. When I received the hat, it finally sunk in that I belonged to a unique brotherhood and that I had accomplished something outstanding. It was a dream come true and better than any medal I ever got.

Receiving the Drill Sergeant Identification Badge bearing the motto, *This We'll Defend*, was just as meaningful, because I knew what I had endured to earn it. More important, the motto symbolized the tradition and responsibility associated with birthing new soldiers and making them patriotic young men and women.

There is a solemnity to putting on the hat and wearing the DI badge. People's lives are entrusted to drill sergeants, and it requires a serious mindset and physical and mental stamina to take 200 raw civilians, instill discipline, form them into a cohesive military unit, and put them in harm's way.

It was nice being done with the course and basking in the glow of having completed one of the most rigorous schools in the military, but better that my family could attend. Although my dad had never attended any of my football games or athletic contests, he surprised me and came to my graduation from Drill Instructor School. It meant the world to me. I had spent most of my life seeking his approval and trying to prove to him that I was a man. To look at the pride on his face that day, I think I passed the test.

ON THE TRAIL

Melinda and I returned to Fort Leavenworth to wrap things up. I had received orders to return to Fort McClellan to serve as a drill instructor with A Company, 787th Military police Battalion, but my orders were deferred until my replacement at the prison was named. Finally, my spot was filled, and the Cannon family said a bittersweet goodbye to Fort Leavenworth.

Since we did the move ourselves, I reported to McClellan to settle into our military housing while Melinda and the girls went to Enterprise city outside of Fort Rucker to stay with her parents until arrangements were complete. Two weeks later, Melinda's parents brought her and the girls to Fort McClellan. We were almost home.

Melinda, Summer, and me at my graduation from Drill Sergeant School.

I was excited about being a drill sergeant, but I was nervous about being a senior drill instructor without having any time "on the trail," a term used to denote field service as a DI. I expressed my concern to my battalion sergeant major and suggested that I work a training cycle before becoming senior drill, but he said, "I don't care—as long as you're wearing those rockers, you're my senior drill sergeant. End of story."

To have somebody come in and take the lead like that was dicey, but the team of drills we had embraced me. I had a reputation coming in, and I arrived like the hard-ass everyone expected me to be. I took care of my drill sergeants, learned the trade, and did the drills that I did not have to do, which earned the respect of the more seasoned drill sergeants. Leadership is willing to do what one does not have to do but leading by example is getting on the ground and getting dirty with everyone else. I even ran the fast group in PT to set myself apart from my peers.

As the senior drill instructor, I directly supervised 14 subordinate instructors, and directed the training of more than 200 soldiers in basic soldiering skills and law enforcement and prison/correctional officer duties during a 16-week course of instruction. My duties entailed scheduling all training and directing drill sergeants in the training of recruits in weapons qualifications, physical fitness, police operations/administration, prison operations/administration, interpersonal communications skills, civil/criminal law classes, and in all practical exercises associated with recruit training. I was also responsible for evaluating the progress and suitability of police/correctional officer candidates and for overseeing the operational budget. Thinking back, I don't know when—or if—I slept.

I did not have the advantage of having previously trained a single recruit, but to lead a unit from Day Zero and to watch them evolve into soldiers as a unit was crazy good. When recruits start a cycle, they watch veteran soldiers march by and wonder if they can ever do that. Sixteen weeks later, they do not recognize their former selves and have become the soldiers they admired. Witnessing the personal and professional transformation of so many young men and women inspired me. Pride and motivation were contagious, and I wanted to share it.

During one training cycle, Melinda's father joined us for Thanksgiving at McClellan. It was his first time there, and I invited him and my mother-in-law to join Melinda and me to eat Thanksgiving dinner at the unit with my new soldiers. When I stepped on the patio outside of the chow hall where the soldiers were assembled, a private yelled, "At Ease!" signaling for everyone to go parade rest as a sign of respect to an NCO. The soldiers stood up straight with their legs shoulder width apart and snapped their hands behind their backs.

A few moments later, my father-in-law arrived, and I called the area "to attention" for him, an honor reserved for officers. My father-in-law was impressed, and I swelled with pride at the precision of my soldiers for honoring him in this way. The act made this senior drill sergeant feel like a four-star general, and I wanted every young man and woman to feel the same sense of respect that I felt. The pride they displayed was not forced rather earned through teamwork and shared hardship. During graduation, it was on full display as proud parents watched their child transition to adulthood and become part of something greater than themselves. Everyone should experience that sense of individual and shared accomplishment and be part of the rising tide that floats all boats.

END OF THE TRAIL

I only conducted two basic training cycles before I decided to leave the Army. Several months earlier, the military began offering early out retirement to qualified soldiers in most military occupational specialties (MOS), but my MOS was excluded. When the Army finally extended the early out option to soldiers in my MOS, I took it. However, not without employing the same due diligence I had used in my 15-year career as a military policeman. I gathered information, asked questions, and sought counsel from those I loved and trusted. I even spoke with retired NCOs and asked what they would do. Given the same option, everyone said they would have taken it. Each had served for 30 years in the military and had to find another career after retiring, but by the time they had retired, they were too old for certain jobs in their civilian career field.

I loved corrections, but I was coming up on 35, and I had heard that a new federal prison was being built about 10 miles from my hometown. Working there for five years would boost my military retirement to that of a military retiree with 20 years of service, and even without the prison job, my family and I would still enjoy the federal health and educational benefits that I had earned in the military.

Family also played a huge factor in my decision to retire. Summer was in middle school, and

A final salute.
U.S. Army photo

The Cannons

Danielle had not started kindergarten, so the transition would be easy for them, and the prospect of not moving again appealed to all of us, especially Melinda. Moreover, Dad had offered to sell us his house in Peoria.

That was the math that went into my decision to leave the military I loved. You can eat, drink, and love Uncle Sam all you want, but one day he is going to tell you to get out of the way and to leave such work to the next man. If I didn't take the offer now, it would not be long before I aged out and someone replaced me.

On June 30, 1995, I retired from the United States Army with 15 years of active duty service. I still loved the Army when I left but retiring early was simply a career decision—the best I ever made.

CHAPTER 11
Coming Home

I have dreamed of making a better life for myself, my family, and my community in every job I have ever had, but I did not expect the genesis of my next career to begin with a chance meeting in an outdoor prison barber shop at Fort Leavenworth, Kansas.

Prior to leaving for Drill Sergeant School in June 1994, I was getting a high-and-tight haircut when Bernie Huggins, a lieutenant at the civilian U.S. Penitentiary at Leavenworth, arrived and sat in a chair across from me. Our daughters knew each other, so we had a connection. He had just received a promotion to leave the penitentiary and to become the disciplinary hearing officer (DHO) at a federal prison being built in Pekin, Illinois about 10 miles from my hometown. I was unaware that a prison was being built there, but I mentioned that Pekin was in my backyard and that with him being black, suggested that he might want to live in Peoria instead. We exchanged numbers, and he said if I wanted to come over to the Bureau of Prisons (BOP), to give him a call. I filed the conversation away and paid the inmate barber. I lightly ran my hand over my head and checked his work in a hand mirror. The popular cut met military regulation and looked good on the streets of Fort Leavenworth, but would it play in Peoria?

THE BIG BOP

I shelved the idea of working for the BOP when the Army did not include my MOS in the first round of the early out retirement program, but when they finally did offer it, I recalled my conversation with Bernie and began considering his offer. I knew I could do it, but I was in the middle of my second training cycle at Fort McClellan, and the window to accept the early out was closing. After completing the training cycle, I called Bernie and asked if there were still openings in Pekin. He said there were and sent me an extensive application that I turned in before leaving McClellan.

Once I got confirmation that I could get in, I arranged an interview and flew to Peoria, where I was met by my dad. In preparation for the interview, I employed the same work ethic and attention to detail that had served me well in the military, particularly when I appeared before military boards. I left nothing to chance. Dad and I timed out everything so I would not be late or miss my interview. I had him drive me to the prison because I wanted to know the precise route to take, where to park, and how long it took to walk from the parking lot to the entrance. A panel consisting of the prison captain, a lieutenant, and an associate warden interviewed me while I was still on active military duty, and I knocked it out the park.

I returned to Fort McClellan about a week later and formally received a job offer from the Federal Bureau of Prisons to become a corrections officer at FCI-Pekin. With an offer on the table, I quickly submitted my official retirement request, received approval, and began out-processing from the Army.

THE RIVER CITY

Melinda and I barely contained our excitement as we rolled along Interstate Route 74 toward Peoria. Summer and young Danielle sat in the backseat of our black Nissan Pathfinder doing whatever sisters do when we crossed the Murray Baker Bridge spanning the Illinois River. A wave of nostalgia swept over me, which was unusual since I had not allowed myself such feelings in a long time. The familiar skyline had always welcomed me home on military leave and symbolically waved goodbye when I glanced in the rear view mirror on the way out of town to my next duty assignment. I loved coming back to Peoria and hated leaving even more, but this trip had a feeling of permanence about it. Melinda felt it, too. It was good to be home.

BACK TO WORK

I had every intention of being a warden one day and retiring from the BOP. I felt like I was one of the best correctional officers in the military, and I was going to transition that mindset into the civilian world. I had taken 30 days terminal leave from the military so I could start at my new job almost immediately, and we had barely settled in at my father's house when I reported to work at the prison as a GS-6 federal employee.

My first day on the job I reported at 7:30 a.m. for an 8 o'clock shift. I always arrived 30 minutes early wherever I went, and most of the prison staff could not believe I would do that, and since I had not yet purchased a uniform from the prison, I wore clothes that lined up with the standard BOP uniform; white shirt, gray slacks, and black shoes.

As with many former soldiers fresh out of the service, the first few months of civilian life can be difficult. After 15 years of regimented military life, I was thrust into a new, undisciplined world consisting of people of many different shapes and sizes with no mandatory physical training program to ensure that BOP employees were in shape and fit to do the job. It reminded me of the old career specialists in the Army with almost 20 years of time in service who were one or two steps above a private and had no desire to progress. The military was a 24-hour job, and there was always something else to do and some way to improve readiness. I don't recall ever working less than a 12-hour shift at Leavenworth, and I would do that for 15-20 consecutive days. Drill sergeant duty was even more intense. We operated in a high-stress environment and often only got two or three hours of sleep a night. I was used to working long days, long weeks, and long months. Doing eight hours at work and not doing something at the end of the day was crazy to me. My worth ethic would not allow it, and I felt guilty not doing more than the minimum. Fellow workers at FCI-Pekin attributed my gung ho attitude to being a rookie and believed that eventually I would come around. That was not in my DNA. And neither was Pekin—to begin with.

MY KIND OF TOWN

"Mom!" shouted a young boy from inside his house. "There's a nigger at the door selling candy!"

I stood on the boy's front porch two feet away unable to speak. I was about 10 years old and he was no more than six, and what he said from behind a screen door stopped me cold in my tracks. A guy we knew in Peoria had come into our neighborhood in the summer looking for kids to sell candy bars, and since I had done it before, a couple friends and I got permission from our moms to go with him and to sell in different neighborhoods to make some extra money. We wound up in a nice residential area in Pekin, and it was the first house I tried. It was also the last. I was done.

Growing up, I was scared of Pekin. It had a reputation for not being open toward blacks; one that I had experienced firsthand. It was no secret that it was once a "Sundown Town," and that legend told of a billboard outside of town warning that anyone who was black needed to be "out of town before the sun goes down." I remember playing high school football games there, and some of the students and adult fans would scream racial slurs and pelt our bus with rocks and soda cans on the way out of town. The treatment was even worse if we won the game. Later, I learned that Pekin once had been the home of the regional director of the Ku Klux Klan who oversaw 40 counties in Illinois.

Pekin was strange in other ways too. It was founded in the late 1820s and named for Peking, the imperial capital city of China (now Beijing), which town elders considered a sister city because they believed it was on the exact opposite side of the world. Sometime in the 1930s, the high school adopted the "Chink" as their mascot, and the sports teams became the "Pekin Chinks," a name that many, especially Chinese, viewed as pejorative and demeaning.

I recall hearing about Pekin's "Chink Rink," a popular roller skating rink, while attending high school, and although the name was catchy, it seemed a little racist to me even at a time when Peoria and Pekin each had a *Sambo's* restaurant. Finally, the school changed its mascot to the "Dragons" in 1981, a good first step at helping change the city's image.

BACK TO PRISON

FCI-Pekin was a medium-high security installation and housed approximately 1100 male and 250 female inmates. The men's side of the house was standard, but the women's prison was designated a federal camp and had no contact with the men. The level of security at the camp was light with no fences, and the camp inmates did all the maintenance. The females stayed in housing units, and each inmate had a bunk, a half wall, and a half locker.

In direct comparison, FCI-Pekin and the USDB at Fort Leavenworth were worlds apart. The USDB was eight stories tall, old, dark, and dirty. FCI-Pekin was two stories tall, new, well-lighted, and clean. The USDB was steamy in the summers and cold in the winters.

Pekin was air conditioned and comfortable all year around. The USDB was military and Pekin was civilian. Despite the physical differences between the prisons, both housed people who had broken the law and whose crimes were serious enough that society punished them by taking away their individual freedom to protect the

public. Right or wrong, fair or unfair, it was not the prison system's function to determine innocence or guilt, only to house and care for the inmates according to the law for the duration of their sentence.

A couple of weeks into my employment, I attended a one-week basic training for corrections personnel at the Federal Correctional Officer Academy Training in Artesia, New Mexico. The academy also trained personnel for the Border Patrol and for the U.S. Marshals Service. Although the training was good, it wasn't anything I hadn't experienced in the military.

WHAT'S MY NAME!

At Leavenworth, inmates called the officers by their rank and the enlisted guards "sarge" or "boss." At Pekin, the inmates called me "C.O.," for "Correctional Officer." I liked the sound of it because it rolled off the prisoners' lips and made me feel like I was in charge, but I was not power-tripping. I had a decent physique and was the talk of the prison when I arrived, but I worked my butt off to prove that I was the real deal. A lot of people were looking closely at me because I had high recommendations from the military, but like with drill school, high expectations came with it.

My trainer at Pekin wanted to show me all the short-cuts, but I had already been that route in the military. I made it clear that since I was a rookie and did not know how everything worked at Pekin, I wanted him to show me everything that I was supposed to do from A-Z and how to do it. But no shortcuts. No easy way out.

A QUIET RIOT

My first several months at the prison were routine, but on October 21, 1995, we had a minor riot, officially called a "disturbance," that coincided with similar disturbances at prisons in Talladega, Alabama; Allenwood, Pennsylvania; Memphis, Tennessee; and at Greenville, Illinois. Inmates at these institutions protested the recent congressional vote that refused to lower drug sentences regarding crack cocaine compared to offenses related to powder cocaine. Possession of five grams of crack resulted in the same sentence as a person convicted of possessing 5000 grams of powder. The inequity of the policy was magnified since most of the people convicted on crack were black. It was systemic racism at its worst.

Two of our eight Pekin housing units rioted. Inmates threw washers and dryers at us barricading the entrance and destroyed whatever they could. We responded by shooting inmates with beanbags and pepper balls and eventually put down the uprising. We then moved the instigators and most violent inmates to the Special Housing Unit (SHU). Although I did not have enough time at the prison to be on the Special Operations Response Team (SORT), I had extensive experience working *The Hole* at Leavenworth, so the prison assigned me to the SHU to help.

Every type of thug known to man came through the SHU during this disturbance, and one especially combative inmate arrived from the housing unit via the five-man Disturbance Control Team (DCT). He was fighting back and giving the team a run for their money, so I jumped in and helped them take him to the floor. After subduing the inmate and holding him down until he was compliant, the team slowly got off the inmate and then stood in a tight circle around him while he laid on the floor. The DCT men were sweating and chomping at the bit hoping to get another crack at the guy, and it would only take one sudden move or insult from the prisoner to re-ignite the situation.

Sensing that the team wanted to give him a serious whipping, I began the process of stripping him out of his FCI-issued khaki uniform in military fashion to potentially save his life.

"Get on your knees and remain quiet," I ordered.

The prisoner complied, and then I fired off a litany of commands in rapid succession.

"Give me your shirt." He took it off.

"Give me your t-shirt.

Unbutton your pants.

Pull them down to your knees." He did.

"Remain on your knees and remove one leg from your pants.

Do the same thing with your other leg.
Remove your underwear one knee at a time.
Do the same thing with the other leg.
Open your mouth." I checked inside.
"Tongue up.
Tongue down.
Tongue to the left.
Tongue to the right.
Tilt your head toward me.
Run your fingers through your hair from the back of your head forward toward the floor."
I checked his ears.
"Head up.
Look left.
Look right.
Look at me."
His eyes were cold.
"Arms out east and west.
Bring them to me—palms up.
Flip them over—palms down.
Hands back to your side.
Lift up your sac." He had done it before.
"Bend over and put your head on the floor.
Grab your butt with both hands.
Spread your butt cheeks.
Now back on your knees!"
All clear. No weapons. No contraband. The inmate was seething. He remained kneeling and naked, and I informed him that he would put on his SHU-issued clothes in the same way he got undressed.
"Remain on your knees and await my instructions!" I barked. The prisoner complied.

"Put on your underwear!
Put on your t-shirt!
Put on your pants!
Put on your shirt.
Put on your shoes.
Now stand up!"

The prisoner glared at me, and if looks could kill I'd be dead. He was so mad at me he was shaking, and he stayed mad at me until I left the prison, but that strip search probably saved him from a physical beat down at minimum and likely prevented him from being charged with violence toward staff and receiving more prison time. I received a lot of praise from peers and superiors for my demonstrated abilities. None of them had ever seen a prisoner stripped out while still on his knees. I believe we did an excellent job quelling the "disturbance" and keeping it quiet.

The riot lasted a couple of days, and although it made little ripple in the news, I was credited for my role

and later named the *FCI-Pekin Rookie of the Year* and promoted.

After I had a year in at the prison, I tried out for SORT. To make the team, candidates had to run two miles in under 15 minutes, successfully negotiate a timed obstacle course, dead climb a 30-foot rope (the most difficult part) and pass a panel interview.

Having been out of the Army for only a year, I was still in great shape and easily made the team. SORT was the civilian version of the military Special Response Team (SRT) that we had at Fort Leavenworth. Although we did fewer forced cell removals of dangerous or non-compliant inmates than we did at the USDB, we stayed busy transporting prisoners by bus, escorting them to court, and training in hostage rescue and sniper operations.

Everyone on our five-man team wore a black paramilitary uniform consisting of boots, helmet, and riot shield, and had a specific number and responsibility during a cell extraction. We went in as a team—and there was nothing nice about it. As one of the larger, more physical, and newest members of the team, I had the #1 position. My job was to rush the inmate, pin him against the well or the bed, and take control of his head. The #2 guy then pulled the inmate's right arm away from the body while the #3 guy pulled the left arm away. The #4 man pulled the lower right leg away and the #5 man did the same with the left leg. Most of us weighed over 250 pounds, which meant the inmate had over a half ton of motivated, energized men on top of him trying NOT to be gentle. The intent was not just to remove the inmate from the cell, but to discourage him, and anyone who was watching or listening, to appreciate how stupid and painful it was to resist. All the while, another guard taped the extraction to ensure the safety of the inmate and that procedures were being followed.

My nickname at the prison was, "Thunder." And it fit. When I took a housing unit, I assembled the inmates during mail call and loudly put out my rules. If the inmates wanted to be left alone, they would follow those rules. This also set the tone with colleagues and established my limits, which I believe prevented fellow team members from doing things to inmates that they might have regretted and contributed to them following proper procedure. After what had occurred in Cell 138, I promised myself that I would do things the right way and be a role model for others wherever I went. Pekin was the perfect place.

Bureau of Prisons
Disturbance Control Training Class #803
Federal Law Enforcement Training Center
January 27, 1998 - February 5, 1998
Artesia, New Mexico

Full Cannon

CHAPTER 12
Email Me

With the addition of the new prison in 1994, community leaders in Pekin were working hard to change the city's image. Approximately 90 percent of the inmate population were minority and so were 15 percent of the guards and prison staff. Although FCI-Pekin warden, David Helman, had brought in several African-American and Hispanic staff, most elected to live in Peoria because of Pekin's reputation. Several staff had been pulled over by the Pekin Police and believed that they were profiled because of race. At the time, only a couple of black families lived in the city, and tension was increasing. Something had to be done.

Helman was an amazing man and an effective go-between with the prison and the city. He understood that social progress was rooted in education, and for it to bear fruit, seeds must be planted in fertile ground at the proper time. And at what better time to begin than Black History Month. Every U.S. President since Gerald Ford believed the same.

On January 30, 1996, President Bill Clinton proclaimed February 1996 as "National African American History Month" and called upon "Government officials, educators in schools, colleges, universities, and libraries, and all the people of the United States to observe this month with appropriate ceremonies, activities, and programs that raise awareness of African American history and invite further inquiry into this area of study."

A few weeks before Black History Month, Warden Helman e-mailed me and other members of the prison Black Affairs Committee and challenged us to engage the community during the upcoming Black History Month. Pekin was ready—and so were we.

SEEDS OF HOPE

The theme of Black History Month for 1996 was to recognize black women and to celebrate their notable contributions to our country. Since I was experienced and comfortable working in schools as an MP in the Officer Friendly program, I proposed that we focus on a program designed for primary and middle school children. The warden agreed.

I chose Harriet Tubman, an escaped slave and the most famous conductor on the Underground Railroad, a network of routes and safe houses taken by southern slaves escaping north before and during the Civil War. Tubman made 13 known trips back into the South and led some 70 slaves to freedom. I shared her story with students at Irving Grade School and Edison Junior High in a way they had not seen.

Dressed in my prison uniform and wearing a wig, I crouched down low and jumped from desk-to-desk depicting how a slave might crouch and hide at stops along the Underground Railroad. My dramatics broke the ice with students and opened their minds to hearing what I had to say. It was also funny watching a 250-pound black man in a wig hopping around the room! But the important and relatable message was that Tubman and other conductors on the Underground Railroad did not do it alone, and that most who courageously hid, fed, and assisted her and others to freedom with great risk to themselves and their families, did not look like her. I explained that while her famous exploits were celebrated by blacks, she could not have done what she did without the help of many white people, and that all people who were part of the Underground Railroad deserve to share in her legacy.

National Portrait Gallery, Smithsonian Institution
Harriet Tubman

The program was well received and the students at both schools were wonderful, but because I was in uniform, the kids wanted to hear more about the prison where I worked and what it was like working with thieves, rapists, drug dealers, gang bangers, and cold-blooded killers, than about a dead lady from the past. Prison culture fascinated them, and many saw "doing time" behind bars as a badge of honor, but I knew it was a badge of dishonor—a permanent mark that every convict would trade for one hour of freedom.

STRAIGHT TALK

Teaching kids about Harriet Tubman and the Underground Railroad was important, but it likely would not save their lives or prevent them from going to prison. My new mission was clear, and what had happened in Cell 138 seven years ago took on new meaning. Although I was a correctional officer charged with keeping people locked up, I had to do more to help keep them out.

Mike Illuzi, the principal at Irving Grade School, and Stan Fitzanko, the principal at Edison, invited me back to give another presentation, and I did a modified version of *Scared Straight*, a juvenile program created in the late 1970s to shock and scare kids into staying out of jail. I called my version, *Straight Talk*, and incorporated it into the prison's school outreach program.

I solicited the help of resident experts, specifically, the inmates of FCI-Pekin. Contrary to widespread belief, most inmates care about the youth and do not want them traveling down the same destructive path they did. They would not wish their world upon their enemies and wanted to share how their attitudes and actions led to prison. Most would say to our youth, "Please don't do what I did." And they meant it.

Understanding that reality, I offered kids a unique message from a different perspective and set of experiences. I explained to the children and young adults that most inmates in the system were not bad people—that they had just made a mistake and were paying for it. Most of them will come out of prison, and we expect them to rehabilitate and rejoin society living peacefully with the rest of us.

I dressed in my prison uniform and talked loud and hard at the kids, often using profanity with the older students. The response was overwhelming, and I soon gave programs at Blaine Sumner and Trewyn schools in Peoria, and I invited Sam Torrence, a senior officer specialist, and Michael Kindred, a former MP and a senior officer, to join me from the prison.

Each principal wrote to the warden stating how well the program was received. Helman summoned me to his office, and I shared what had happened.

"When are you doing the next one?" he asked. "I want to come."

I set up the next program at Von Steuben, my old middle school, and it went over big. The warden attended, and when we returned to the prison, he bought us lunch at the staff dining facility.

"You all did a wonderful job," he began, "but pull the cursing. You can't get respect by using disrespect."

He was right because the message was real. All I had to do was to speak the truth, so I stopped cursing and began wearing my DI "Round Brown" hat as part of our reality check to depict to audiences how a youth boot camp environment might exist. This was part of the larger aim to dissuade wayward youth from escalating negative behavior and motivating high-performing youth to stay in their lane.

Kids love the hat and it is a signature piece of my presentations today, which are topic driven and tailored to the age and audience profile. For example, I might not present *Straight Talk* the same way at a school on the south side of Chicago as I would at a rural high school. The topics are the same, and the message is audience driven—for it to be well-received, it must be a thought-provoking, collective delivery that reaches the individual. I want each student to walk away not feeling that the presentation was a waste of time.

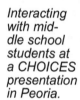

Interacting with middle school students at a CHOICES presentation in Peoria.

Kids love music, and no presentation is given without it. It is the emotional gasoline that I use to draw fire from kids, understanding that if they allow lyrics to get them out of character, it's the same as picking the wrong friends. As the prison's school coordinator, I had a real opportunity to interact with the teachers and students regarding their needs, which included providing role models, mentors, and people who cared.

Within three months, the program had gained the attention of many area schools and law enforcement agencies. The warden received several requests to extend the program throughout the year and for us to assist the Peoria Police Department in developing *Cops For Kids,* an outreach program to help bridge the gap between law enforcement and the youth of the community.

RETURNING POINT

I was about a year into *Straight Talk* when U.S. Congressman Ray LaHood's office called and asked if Ray could attend a program. Ray was a former schoolteacher and was elected to Congress in 1995 to represent the 18th Congressional District, which included much of central Illinois. When the warden got the request, he personally made the arrangement and asked if I would choose a familiar school with a new group of kids, so I returned to Pekin Edison.

The presentation was a hit, and the warden looked like a genius. After that session, he asked if I had ever considered using female inmates since they were a lower custody level with less risk, and although I had wanted to do it, I had not asked, but he opened the door and cleared the way. Later, as the program evolved, I began using male inmates. Warden Helman recalls the beginning of the program:

"At an earlier stop in my career as Drug Abuse Treatment Program Director at the large federal women's prison in Alderson, West Virginia, I had overseen a community outreach program whereby carefully selected and counseled inmates would with direct supervision exit the prison to schools and other community gatherings to share life experiences. This was not

'Scared Straight,' the largely unsuccessful effort in some prisons to foster fear and intimidation in the presence of youth. I would have none of that. This was not to be a sensationalized activity but a routine one that folded with the rehabilitative function of the others.

The Alderson experience was based in mutual respect, empathy, civil exchange between inmate and youth and the fostering of the human relationship. For the inmates, the self-reflection provided immeasurable value. For youth, the exchange afforded an opportunity to meet a very diverse group of people in the midst of troubled lives who often grappled with daily problems not unlike some of their own. It was time to give it a go at the women's prison at Pekin. Carl Cannon was the officer to lead the effort.

This was not the job for every correctional officer although some sharing Carl's passion for making a difference joined this small cadre in its work. Several female officers stepped forward and were essential in supervising female inmates. The program had to be well organized, airtight in security and skillfully led. Taking inmates from prison to town is met skeptically by many in the public so it must be done right.

The program leader must work closely with diverse constituencies and please the warden. Sound communication and team building with prison staff, supervisors, inmates, teachers, school officials, community law enforcement and news media were required. Foremost, this point person represented the United States Department of Justice.

Because of Carl Cannon the youth outreach effort achieved great success and was richly regarded in the *community. At times, requests for programs were more than staff time permitted.*

To be sure some of the more traditional thinkers in the officer ranks believed Carl's team was being distracted from their primary duty, may be attempting to gain favor with the warden or were coddling inmates needing punishment not coddling."

I started with three female inmates who I believed had pure motives and who were good for what I needed. They agreed that they would present their stories to middle and high school students by telling the truth, the whole truth, and nothing but the truth, and that their purpose for doing so was not to self-promote or to be pitied. The inmate presentations were not the standard "hit and run" assemblies where a speaker comes in, delivers a message, and leaves. Rather, they used a "hit and stick" approach that made an immediate and lasting impact.

My first prisoner was a short, middle class white girl from a small town in southern Illinois—inmate #98250. She was doing time for taking part in an armed bank robbery with her black boyfriend. I selected her for two primary reasons; one, she had no prior criminal history, and two, because she did not look much older than a typical high school student. She could relate to teens on their level, which was key, because they

FEDERAL BUREAU OF PRISONS

98250　　　　JUN 16, 1995

could envision themselves being in a similar situation.

Her story centered on picking an abusive boyfriend, not listening to her teachers and parents, and not trusting her instincts that this guy was all wrong for her. She told students of how her boyfriend beat her and then had her drive him to a bank that he robbed without her knowing it while she waited in the car. The next thing she knew, the police were knocking at her door and arrested her, which may or may not have been true.

"I didn't know he was going to rob that bank," she told the judge. "And then he turns it around and says it was my idea!"

She got 12 years.

The second person was inmate #83351, a black woman in her mid-30s from inner city Detroit. She was doing time for the distribution and use of crack cocaine and for violating the Federal Racketeer Influenced and Corrupt Organizations (RICO) Act related to gang activity. I selected her because she could relate to inner city youth and street life. Her raw, unvarnished story centered on being raised in a life of poverty, dysfunction, and violence, and stripped the audience of the excuse that there was no way out of that life.

FEDERAL BUREAU OF PRISONS

83351   OCT 19, 1994

"I went from the outhouse to the penthouse to hell in prison," she snarled. "Don't be a crash dummy like me! I hit that wall, but you don't have to!"

She mesmerized students with her gut-wrenching story and by her passion to keep them out of her world.

The third person was a white grandmother in her late 50s, inmate #23389, who came from rural America and was doing time for fraud, drug distribution, prostitution, and drug possession. I selected her because she looked and sounded like a grandmother. She related that she had done everything for which she had been sentenced, and more, and that her legacy to her daughter was a similar life of dysfunction. Her sweet, motherly demeanor belied her crimes and baffled youth as to how she could be locked up. She offered the message that we are all just one mistake away from losing our freedom, and that giving up control of our lives often begins with picking the wrong friends, making the wrong acquaintance, or using a mind-altering substance.

FEDERAL BUREAU OF PRISONS

23389   NOV 1, 1994

The inmates' messages were so powerful that on one occasion at Roberto Clemente High School on the west side of Chicago, the lunch bell went off during the presentation, and not one student left their seat. Ten minutes later, I tried to conclude the presentation but the administrator said, "Leave them alone, they've never done this before."

The inmates give kids who are enamored by a Hollywood version of prison life a dose of truth and harsh reality, and who better to teach our youth than someone who has been there, done that, and regretted it?

Make no mistake, the women who shared their stories, and others not mentioned, saved lives. They did so with their testimonies while enduring the humiliation of wearing their prison issued green uniform shackled in chains at the waist, hands, and ankles. Could we do as much?

An inmate tells her story at a school assembly.

1999

In April 1999, Warden Helman retired from the Bureau of Prisons after 26 years of federal service. He was a driving force in the creation of CHOICES, my new outreach program, and a champion of our work. Moreover, he believed in me and gave me the latitude to flourish within the system. He went on to say,

"As warden, I sought people with the necessary skills, education and training to be a correctional officer, nurse, cook, tradesman or teacher and looked to

hire those having a broader perspective of not merely securing prisoners but in making a difference in their futures. I struck gold with Carl Cannon.

Carl's exemplary military service matched the skills needed in a correctional officer. Inmates respect good order, structure, and clear, honest, and fair directives. They received these from Officer Cannon, whose uniform appearance and adherence to the necessary rules that keep good order, were impeccable.

My proudest moments from which I do not shy from trumpeting were spent with Carl and his colleagues who shaped one of the finest teams of correctional officers ever assembled in the Federal Bureau of Prisons.

As we moved ahead after the first year, we were able to develop program initiatives to my liking.

With the basics of security, sanitation, safety, food service, health care and work programs in place we could move on. I consider my collegiality and friendship with Officer Carl Cannon to have been one of the richest professional relationships of my life."

Warden Helman not only encouraged and supported me, he also defended me against attacks from inside my own organization. Unknown to me, a member of the team connected to CHOICES had become jealous of the personal attention that I had received and wished to see the program abolished. I learned that this person had been criticizing me and the program for months. When Helman retired and the new warden came in, the attacks increased. The new warden didn't know me from a hill of beans and was unaware that I set up my own presentations, but based on false and malicious complaints accusing me of utilizing prison resources, inmates, and time, he said, "You can't do CHOICES anymore."

I was stunned, and internally decided at that moment, to become my own man with CHOICES, and to break from the prison outreach program. "Okay," I replied coldly, as I considered my next move. And that's all I said.

I had spent a career in the military following the rank structure and knowing when to shut up. Now was not the time to argue. I was coming up for review, and the BOP was pushing me to be a lieutenant. I was at the top of my game, and I had a future in the BOP if I wanted it and played the game according to the rules. But did I want it?

In four years, I had developed and grown CHOICES into a recognizable program that had reached thousands of students. The staff and inmates, including a few high-ranking white supremacists, respected my honesty, fairness, and what I was trying to do for children and young adults. And that spoke volumes.

Even while doing the outside work I was still making a difference at the prison. I had orchestrated a successful recruiting trip to Fort Leavenworth that netted a record 20 new BOP applicants and I had helped quell a riot. Also, I had just been recognized for running the SHU for nine consecutive months without a major incident on my shift and was credited for the exemplary sanitary condition of the unit. This was followed by a VIP visit from the Director of the Federal Bureau of Prisons, Ms. Kathleen Hawk, who presented me with a letter of commendation.

Kathleen Hawk, Director of the BOP, visits FCI-Pekin.

Several months later, Captain Huggins called me and said that the warden of FCI-Memphis had contacted him inquiring if I would be interested in an open lieutenant's position—to which I refused. My family and I did not want to move again, and keeping young people out of the system was more important to me than keeping them in or climbing the BOP ladder.

RED LETTER

Because the new warden forbade me from doing my CHOICES presentations, I called Peoria attorney Don Jackson, head of the local NAACP. Don and Illinois State Senator, George Shadid, had attended one of my presentations at Trewyn School given without inmates, and after the presentation, they publicly remarked that "This is the most powerful presentation students would ever see" regarding making good choices, and promised their support.

Don even referred me to his partner, colleague, and friend, Stephen Thomas. Stephen embraced the

CHOICES concept and led the effort to obtain a 501c3 not-for-profit status from the IRS free of charge.

When I informed Don about the warden's order, he was outraged and responded by writing an eloquent response on our behalf to the warden on NAACP letterhead. The letter approached the new warden from a legal perspective and dressed him down for trying to muzzle my 1st Amendment rights. He further related and advised that it would be in his best interest to not interfere with my continued service to the youth of our community.

The warden backed off, and I am forever grateful to Don and Ernestine Jackson, and to Stephen and Elaine Thomas, for their friendship and encouragement during the early days of CHOICES. They probably did not realize how important their belief in me was and how many children they helped, but I hope they know now.

Don Jackson and Elaine & Stephen Thomas.

ESCAPE TO THE FUTURE

Although the new chain of command had wanted to check me the past 18 months, they did not want to battle the NAACP nor did they want to surrender the good press they were receiving because of CHOICES. However, in late October 2000, events beyond our control started a chain reaction that changed the trajectory of my professional life.

Using a homemade grappling hook, two Hispanic prisoners from the housing unit adjacent to the one I was working at as a correctional officer, climbed over the fence and escaped. It occurred on my Friday, the last day of my week's work, and I was annoyed that we had to work forced overtime to try and recapture them. We had done a head count at 10 p.m., but couldn't find them, so we locked down the entire prison and implemented escape protocol.

I was assigned to an escape post in a cornfield with another man from Pekin, and we parked along an embankment in a prison sedan armed with 9mm pistols and .12 gauge shotguns. After several hours on lookout, I had to take a leak, and when I went behind the vehicle, I slipped and severely pulled my right groin muscle. I remained on guard that night, but by the time I got off work, my leg was swollen, and I could barely walk. My injury was so severe that the doctors put me on convalescent leave for two weeks. When I went back to the doctor, he put me on two more weeks. The longer I was out, the more I did not want to return. Working at the prison had lost its luster.

My injury was a blessing in disguise. While recuperating, I used the down time to go out and speak to kids, and when I returned to work, I used my seniority to get shifts that freed up my days to do school programs. Working second and third shifts and on weekends was tough on my family and made for long days, but the kids were worth it.

As for the escapees, they got away and remain the only inmates ever to have successfully escaped from the prison. One was later caught in Memphis in 2008, and the other was shot and killed in Mexico following a kidnapping. Justice may take a while to come, but it comes eventually.

RETIREMENT

In early 2001, I retired with over 20 years of combined military and federal BOP service. I had earned my pension and was now excited to begin a new chapter in my life. A brief career that had begun in a place that I had long-feared and never understood, ended in a city that I had come to enjoy and admire.

Coming in, I did not want to get lost in Pekin. Little did I know, that six years later, it would be the city where I would start CHOICES, be embraced by children and their parents, and become lifelong friends with some of the finest people I have ever known. Somewhere along the way, I had quit judging the city and everyone in it based on childhood experiences and on what others had told me. I had grown and given them a chance to prove that their community did not deserve the labels of the past, but instead embraced the hope of a better future.

Go Dragons!

CHAPTER 13
C.H.O.I.C.E.S.

BOYS and GIRLS CLUB

I took a $20,000 a year pay cut to leave the prison to work at the Boys and Girls Club of Peoria as the Teen Reach Coordinator, where I would serve middle and high school age students residing on Peoria's Southside and the kids living in the Harrison Homes housing project. The inner city housing area was the scene of the recent murder of a rising high school basketball star that had deflated the spirit of the community. The tragic murder occurred at a time when the city should have been celebrating the pride of the Southside, Peoria Manual High School, which only a few weeks before had won its 4th consecutive boys state basketball championship and achieved the number one ranking in the nation. Rather, it was a stark reminder that the area was saddled with the highest crime rate in the city and that the suffocating effects of systemic and generational poverty were widespread and real.

In my new job, I seized the opportunity to do more than just hit and run programming. I was on the front lines working with youth where I could best deliver, demonstrate, and secure the message of hope to those who needed it. It was the best work I have ever done.

The Boys and Girls Club already had a national programming concept in place when I arrived, but I shook things up and implemented the old school concept of RESPECT in all things. It had worked so well in our outreach presentations that I applied it to the everyday operation of the facility. Kids were not allowed into the club without demonstrating proper respect for self and others. No sagging pants, swearing, mean mugging, horseplay, and/or gang banging.

Because we established respect at the forefront of our programming, I was able to organize and reintroduce league basketball, indoor soccer, double-dutch jump-roping, dance, a traveling gymnastics tumbling team, and other activities for kids. To do the fun stuff, kids had to have a good day at school/home and participate in the age-based after-school tutoring programs we sponsored at the club. In short time, conduct issues in the community and at home declined and performance at school improved.

Although I planned to work at the Boys and Girls Club forever, I spotted a photo in our local newspaper of a big hole in the ground where the new 118,000 square foot Peoria Park District (PPD) RiverPlex Recreation and Wellness Center would be built, and my plans changed. It was a huge joint project between the park district and OSF Hospital, and I considered it a potential employer for several teenagers in the Boys and Girls Club.

I approached the RiverPlex general manager at her park district office about interviewing some of my youth for part-time entry level jobs, and promised that I would personally prepare them for all aspects of employment, including the interview process, dressing for success, and effective communication. I also vowed to work with them on soft skills, social skills, and life skills as they pertained to the workplace.

While there, I skimmed the jobs board and noticed a posting seeking a full-time recreation professional with a bachelor's degree and experience. I didn't think much about it at the time and moved on to the part-time postings that applied to my kids. Those jobs only required that applicants be 16 years of age or older. I returned to the Boys and Girls Club determined to get my young people ready for the process as soon as the RiverPlex opened.

The next day, I received a call from the park district HR manager informing me that she had a discussion with the RiverPlex GM regarding job opportunities for my youth. She related that the park was interested in supporting my efforts but pivoted the question to me.

"Are you interested in working for the park district?"

I responded in kind. "I saw the jobs board, but I don't meet your minimum qualifications. I do not have a bachelor's degree."

"Just interview," she replied in a reassuring tone. "You have nothing to lose."

I paused, and the delay was noticeable.

"Don't answer now," she added quickly. "Think about it tonight and call me tomorrow."

I could not wait for tonight and thought about it all the way home. I prayed hard about what to do, and at the end of my prayer cycle, I decided to role model what I had been telling the kids to do. I was talking the talk, but it was time for me to walk the talk.

The next day, I called the HR manager and agreed to interview in the park district board room at Glen Oak Park. That night, I researched the history of the Peoria Park District and the RiverPlex, and learned that the PPD was the oldest park in the State of Illinois, and that construction of the RiverPlex was controversial, with much of the blowback coming from private gym owners who did not want another local competitor. The media focused on the conflict but did not share the market analysis revealing ample room for coexistence and more competition.

Armed with an arsenal of information, I dressed to the nines and rehearsed my answers to what I anticipated the board would ask. On the way in, I dropped by the Boys and Girls Club to role model how to present oneself and how to prepare for an interview.

Bonnie Noble and me at the RiverPlex.

But I had not prepared for everything. While the three-person panel was questioning me, a distinguished looking woman walked in and interrupted.

"I'm Bonnie Noble," she said. "I am the Executive Director of the Peoria Park District. Before you leave, would you please stop by my office?"

When she left, I went straight into fright night. I had been around generals, sergeant majors of the Army, state governors, and even murderers, but they didn't scare me. Bonnie scared me! She was a legend in the Peoria Park District and had held about every leadership position up through the ranks beginning in the early 1970s. The district had even received the 1994 *National Gold Medal Award for Excellence* under her watch. She was an outstanding leader and an even better person, and later, she would play a significant role in the growth of CHOICES and beyond. Fortunately, PPD board members Jackie Petty and Robert Johnson had spoken to her privately on my behalf. If not for them, I would not have gotten an audience with Bonnie.

The panel thanked me for my time, and as I was leaving, they pulled me back.

"We have one more thing," added the chairperson. "We would like for you to write a program from scratch through implementation."

"I can do that," I said confidently. "When would you like it by?"

"Now," said the chairperson. "Just write it out longhand. That will be fine."

There was nowhere to hide. Although I had no problem writing a program, I was embarrassed by my handwriting. I pleaded with the panel to let me use a typewriter or computer, but they insisted that I put pen to paper.

Three hours later, after several retries, I presented a viable program, but I thought I had no chance of getting hired because of my poor handwriting, caused in part by exposure to nerve agent on Johnston Island. Several months into my tour, I was evacuated to a military hospital in Honolulu and had a brain tumor removed.

The next day after the interview, Carol Kiethly, the park HR superintendent, called and offered me the program coordinator position.

BETTER CHOICES

I was thrilled with the offer, but I struggled with it. Leaving the Boys and Girls Club was a gut-wrenching decision that could have a negative impact on the children I was trying to serve, and I prayed hard over it.

The next day, I was at peace. I realized that the enormous RiverPlex facility, located near the Taft housing project on the Illinois River, was an incredible tool that had the potential to reach more kids, especially if linked with my burgeoning CHOICES Youth Outreach program. It would be the perfect centerpiece for growing the program and would provide kids a large, safe venue with basketball courts, a pool, a weight room, classrooms, a kitchen, and more.

I was all in, but I would have to wait another four or five months for construction of the facility to be finished, and once it was, I used volunteer inmates from the state work release center out of downtown Peoria to help with the move in. Al Thompson, whom I knew from working at the prison, was one of the staff members at the center, and had it not been for our relationship, the move would have been more costly and would have taken longer. We were the muscle that moved the machines into the facility and helped open the door.

In May 2001, I started as a recreation programmer at the RiverPlex, and my sole job was organizing birthday parties, Easter egg hunts, and social functions of every kind. I was doing typical park recreation work when my boss, Brent Wheeler, a young and energetic innovator, challenged me and my colleagues to program outside the box. With his blessing, I created *Days of Hope*, an incentive program that rewarded kids with a free day of play at the RiverPlex pool and gym after they attended a school assembly, listened to a presentation, and recorded two months of negative-free behavior at school.

The Peoria RiverPlex.   *Peoria Park District photo.*

This initiative gained immediate publicity for the park district and helped feed the engine to generate more ideas and innovative programming. It also gave teachers a tool from the PPD that encouraged and rewarded good behavior from many kids who had rarely shown it.

HULK HOGAN

The RiverPlex had been open less than a week when a local mom was driving downtown and her young son spotted Hulk Hogan, a famous professional wrestler, walking outside the Civic Center where he was scheduled to wrestle later that night. The kid pointed Hogan out to his mom, so she stopped and asked if he needed anything.

"Yes, ma'am," Hogan replied. "I want to go to a place called the RiverPlex."

The woman offered him a ride and brought him to the RiverPlex to the thrill of her son. Everyone recognized Hogan immediately, and a crowd began forming. I asked what I could do for him and if he would mind taking a few photos.

"Look, brutha..." he said in character. "All I need is an hour, brutha! Give me an hour to work out, and I'll give you anything you need."

I cordoned off the entire weight room, and a crowd watched him work out. I had been a professional wrestling fan since I was a kid and had followed him during his heyday in the 1980s when he was the biggest attraction on the planet, and it was a thrill to meet him.

Hogan was a huge man and was renowned for his strength. As an avid weightlifter, I appreciated how hard he worked out. I had been lifting for a while, and had injured my shoulder bench pressing 505 pounds, which wasn't too shabby, but when Hogan shook my hand, I felt just how strong he really was. His hand swallowed mine. After the workout, he kept his word and stayed and took pictures. He then gave Brent and me tickets to the wrestling match that night. The job had its perks.

Hulk Hogan and me.

Brent and I soon elevated up the ranks at the RiverPlex and took over exclusively recreation, while another person took over the fitness side of the operation. Over the next year, recreation exploded, but fitness still struggled. Brent then became the overall general manager, and I was promoted to General Manager of Recreation with the added responsibility of maintenance and membership services, which had not met projected monthly goals since the facility opened. In my first month of running membership, the RiverPlex met its membership goal for the first time, and I met that goal for 15 straight months.

In that position, I had the flexibility to hire workers and to make it fair for everyone. I hired salespeople, shift leaders, custodians, recreation attendants, and diversified the workforce. I even started doing River-Plex commercials and promotional work to expand our reach. My premise for growth was based on the park district partnering more effectively with school districts to motivate the previously unmotivated, and the park supported me in that effort. Brent was soon promoted to Superintendent of the RiverPlex and later Deputy Director of the Park District, and he encouraged me to keep the ball rolling.

Although I was growing CHOICES undercover and still finding ways to talk to kids, my new position at the RiverPlex made it more difficult to find time to visit schools. But with the continued help of two great friends, I hoped that the park district would eventually take notice and jump in to help.

LEW and JERRY

Fellow correctional officers Lew Westercamp and Jerry Stoneburner made a difference in everything they did. Fortunately, they believed in CHOICES and in doing whatever it took to provide kids with a future.

Lew was a guru in corrections and the man who trained me. He was the most honest correctional officer I had ever met—military or civilian—and would have been a great fit as one of Elliot Ness's Untouchables. He was square with everyone and did everything by the book—partly because he knew the book better than anyone. Because of him, I wrote an operational manual for the FCI-Pekin Control Center detailing every function within the prison, and had I not left the prison, it might still be in use there today.

Lew was the most dynamic control center officer in the BOP. He could juggle a hundred things at once and not miss a beat on anything. Although he was not one of the founders of the Prison Outreach Program that evolved into CHOICES, he became an integral part. He genuinely enjoyed helping kids, and people respected him for it.

Jerry Stoneburner was my best friend and sharper than most. He was a graduate of Pekin High School, which endeared him to me even more, and he had a flair for the dramatic. He strongly believed in what we were doing even when people were telling him that CHOICES was a waste of time. Jerry was his own man, and if he believed in something, he threw himself into it. When he gave his presentation, everyone knew he was serious and was not to be played with. He was a staunch supporter, and when the new warden tried to shut me down, he had my back.

By 2001, CHOICES had built a good reputation, but word of the program began spreading like wildfire and we had to expand our game. We developed two similar but distinct types of CHOICES programs as part of a three-phase initiative.

The Phase I program was a basic presentation where a middle school or high school principal contacted us and extended an invitation to present. Schools paid an honorarium to cover expenses and to increase programming. Time permitting, Lew, Jerry, and I went to the school and presented the program, usually during an assembly, and tried to get kids thinking about their decisions and how they positively or negatively affect their lives.

The Phase II program built upon Phase I, and depending on the school and the profile of the students, incorporated inmates from the State of Illinois work release program who interacted directly with students and shared their stories to help keep youth from making the same mistakes they had made. Phase III is an awards program based on selection and adherence to phases I and II.

Although the presentations differed, they followed a general format that addressed core elements. The strength of each presentation was how clearly and dramatically we expressed it—which as former military and correctional employees—came easy. The following are examples of each phase of the CHOICES program:

PHASE I
– *THE UNGUARDED MOMENT*
—The unguarded moment is the moment when youth are most vulnerable to making poor choices that

might have serious and lifelong consequences.

ENTER CARL

The music blares as I enter a school gym or auditorium dressed in a black tactical uniform, boots, and my Army DI hat. I am loud and ensure that everyone hears me. I introduce myself as C-O—Correctional Officer.

Going "Full Cannon" to save lives.

"What's my name!" I yell with as much bass as I can muster.

Most kids answer timidly at first, "C-O."

"What's my name!" I yell even louder.

"C-O!" They yell back.

I have their attention. I share that the goal of the presentation is to save one life, and that there are over two million inmates from all walks of life incarcerated in America who regret the poor choices they made to get locked up. I further explain that while poverty, geography, and/or family dysfunction are contributing factors to incarceration, not everyone who experiences them is destined to go to prison.

I drive home the point that as bad as those factors are, life can be worse in prison, in a harsh environment where every move is watched by predators and controlled by a person like me. I explain that only by putting themselves in that position will they understand that they could have, should have, but did not listen to someone in the room who loved them.

"What's my name!"

"C-O!"

"Who in this room loves you and proves it every day?" I ask, causing them to think. "What about your teachers—people who tell you what you NEED to hear, NOT what you WANT to hear?"

I go on to say, "In America—unlike in some countries—teachers are the surest and least painful way of offsetting those negative factors. If you listen to them, you'll gain knowledge, and in America, knowledge is power. What's my name!"

ENTER JERRY

"What's my name!" Jerry shouts, demanding the same response from the students. He then introduc-

es himself and shares his background, professional experience, and role in the youth outreach program concept.

He tells a story about a little boy (himself) and how he overcame hardships in his life, emphasizing that if some of the people who have been dealt a bad hand in life

Jerry Stoneburner

don't reshuffle the cards, they stand a good chance of calling someone like him, C-O.

"What's my name!"

ENTER LEW

Lew takes center stage. "What's my name!" he asks, echoing Jerry and me.

He introduces himself and begins by explaining to the audience that everyone is labeled by race, neighborhood, intelligence, beauty, athleticism, or by whatever mindset the labeler has and by whatever valid or invalid label they choose to assign. He then asks the audience if it is better to be labeled as "ignorant" or "stupid," and explains that everyone is ignorant or unaware of something, but that knowledge can reduce or even cure ignorance. He reminds students that ignorance of the law is no excuse and segues into the second part of his question—

"Are you stupid?" he asks. "We define stupid as knowing that something is wrong or bad and choosing to do it anyway. That is also the definition of a fool. Are you a fool? Or do you choose a friend who is a fool? If so, doesn't that still make you a fool? That defines the youth outreach program called CHOICES.

What's my name!"

The program transitions back to me, and I share that an inmate asked me to tell students about what he called the "*Unguarded Moment.*"

He explained that "all our lives we've been conditioned by parents, teachers, and society, and that they have proven a genuine love for us since we were knee-high by conditioning us to 'beware of strangers.' But no one conditioned us to 'beware of friends.' Very few strangers offer us the opportunity to go to prison."

The story hit home. I then asked the kids, "Who do you have on your right and on your left? Are they friend or foe? Are they looking out for themselves or for you? Over two million people in this country might say that they had the wrong person on their right or left.

What's my name!"

Jerry and I then engage the audience in role-play and talk straight with them about life issues with the purpose of educating them about the real-life consequences of their day-to-day decision-making. During this time, we reinforce good behavior, recognize the academic achievement and appropriate goals of the stellar student, and encourage the struggling student to make good and healthy choices.

The student already making poor choices will understand that there are consequences to those choices, and he or she will be held responsible. We encourage students to become self-controlled, self-motivated individuals who are aware of negative peer influence.

PHASE II
– BEEN THERE, DONE THAT

Jerry then transitions to Lew. We march in a few shackled inmates in bright jumpsuits, and they stand in front of the audience until called on to speak. During this phase, present or former inmates interact with the students and share their emotional accounts that focus on the hard lessons they learned from failed relationships, dependence on others, substance abuse, and disrespect for parents and teachers.

This phase of the program is especially effective, as it provides an emotional link between the adult inmates and the audience in an honest, positive, inspirational manner that strips away the false facade of prison. This phase benefits both the inmates, who can see they are making a difference, and the students who cannot dismiss the reality and truth of the presentation.

The format is not intended to "scare straight" the student as a deterrent to poor choices. We consider

Sharing that "Respect is a Two-way Street" with students at a CHOICES assembly. Photo by Ching Zedric.

that a suspect approach. While hard-hitting dialogue combined with drama and emotional personal accounts is key to gaining the attention and thought of each and every student, the exchange respects the student as a young adult and stresses the virtue of making mature adult choices. Sessions always close with officers offering words of support, kindness, and encouragement.

Jerry then transitions back to me, and I give an overview of poor choices emphasizing the prisoners

THE RESPECT PLEDGE

WHAT IS YOUR NAME?
HOPE.

WHO DO YOU SERVE?
MY COMMUNITY.

HOW DO YOU SERVE?
WITH RESPECT.

HOW DOES RESPECT WORK?
IT'S A TWO-WAY STREET--
FROM ME TO YOU--
AND FROM YOU TO ME.

WHAT IS YOUR JOB?
TO GET AN EDUCATION.

HOW DO YOU GET PAID?
GOOD GRADES.

WHAT IS YOUR NAME?
HOPE!

--CARL CANNON

and their chains. I assure the students that we are not there to entertain them, but to save them. I conclude with a *Respect Pledge* that had just rolled off my tongue during one of my first presentations at a middle school in Mt. Vernon, Illinois. The students were above me looking down and it was powerful. It was what God intended.

An inmate speaks to students.

PHASE III
– LAW ENFORCEMENT INCENTIVE AWARDS

I then conclude with an explanation of Phase III, the *Choices Youth Outreach Community Law Enforcement Incentive Awards* program, which recognizes students who make good choices and who embody the CHOICES theme of self-motivation.

The Phase III program combines all phases and requires a greater commitment from the school and from the students. By enlisting corporate and community support, the program enables educators to identify hundreds of 8th grade students and to select award recipients based on newfound school effort and outstanding decision-making skills. The identified students have experienced the first two phases of the CHOICES program in their schools, and the educators who deal with them daily, attribute their improved attention to school and citizenship to the effects of the CHOICES presentations.

Typically, we receive an invitation from a school, such as in Kansas City, Missouri, where my brother Bill worked, and he would arrange everything. Jerry, Lew, and I would travel to Kansas City and give the CHOICES presentation to several schools over a few days, and at the conclusion of the program, announce that two 8th grade students, one boy and one girl, would be selected by their respective teacher(s) to represent their school at the annual *CHOICES Youth Outreach Law Enforcement Awards Ceremony* in Peoria. We asked that schools base their selection on need and effort—not on a student's final letter grade.

Nominated students and their parents were notified of their selection and recognized at their school's end-of-year assembly. Between Jerry, Lew, and me, we returned to each of the schools and announced the recipients. As a bonus, each recipient got to select a friend to take part in the award day activities in hopes that they would enter their freshman year with a supportive friend.

The recipients and their families, along with select-ed friends, were invited to Peoria for the ceremony at the RiverPlex, where they were awarded a gently-used desktop computer and treated to a three-hour shopping trip to the local JC Penney store. Each recipient was credited $500 for school clothes and school supplies for their upcoming freshman year. Parents and friends accompanied the students and helped select clothing that met their school's dress code and our criteria. All dollars not spent were turned back in.

Following the student shopping experience, we treated each recipient and their party to an all-they-could-eat mix-n-match dinner at the Northwoods Mall food court. Afterward, the parents took their child's clothing back to their place of lodging, and Peoria Charter Coach provided first class transportation of the recipients and friends back to the RiverPlex for a 7 p.m. lock-in that included all night access to swimming, basketball, volleyball, rock climbing, inflatables, music, dancing, candy, pizza, soda, and more. For eight hours the kids thought everything was about them. But it was all a set-up!

At approximately 3 a.m., we shut down all activ-ities and assembled the students in a large circle in the RiverPlex Arena called the "Circle of Hope." For the next two hours, we required each student to share the worst thing and the best thing that had ever hap-pened to them. Some had witnessed murder. Others had been raped. When one kid said that his dog dying was the worst thing that he had ever seen, some kids snickered.

"Don't you laugh at him!" I barked, talking to ev-

Award recipients receive a police escort to the RiverPlex.

eryone in the room. "How can we laugh when his dog might have been the only positive thing in his life? How can we laugh at someone else's pain without knowing what's behind it?"

The goal of the exercise was to help kids recognize that as bad as their lives may have been, someone else has been through worse, and to understand that they can fix or improve any situation.

Many kids were initially shy and uncomfortable sharing personal information with strangers, but once everyone had spoken, they knew something about everyone else, and there were no strangers. In a sense, each kid had become part of a new family with relatives throughout the community and in other parts of the country. For many, it was the most inspiring two hours of their lives, and what began as a day of celebration and play, ended as a day of hope.

~

AWARDS PROGRAM

The CHOICES Awards program evolved from an inauspicious beginning in 1999, when we held the first formal congratulatory ceremony in center court of the Northwoods Mall in Peoria, to a full-scale production at the RiverPlex a few years later.

Initially, the mall was convenient because we shopped for the graduates at the JC Penny store there. The mall wanted the positive publicity, and we wanted a venue with exposure. The partnership was mutually beneficial and the beginning of a long relationship. We also held lock-ins for the kids at the nearby Landmark Recreation Center that included bowling, music, wal-ly-ball, and other activities. We limited it to about 15 graduates, and each recipient got to bring a friend.

In May 2002, we held our first *CHOICES Awards Ceremony* at the RiverPlex. The park district did not know that I was doing it, but they would soon. Fifteen proud graduates stood at the ceremony in the main arena and were joined by about 30 friends and family. Unlike later graduations, there was no music, no important guest speaker (only me), and no publicity. I did

not want to draw any attention, but the program kept growing, and within a few years, it featured an honor guard, music, spotlights, dignitaries, television and print media, and hundreds of guests.

Congressman/Secretary of Transportation Ray LaHood, Caterpillar CEOs Doug Oberhelman, Glen Barton, and Jim Owens, and other noted civic and business leaders, including four Peoria mayors, presided at subsequent ceremonies. News anchor Christine Zak, the grand dame of WEEK-TV, the NBC Peoria affiliate, emceed a few early programs, and because of her dedication to kids and extraordinary talent, the program received state-wide attention. She gave the program credibility and ensured that the accomplishments of our kids would be publicly recognized.

ADULT AWARDS

Kids should not have all the fun. CHOICES would have been impossible to maintain without the help of

Above: Christine Zak. Opposite: Pastor Spencer Gibson directs the New Hope of Deliverance Choir at a CHOICES awards program.

generous and caring people from all sectors of the community, and I sought to recognize those who exemplified what was best in all of us. In our first year, I only gave one award.

TEACHER OF THE YEAR

The *Suzi Russell Teacher of the Year Award* was the first award given at the CHOICES Awards program beginning in 1999. A dynamic and beloved educator, Suzi taught for more than 20 years at Calvin Coolidge Middle School in Peoria and touched the lives of many students and staff. She died of cancer in September 1998 after a valiant 10-year battle, so I asked her husband, Dr. Scott Russell, if I could honor his wife by presenting a Teacher of the Year Award to someone within the CHOICES community who had gone above and beyond to help students. He presented the first award in 1999 to Larice Joseph, a friend of Suzi's, and it has been awarded every year since. My goal was to make it perpetual, and we have been true to that end.

Suzi Russell

David Helman

PRINCIPAL OF THE YEAR

In 2000, I added the *CHOICES Principal of the Year Award* after David Helman, the former warden of FCI-Pekin. His retirement ceremony was held at the Pekin Elks Club, and I attended and announced the *Principal of the Year Award* would be in his honor. He was the most innovative law enforcement officer I have ever met and was everything but "Hug a Thug."

In the eyes of the inmates we might be that last chance to have a role model, so somebody had to do it the right way, and he did. For no other reason than safety, he made the prison less dangerous, and the effect was immediate and lasting for everyone. He made it his mission for area law enforcement agencies to prioritize and integrate juvenile intervention in their daily vocation. He challenged his prison staff to offer their support to these efforts and other social concerns. I wanted the award to recognize a principal that reflected Dave's leadership, and through the years the program has honored many outstanding principals who have made a difference.

COMMUNITY SERVICE AWARD

The impact that Henry Holling had upon the CHOICES program was immeasurable. As manager of the Caterpillar Foundation and one of the first supporters of CHOICES, he advanced several youth-related community programs. In honor of his work, I established the *Henry Holling CHOICES Youth Outreach Community Service Award* recognizing individuals for significant work with kids. Henry was a blessing and one of the finest people I have ever known.

LAW ENFORCEMENT AWARD

Peoria County Sheriff Charles "Chuck" Schofield became the 54th sheriff of Peoria County in 1994 after serving with the department for 32 years. He had volunteered in the early days of CHOICES and was a huge supporter of the concept. In June 2002, he suffered a fatal heart attack. The next year, I established the *Chuck Schofield Memorial Law Enforcement Award* to be presented to a cop who was doing more public service by modeling and growing the next generation of youth rather than just policing them.

As the CHOICES program grew, we included additional awards to recognize the contribution of corporate and civic leaders and dedicated volunteers who, through their work with youth, made a substantial contribution to the advancement of youth related community programs. Their selfless contribution of resources, time, and love has made the difference in the lives of many kids.

HELP FROM MY FRIENDS

The awards and formal recognition were significant in the growth of CHOICES because they heightened awareness of many of the issues that young people face and increased financial support from the private sector.

Corporate support was vital in the early days of CHOICES and ensured that I had the resources to operate and to grow the program. The Caterpillar Foundation was among the first and more significant supporters. The Biefeldt Foundation, headed by Carlotta

Biefeldt, was also a major donor. The foundation funded the AquaPlex, a $5 million addition to the RiverPlex, which was an amazing component of CHOICES and key in my ability to offer kids healthy and fun programming.

Apart from a couple major contributors, Lew, Jerry, and I were always hustling and were mostly on our own. We tried to get a $250 scholarship from each school to keep the program going, and the more exposure we got, the more awards that followed.

At the end of the day, nobody wins an award without the help of others. Although I was the front man and the face of CHOICES, Jerry, Lew, Bonnie Noble, Brent Wheeler, Matt Freeman, and scores of others share in the awards and in the growth and success of the program. Their tireless efforts, professional and personal support, and commitment to helping kids are testaments to the power of love.

Opposite page: Chuck Schofield. Above: Former Peoria Mayor, Jim Maloof (center) with CHOICES recipients.

Full Cannon

CHAPTER 14
Let Me Find Out!

I have a goofy side that I rarely showed as a military policeman and prison guard. In my professional life, I needed to be taken seriously and respected—if not sometimes feared. When I became a senior drill instructor in the Army, I came up with the catchphrase, "Let me find out!" that filled both needs and fit my personality. I delivered it with a command voice to let people know I was coming at them and that I was serious. When I gave an instruction or a command, I expected it to be carried out, and if it wasn't, a price would be paid. In the military and corrections environments, strong leadership is based on respect often demonstrated by a strong voice and the ability to "walk the talk."

To family, friends, and co-workers "Let me find out!" was funny, but to military recruits, subordinates, inmates, and others, it implied that I was going to find out what they didn't know or what they were hiding. And when working with at-risk youth during CHOICES presentations and on the street, both positions are dangerous.

THE THREAT

All kids are at risk from something, and they are bombarded daily with choices that can affect them for the rest of their lives. A child can make the right choices every day and then fall prey to the unguarded moment that changes their life trajectory. One poor choice can erase years of good ones and destroy their future in a second. Poor or absentee parenting, lack of positive role models, peer pressure, drugs, gangs, apathetic educators, and myriad other factors contribute to a viral mix that, when coupled with poverty, can be lethal. My mission within CHOICES (and later programs) was to reach out to those kids drowning in poverty and dysfunction, or who were vulnerable to other attacks, and to pull them up and out and to give them a fighting chance at leading safe, healthy, productive lives in which childhood dreams were possible.

Poverty was our number one enemy. The embarrassment of it is real and not confined to an urban setting. Early on, Jerry and I spoke to poverty as a significant obstacle for kids to overcome but not as an excuse for making poor choices. During his part of the CHOICES program, Jerry told a story of a little boy (him) who lived in the dysfunction of poverty in a rural area, and that surprised me. I had always considered poverty to be inner-city condition, but I discovered later that it was also prevalent in rural and suburban areas with the same devastating effect.

As CHOICES evolved, I also realized that many of the disadvantaged kids from the rural areas lacked programming that they needed as badly as the urban kids. They were often left out, and it was costing them part of their lives. We then expanded the program into those areas and the parents, educators, and principals loved it. I was all in.

TWO MINUTES

The goal of every CHOICES presentation was to save lives—and I had two minutes to do it. If the first two minutes were interesting and appealed to the kids, they'd give me a third, fourth, and fifth. If those first minutes were good, they bought me 90 minutes to say what I needed to say and what they needed to hear.

It all began with music, which helped me get my swagger on and to hype up the kids to get them out of character. It's easier for ghetto kids to cut loose and revert to the ghetto, but often harder for the white kids, so I changed the approach according to the makeup of the kids and the school. I found that music was the lowest common denominator, and as I marched into their gym or auditorium, I did not mix with my staff or the school administration, but spoke to every kid in hopes that my message would save one. And while my message was to everyone, it was specific to the kids it hit home with and gave them a fighting chance. Let me find out!

NOBODY'S FOOL

Kids are kids, but I can smell a thug. The culture is in my mind before I speak, and I know who I'm going to address before they do. Working with all kids, I set the ground rules early. "I ain't no Tonka truck!" I snarl, as I hard-eye those I suspect will be disruptive. "I ain't nobody's toy! I ain't playin' with you!"

The troublemakers, show-offs, and thugs were usually the ones sitting next to the kids that wanted to be reached, and sometimes they had to be removed to save the others. I wanted to serve warning to the good kids not to fall prey to the knucklehead. Neither a city kid nor a suburban kid wanted me singling them out or climbing down their neck in a crowd of their peers. Not many stood up once I confronted them, but occasionally, some kid in the audience would try to disrespect us and start clowning, which is a prison term for disrespecting someone, so we warned them early that we weren't going away because they got stuck on a four-letter word called "cool."

At the start of each presentation, I might say, "If I call you out, stop at the bathroom, look in the mirror, and point your finger at the reflection. There's no one to blame but yourself."

If I say to an audience, "On my count of three, everybody laugh at him or her on their way out," and if everybody bursts out in laughter, that fool wants to crawl under a rock. That says to everyone else, "He ain't getting me like that!"

I further explain that the embarrassment doesn't end there. Ten years from now someone will say, "Remember when that black guy clowned you at school?"

I ain't playin' with you!

Message sent. Message received. I only had to do it a couple times with hundreds of thousands of youth, and I believe that if it did not make them think, it made many of those around them listen more carefully. Not checking such behavior does children a disservice and fast tracks them to more dysfunction, possibly prison, or worse. A consequence given early is better than one suffered late, because late is often too late.

After every presentation, many students and staff in the audience would say that the CHOICES assembly was the best they had ever seen, and for some kids, it might have been the first assembly where they did not get into trouble or get removed. These presentations were necessary and valuable because they truly served the disadvantaged.

By the end of the 2003 school year, we had presented to more than 125,000 students throughout central Illinois and beyond. And we were just getting started.

BREAKING OUT

I rarely took a morning off during the week, but I had been busting my butt around the clock for three months helping to open the RiverPlex, and I needed a breather. It was a pleasant Tuesday morning, and the warm September sun streamed in my bedroom window. I flipped on the television and sat stunned watching a commercial airliner crash into the North Tower of the World Trade Center in New York City. Initially, I thought it might be an accident, but minutes later, a second plane slammed into the South Tower resulting in the destruction of both. I knew we were under attack. A third plane targeted the Pentagon, and a fourth attack was thwarted when passengers overpowered the hijackers and brought the plane down in a field outside Shanksville, Pennsylvania killing everyone on board. Life for everyone changed on September 11, 2001.

COURT TV

Two years after 9/11, I stood on stage at McCormick Place in Chicago waiting to receive the *National Everyday Heroes Award* from *Court TV* for my work with CHOICES. I don't know how they found me or how I was nominated. I simply received a letter at the park district informing me that representatives from *Court TV* would be presenting the award to me and a few others on their awards show, including Lisa Jefferson, the GTE Airfone operator who took the call from Todd Beamer, a passenger on United Flight 93 who tried to take control of the airplane from terrorists on 9/11 and prevented them from crashing the plane into either the White House or the U.S. Capitol in Washington, DC. It

Representative from Court TV presenting me with an award. Photo courtesy of Court TV.

was Lisa who recited the *Lord's Prayer* with Beamer in a moving act before he and several others bravely forced the plane into the ground potentially saving thousands of lives and preserving cherished institutions of our government.

After the program, I met billionaire Mark Cuban, the cable TV and tech giant, who was incredibly gracious, but meeting Lisa was the highlight of the evening. Her touching and inspirational act on 9/11 was just what my CHOICES kids needed to hear, and in turn, she was intrigued by them and offered to help. Several months later in May 2004, she came to the RiverPlex and told her story to the graduates of the third CHOICES class, replaying the recording of her and Todd's conversation, which I broadcasted throughout the arena. It was so still that you could have heard a pin drop.

The 2003 *Court TV Award* was the capstone of an incredible year for CHOICES, and people were beginning to take notice of its progressive approach to helping kids. Earlier in the year, Illinois Attorney General Lisa Madigan presented me with the *Illinois Attorney*

General Peace Keeper Award for our efforts in helping to keep youth out of the system, and CHOICES was again recognized when I received the *Peoria County Association of Police Chiefs Citizen of the Year Award*.

This was important because local law enforcement executives applauded the work we did in preventing crime, and as a former policeman, I valued recognition from the people serving on the front lines of public safety. But receiving the prestigious *National Parks and Recreation Association Humanitarian Service Award* for 2003 was the greatest feather in the program's cap. I accepted the award in St. Louis at the National Conference with Melinda, my mom and her husband, Jerry and his wife, and other members of the Peoria Park District in attendance supporting me.

NATIONAL CARING AWARD

As good as 2003 was, 2004 was even better. Somehow, the Caring Institute, an international non-profit organization dedicated to the principles of caring, integrity, and public service, heard what we were doing and informed me that we were selected as a potential recipient of their national award. They sent a film crew to Peoria and interviewed me and some of the people I had been working with and we did a photo shoot with several children at Calvin Coolidge Middle School. A few weeks later, they announced that I had received an award and that I would be inducted into the Hall of Fame for Caring Americans housed in the Frederick Douglass Museum in Washington, DC.

The Caring Institute flew Melinda and me out, and Jerry and his wife, Tracy, accompanied us, while my assistant, Carrie Wahlfeld, and her husband, drove to DC, where the Caring Institute staff gave us a private tour of the Hall of Fame and we viewed photos of other inductees, including Oprah Winfrey.

That afternoon, the Caring Institute selected me to be interviewed and to appear on a national radio broadcast concerning my induction and on the CHOICES program. They also informed me that I would appear on the cover of the upcoming December 2004 edition of *Caring*, the institute's national magazine. This was significant for CHOICES because it was the first time it was showcased on a national stage.

The induction ceremony was held that evening at the Ronald Reagan Center and was one of the most elaborate affairs I have attended before or since. I chuckle when I recall how out of place I felt during the formal dinner when I got a bowl of soup with no soup in it. The bowl only had one small cracker in the center of it, and I must have looked relieved when the server came to our table and delivered the soup. I had not done much fine dining in my life, and had it not been for Carrie running point during the entire Caring Institute process from start to finish, I would still be trying to figure out which fork to use!

Carrie and I had met while serving on our respective middle school PTOs. She was president of the PTO at Northmoor School, where her daughter attend-

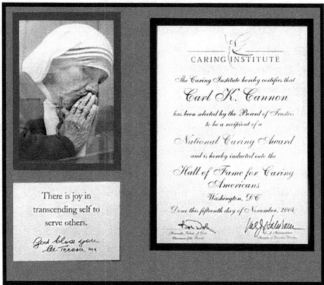

The National Caring Award.

ed, and I was vice-president of the PTO at Franklin Middle School, where Danielle attended. We each had spearheaded efforts to involve our respective schools in the Edison School concept and shared an educational philosophy about kids.

I appreciated her passion and I invited her to work with me on CHOICES. She was smart, hard-working, motivated, loyal, had extraordinary organizational ability, and was committed to kids—all traits I admired and needed. One of her first projects was attending to the myriad details involved with the *Caring Institute Award*. Carrie remained with me for several years and was a vital part of most every project and program. When the park district expanded, she came on as a part-time employee and later joined the park as a full-time employee in another department. I hated losing her.

The cover of Caring Magazine featuring me and students from Calvin Coolidge Middle School. Photo courtesy of the Caring Institute.

Full Cannon

Let me find out!

CHAPTER 15
Family Matters

It was a lot to take in. I stood on the stage of Ford's Theater in our nation's capital and cast my eyes to the booth where President Abraham Lincoln was seated 140 years earlier. The Civil War had just ended a few days prior, and I imagined our weary president enjoying the play below him after four bitter years of conflict.

The National Caring Institute had invited me back to Washington to emcee a program on Frederick Douglass for middle school urban youth as part of Black History Month. I was dressed in a suit and tie which was the first time I had ever given a program in such, but the purpose was serious, and I needed to be a role model and respect the environment I was in. As the children took their seats, I looked for myself in their faces when I was that age. Standing on that stage in front of 500 youth that looked like me was humbling. I savored the moment and considered how far I had come.

FAMILY CANNON

My 3rd great grandfather, Brown Cannon, was born a slave in Philadelphia, Tennessee in 1830, and it is told that his parents were brought to this country from Africa on a slave ship. A sobering thought, that only five generations removed, my family was in chains being bought and sold as chattel. His son, Brown Cannon, Jr., was born in 1848, but it is unknown if he was born free. His wife, Nancy (Foster) Cannon, was a mulatto, and hailed from South Carolina, as did her parents, but she not read nor write.

For many African-Americans, slavery is difficult to embrace as part of a family's history because there is a shame attached to it, and tracing family history before emancipation is difficult at best. We never discussed slavery and lineage in my house growing up, and al-

Family photo of Brown Cannon, Jr., his wife, Nancy, and their children.

though my dad talked about his father, he seldom spoke of his grandparents or mentioned earlier generations. What we have learned about the history of our family has come from a few state and federal census records and from an old Bible or two.

Philadelphia, at the time a small town of about 650 people located 40 miles southwest of Knoxville, Tennessee, and 80 miles northeast of Chattanooga in the Sweetwater Valley, was an agricultural area a few miles south of the Tennessee River founded in 1822. It was mostly inhabited by poor white farmers, some free blacks, and a few landowners with slaves.

The area was important to the British during the French and Indian War as an early outpost in the Cherokee Nation, and later to both sides during Civil War, because of the railroad that ran through it between Knoxville and Chattanooga bisecting the Confederacy.

Although the area was strongly pro-Union and a stop on the Underground Railroad, it was largely ignored early in the war. However, as Union forces advanced further into eastern Tennessee in the fall of 1863, the depot near Philadelphia gained strategic importance and was the site of a skirmish, referred to as "the Affair at Philadelphia," that resulted in a Confederate victory, but the minor engagement had little impact on the war.

1F   28
AFFAIR AT PHILADELPHIA
—— Oct. 20, 1863 ——
Here, in the cavalry action following the Battle of Chickamauga, the Confederate cavalry regiments of Dibrell and Morrison attacked Wolford's cavalry brigade, captured 700 prisoners, 6 mountain howitzers, 50 wagons loaded with stores, 10 ambulances and a quantity of horses and mules. The Federal survivors fled to Loudon. Personnel casualties were small.

Full Cannon

My thoughts returned to President Lincoln, who had issued the Emancipation Proclamation in 1862 that freed all slaves in the South and paved the way for family member, John L. Love, to enlist in the Union Navy with the rank of "First Class Boy" in August 1864 at 18 years of age. Previously, Love had served five months as a 17-year-old "Second Class Boy" on the *USS Lexington*, a timber-clad gunboat. He was born a slave in North Carolina but either escaped or was freed and went to Cincinnati, Ohio and enlisted. He then spent the remainder of the war aboard the *USS Exchange* patrolling the Mississippi River and its tributaries, convoying Union Army transports, shelling enemy shore batteries, and repelling guerrilla attacks on Union camps. He must have been as proud to serve his country at that time as I was to serve mine over a century later.

The USS Lexington during the Civil War.

Mom knew a little more about her family. Her paternal line came from Tennessee and Kentucky, and her great-grandmother, Mattie Dawson, was a Native American from the Creek/Muskogee Nation in Oklahoma. Born in 1856, she married Sam Gasper, who was

Above: Sam and Mattie Gasper. Below: Mom and her father, Samuel Daniels.

likely born a slave in Alabama in 1840, before moving west and living out his life in Navarro, Texas. It was relatively common for freedmen and other blacks to travel west to escape the South and to intermarry with Native Americans, which makes

it even more difficult to trace family history.

It is more important than ever for young people to know their family history and to recognize the importance of tradition, which is the foundation upon which their house is built. In this age of information and greater social inclusion, it is easier to cobble together family history and to address family secrets, but few people are alive who knew them. When I was young, it was okay to be a *Negro*—then it wasn't. Then it was okay to be a *Black*—then it wasn't. Then it was okay to be *African American*—then it wasn't. We live in an ever-changing landscape that is difficult to navigate, but it's really where we each land. It's not the label—it's who's wearing it.

My dad had accompanied me on the trip, and it was meaningful for him, too. It was a gray, wet day, but nothing could dampen our spirits. Guides from the Caring Institute met us at our

hotel and took us to Ford's Theater, where representatives from the U.S. National Park Service gave us an overview of the stage below the booth where Lincoln was shot and where his assassin, John Wilkes Booth, jumped onto from the balcony and broke his leg before escaping out a nearby door.

The BHM program consisted of an actor's portrayal of Frederick Douglass, and I had the duty of introducing him. As the kids were coming in and being seated, I gave my presentation and then in-

Opposite page top: Cousin Fred. Bottom: Mom and my grandmother, Elizabeth Daniels. Top: Grandma Excenia (Woods) Cannon. Bottom: Unknown Cannon boy.

My great-great grand-mother, Nancy Cannon.

troduced the actor depicting Douglass becoming great friends with Lincoln and later being appointed the first African-American U.S. Marshal in the District of Columbia by President Rutherford B. Hayes in 1877.

When the kids left, the grateful Park Service rangers gave us time to understand and appreciate where we were. For me, Ford's Theater was historical holy ground, and the rangers sensed our reverence and offered to give us a private tour of Lincoln's booth. Just being in the theater was inspirational, but to go up the stairwells that were off limits and to stand in the booth where everything was essentially untouched since the day of the President's murder, was surreal. I loved history, but being allowed to walk through like I did, connected me with my country like nothing else, and it helped solidify the belief that, despite periods of collective and individual darkness, we are a good and just people. The tour I experienced with my dad will forever be part of my life.

HALL OF FAME

There are two professional occasions that are most meaningful in my life. The first occurred in 2001 when the Central Illinois African American Committee presented me with a *Dr. Martin Luther King Drum Major Award* for my early work in creating CHOICES. The award recognized that the program was promoting a civil rights message of justice for all young people. Having grown up during the Civil Rights era, the award meant to me that I was living up to what Dr. King hoped would be the battle cry across the nation and that I had received internal recognition from my own community, which was often difficult.

The most significant moment occurred in 2005 when I was inducted into the *Central Illinois African American Hall of Fame*. I was honored to be inducted with Larry Ivory, one of the founders of the National Black Chamber of Commerce and its current national chairman, and to deliver the keynote address, which I believe to be the best I have ever given. I had help writing it from my brother, Bill, which made it even more personal. The Hall of Fame is in the upper level of the Proctor Recreation Center and is a lasting testament to those who dedicated their lives to making the community a place of opportunity and equality.

MY GIRLS

Where does a decade go? A lot had happened since the Cannon family crossed the Murray Baker Bridge on its return to Peoria. I was knee-deep in CHOICES, and Melinda was my rock. She worked part time, raised the kids, and helped me with anything and everything. Coming from a military family, she was used to frequent moves, long hours, separation, and controlled chaos on every front. That was our life, and she was okay with it. From the moment we met, she knew that I was all about reaching out to kids, and she just thought the long hours were the norm. She understood that life doesn't always happen on a time schedule or as planned.

When we came back to Peoria, my job was to get Summer enrolled in a good public middle school, but when we approached the building, I spotted a bullet hole in the front glass, which I interpreted as a bad sign. We then entered the lobby and were ignored by the secretary for several minutes despite being the only people there. "Let's go, Summer," I said gruffly.

I was angry and did not want my daughter to have to put up with that, so we went home and I pulled out the phone book and started looking for alternatives, but all were too expensive. Eventually, I found South Side Catholic. I had never heard of it, but I soon located it next to an old church. I rang the doorbell and Sister Judith Ann answered. She explained that they were a private school sponsored by the local diocese of the Catholic Church and then she outlined the curriculum. "I want to enroll my daughter today," I stated boldly.

The sister locked eyes with me. "We need to interview your daughter first," she said, looking like a gunfighter squinting into the sun.

I blinked first. I was scared to death that I had not prepared Summer for this level of schooling, but I knew that I had to go home and bring her back to interview. Sister Judith Ann was also the principal and did not let me stay in the room during the interview, but when Summer came out smiling, I knew all had gone well. Summer graduated first in her class in her 8th grade year.

I was very involved in Summer and Danielle's education. I wanted Summer to attend a private high school, but it was too expensive, so she attended Peoria High, my alma mater. I was worried about her attending PHS, so I wrote an introduction letter and, much to her embarrassment, attended the PHS Freshman Meet the Teacher Night. I went from classroom to classroom introducing myself and delivering that letter. I related that, "I did not want to find out how my daughter was doing on payday. I want to know what she is doing and when she is doing it in real time."

I made a personal visit to each of her teachers her first three years of high school. I was going to skip it her senior year, but she said, "No, you're not!"

Not surprising, she was the first of my parents' grandchildren to go to college. In 2004, Summer gave birth to Logan, our first grandchild. He was a blessing that we did not expect and was the son we never had. Nothing could compare to becoming a grandparent and welcoming a new member into our growing family.

In 2005, my little Danielle was not so little. She had begun her freshman year at Peoria Richwoods High

School and became active in everything. She ran track, took karate and kickboxing, and enrolled in JROTC, but she would get upset that I was spending too much time on CHOICES and at work. As she grew older, she

Summer and Logan

Opposite page:
   Summer and me.

understood that there were kids worse off than her, but I sometimes felt guilty that I had given too much time to other kids and not enough to my own, especially to her. Whenever we went out in public as a family, people greeted me, which I loved, but I often worried that my girls felt left out or pushed aside. Years later, I read something each had written:

SUMMER: *"I know many people who grew up without a dad. I'm beyond blessed not to know what that's like. Not only do I have a father who was present, but I have a father who is caring, passionate, has my back, and I can reach out to him no matter what the issue is, day or night. Even when I make a mistake I can always 'come home to Dad."*

DANIELLE: *"Dad has made a tremendous impact on people by leading with his heart. I have seen people drawn to him and cling to him. I have seen him inspire others and bring them to tears of gratefulness. Also, he doesn't just talk the talk, he walks the walk. I have seen so many of his ideas come to fruition—and it all points back to my dad's love for people and a desire to make a difference and improve the lives of others. Growing up it was pretty hard. I remember being jealous, angry, and annoyed at times. In 5th grade he missed a dance program I was in and I was devastated. I remember looking at my mom in the audience and even her face screamed, 'Where is he!' When we got home, he was there. I was in tears the minute I saw him. He brought me a card and apologized that night. He explained that he needed to help someone at his job right away.*

I remember thinking that the person he helped must've been pretty important, but I couldn't decide if they were more important than me or not. Up until that point he had never let me down.

When I was a toddler through grade school, being dad's daughter was the coolest thing in the world, most times. A lot of people (kids and adults) were amazed at who my dad was and ad-

mired him. This made my life pretty easy, but in middle and high school it was less cool. I got teased at times, nothing I couldn't handle, but it still bothered me. Today, it's the coolest thing in the world. My childhood was everything it should've been. Looking back, it wasn't perfect, but both my mom and dad did everything to make sure that I had what I needed. I wouldn't change a thing. My dad is one of a kind and I am proud to be his daughter."

Pardon me while I cry.

My girls.

CHAPTER 16
ELITE

TOO MANY MURDERS

Sixteen homicides in one year was sixteen too many. Peoria was reeling and all crime was on the rise. If we did nothing, it would multiply. With civic and elected leadership doing what they could, the wheels were already in motion to find a way to mitigate the situation, but I had to do something more to help.

On a cool morning in late fall 2006, my daughter, Summer, was working on the computer in my home office when she heard someone knocking at a side door just off the kitchen. She assumed it was a young person wanting to speak with me, but she would not answer the door since I had told her never to answer it when home alone. Kobe, our dog, barked until the knocking stopped and Summer returned to work. A short while later, a loud boom startled her and she went toward the kitchen to investigate and came face-to-face with a young man who had just kicked in the door and was clutching her purse that she had left on the kitchen table. The man turned and rushed out the door, and Summer went after him. Thank God, she did not catch him and returned and called 911 and me.

I was in a meeting at the RiverPlex and raced home. When I arrived, the police were already there and Summer was giving them a description of the suspect—a young black man wearing a black hoodie, blue jeans, and white tennis shoes. Within 10 minutes, the police did a street lineup of four or five people fitting the description. Summer did not implicate any of them, but the profile allowed the police to round up that many people in a small area within a few minutes. That the police could pick up so many fitting the description during a school day spoke to the community at that time. My thoughts turned to the hoodie. *What if young people dared to be different, and what if they dared to wear a white hoodie instead of a black one?* That initiated my "Dare to be Different" approach.

That night, I attended a public forum in the packed basement of the Riverside Community Church. The mood was serious, and I got up and spoke about what had happened in my own home earlier in the day. "It's personal now," I said, sharing the emotional weight of the event. "My daughter could have been one of those victims!"

The next day, the break-in house made headlines in the local newspaper, and Peoria mayor, Jim Ardis, asked me to speak at an upcoming forum on a *WTVP* simulcast as part of his community forum against crime that included the Peoria County State's Attorney, a local pastor, the Peoria Police Chief, and the Peoria County Sheriff.

The forum had a live audience, and I felt good about myself sitting on a panel with such leaders, but my ego trip was short-lived. People in the audience asked tough questions wanting real answers, but all we gave them was the same tired old lip service they had been hearing. After the show, I sat in my car outside the studio feeling guilty that all I had done was run my mouth. I started thinking about what I could do to help the kids in the community get off the streets. It was time for action.

STANDING VIGIL

Before the end of the year, Peoria experienced its 17th homicide, and I made another direct public appeal to help curb the violence by holding a prayer vigil in the community where the victim had lived. I had done so for each of the previous homicides, and the vigils were an outcry against those in the minority who were perpetrating the crimes. We were trying to grow responsible kids, but they were being endangered by a criminal element that contributed to the destruction of our community and besmirched the good name of the city. Younger violence was increasing, and we had to respond.

Holding a street vigil in Peoria.

Before each vigil, I approached the family of the victim and asked if I could honor their loved one in a public gathering lasting less than an hour at the site where the murder occurred. It's a tough knock on the door asking the mother of a murder victim permission to speak about their child. I had earned credibility in the community, and the family appreciated the gesture. It was their chance to heal, to take back control of their lives, and not to be victims. It was a restorative way to

Mayor Ardis speaks at a vigil. Opposite page: a family mourns the loss of a loved one.

turn the loss of their loved one into an opportunity to save another family from enduring the same grief.

Once I had the blessing of the family, I issued a press release and put a call out to my CHOICES (and later ELITE) community, which included family members, friends, media, Mayor Ardis, law enforcement, and other interested citizens.

For years, the CHOICES program carried uplifting and motivational signs during its graduation march, and we distributed them to people at the vigils to convey a

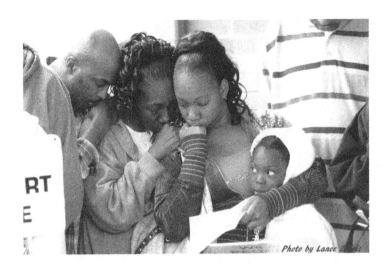

Photo by Lance [...]

powerful message of hope and solidarity. We started on time, and the community showed up and stayed on script. We gave God most of the time, and I had a clergy member open and close with a prayer. The mayor then spoke for a couple minutes against violence. I did not make those prayer vigils political showcases. No "D" No "R" (democrat or republican), just community.

Instead of people facing inward, I had them face outward to warn those who were perps that we would be looking for them. I used a sound system to amplify the message, "Enough is enough! Can you hear me now!"

After holding 17 vigils in one year, I was emotionally drained and physically exhausted. Although I felt obligated to the community to do them, I questioned their effectiveness, and after mulling it over and committing considerable time in prayer, I passed the torch to Pastor Harvey Burnett, a friend and well-known lay minister. Harvey was respected for his street ministry and had

worked with local law enforcement in successful community drives to put guns down and to turn them in. He was the right man to lead the charge, and I was determined to support him.

Another reason I stopped leading vigils was because those I wanted to reach were receiving the message in the wrong way. Thugs and at-risk youth began seeing them as rites of passage and a public opportunity to pay homage to their fallen by wearing t-shirts bearing the victim's face or other messages. I saw this as dangerous, and it made it easier step aside and to remain focused on prevention. Many people had endeared themselves to the notion and process of a having a vigil, but not to the message, and the absence of such vigils left a void to some. I never got blowback from gang members or suspected perpetrators for holding the vigils because they respected that I was consistent in telling them that, although the consequences for their actions would be delivered out of love and concern, they ultimately would be delivered.

I am a man of faith, and I think the strength of who I am is that faith. I do not push it on others, but I am mindful of it. The hardcore black man exterior that ev-

Opposite page: A mother and child support the family of a victim at a vigil. Above: The sign says it all.

eryone sees is just a little spirit that tells people what they need to hear. After one vigil, this prompted a reporter to ask, "Why are you doing this? Prayer is not doing any good."

"If prayer doesn't work," I said, "we have no chance."

Abraham Lincoln was a wise and sensible man, and I often looked to his words for answers. In December 1861, six months into the Civil War and on the verge of issuing the Emancipation Proclamation, he addressed Congress:

"The dogmas of the quiet past are inadequate to the stormy present. The occasion is piled high with difficulty, and we must rise with the occasion. As our case is new, so we must think anew, and act anew. We must disenthrall ourselves, and then we shall save our country."

The Peoria of 2006 had changed since the Civil War, but the people of that time and this shared the need for a new and different way of thinking and acting to address our problems. Unemployment, lack of opportunity, poverty, drugs, violent crime, and other issues were the enemies, and their target was our youth. It was time to act anew.

ACTING ANEW

A young skinny white girl in a skimpy string halter top, dirty blue jeans with holes in the knees, and flip-flops sat waiting for me in the conference room of the RiverPlex. I was mad the moment I saw her. "Why are you here?" I chirped, as I scanned a messy handwritten application checkered with omissions, misspellings, and errors.

"I want a job," she snipped, unaware that she was being short with the person who might hire her.

I sat and leaned across the table. "No, you don't, young lady," I scolded. "Just look at you. You're not serious about a job."

That's when it dawned on me that there were a lot of young people like her who wanted to work but who did not know where or how to begin finding a job. I recalled the frustration I felt in the parking lot after the mayor's program on crime. I felt as helpless then as she did now. She did not know the first thing about how to fill out an employment application, how to dress for success, or even how to stand when a potential employer enters the room.

And why didn't she know? She had not been taught. If I were to get kids off the streets, out of the alleys, and to save lives, I had to offer them something of value that would lead to something of even greater value. Hope. Skills. And respect.

I went to work the next day and approached my boss, Brent Wheeler. "I got it!" I said excitedly. "What if we taught young people how to get jobs? What if we helped get them jobs? And how can we make this work?"

Brent's eyes lit up. "How can we make this bigger?"

I had all the approval I needed, and I ran with it. I talked to anybody who would listen and began formulating a plan to develop a new jobs program tied into CHOICES—one that I could take into the schools to reach the unreachable. It was risky and bold. And I would need volunteers. A lot of them.

VOLUNTEERS ALL

Volunteerism is the lifeblood of most social programs. Without it they will die. It is also one of the most fulfilling and self-rewarding acts that a person can do if their heart is pure. Giving of oneself without seeking reward or having a personal agenda is uplifting and restorative to the soul.

I attract most of my volunteers through my own attitude. If the head of a program or a leader isn't enthusiastic about what they're doing, it's unrealistic to think that the volunteers will be. They must be given the chance to use their volunteer fever and spirit. It was important for me to exude enthusiasm and to be consistent. I was blessed with an internal excitement that I could pour into others despite their different personalities.

I recognized that each volunteer needed a different lane, and I allowed them to experience their own success by helping a child. People want to make a difference, and I tried to encourage them to help by utilizing their unique personality, experience, and love. I had to find a person's fit and put them in a position to maximize their talents and gifts in a way that allowed them to be a caring adult that recognized that in every audience there is a kid sitting in silence that needs them.

Every graduation, those volunteers meet those kids on the stage, and the love is undying. There's a bond that will last beyond today. We've got volunteers that know things about their kids that I will never know. If it's good and contagious and doable, I supported it.

The shelf life of a volunteer is 3-5 years, but over time, our volunteer force has grown exponentially. Our

Sally Klabunde, Al Thompson, and Hugh Sizemore share a laugh at an ELITE event.

young volunteers bring immense energy and are a good fit with young people because kids want mentorship and direction from young adults that they can better identify with. However, young volunteers often are the first to leave because they are evolving in their own careers and are more transitory by nature. And although young volunteers in their late 20s and 30s have more focus, they also are more involved with raising their own families. Conversely, older volunteers are sometimes best because they bring more knowledge, patience, and experience to a project and are more settled. However, they often lack the energy and endurance of younger volunteers. But that doesn't mean they can't shift roles and better utilize their wisdom.

Volunteerism also has its detractors. Some say that without financial motivation, it's hard to retain volunteers, but I've found that if volunteerism is utilized in spurts, volunteers see the immediate fruits of their labor and remain and evolve into other areas.

Volunteers become an issue when they bring an agenda. They may have great skills and something to contribute, but other adults and even the kids know when they have an agenda or personal motives. Generally, they weed themselves out quickly when they discover that their needs do not align with those of the organization or serve the greater good, which at the end of the day, should be the goal of every institution and its members.

On October 10, 2006, a small, eclectic group of volunteers met at the RiverPlex. Some had little idea why they were there and others less than that, but all wanted to help.

Hugh Sizemore and Sandy Klabunde worked together through the Riverside Community Church Youth Ministry and had come to me at the RiverPlex seeking day passes for disadvantaged kids at the Taft homes. I didn't know either, but I offered to trade day passes in return for their presence at the meeting. Hugh was employed at Caterpillar and had worked in upper management at McDonald's. He had also worked as a social worker in his hometown of Detroit and was due to retire in a few months. Sandy was a renowned sculptor whose works appeared in more than 20 galleries throughout the country and had worked with kids at Irving Elementary School.

I also invited Cheryll Boswell, the Executive Director of METEC, a not-for-profit community development corporation that provided credit counseling, and administered and promoted home ownership programs, social outreach for families, and job training and education for youths. She had a strong Caterpillar management background and brought a high level of expertise teaching people about finances. She was quite an asset.

I met Mary Arnold on the phone while discussing birthday parties. She was working at Peoria Flag & Decorating Company and had been a committed volunteer for CASA (Court Ordered Special Advocate for Children). Since we were reaching out to the same kids I had in mind for our CHOICES program, I convinced her to attend the meeting, as I did my Aunt Rose, who had called about something unrelated. I shared with her what I was doing, and she jumped on it. Rose had a tough life and a big heart for the kids we were targeting to help.

Charles Stewart was one of my shift leaders at the RiverPlex, and he had reached out because of something he wanted to do with disadvantaged kids. He was already working with students at Manual High School, and I knew how well he interacted with youth.

The final attendee at that first meeting was the co-author of this book, Lance Zedric, a historian and fellow Army veteran. We had met just three days prior at *An Evening With Anna Chennault*, a civic event arranged by Stephen Thomas and his wife, Elaine Chao Thomas, that honored the wife of Gen. Claire Chennault, commander of the famed *Flying Tigers* fighter unit that flew with the Chinese Air Force prior to America's entry in World War II.

Elaine was the founder of the Peoria *Joy Luck Club*, a social organization comprised of women from different countries and cultural backgrounds, and was a friend of Lance and his wife, Ching. They were part of the planning committee and had accompanied Stephen and Elaine to the event. Lance told me that he was a special education teacher at the Children's Home and that he had attended one of my CHOICES programs, so I knew where his heart was. We've been friends ever since.

Within a week, more people volunteered, and by the end of the year, a complete staff had been assembled. Carrie Wahlfeld-Bottrell, Sherry Cannon, Tony Jenkins, Diane Cook, Jerry Stoneburner, Kathryn Timmes, Al Thompson, Jamie Powers, Pastor Claire Underwood, Shaleese Pie, Rev. Alphonso Lyons, DeMario Boone, Laura Lee, Bernice Young, Brent Wheeler, Agbara Bryson, Nichelle Ritterhoff, Connie Sullivan, Keith McDaniel, John Lewis, Gary Martin, and my dad were the core group in the beginning of the CHOICES Jobs Training Program. Some stayed and some left, but all contributed.

WHAT'S IN A NAME

The CHOICES Youth Outreach Program had existed for over a decade and was well known, but the new CHOICES Jobs Training Program needed to set itself apart and establish an identity. The group tossed around several ideas over the next two weeks, and at our meeting on October 25, just two days after a teenage invader had kicked in my front door, Lance proposed that the new CHOICES Jobs Training Program be renamed the *ELITE Youth Program*, with ELITE being an acronym for "Economic Leaders Integrating Trained Employable Youth."

The name reflected not only the goal of getting business leaders to employ kids that were already trained in soft skills and who were ready to enter the work force, but that they were quality kids. The name stuck.

The next couple months were busy and exciting. We developed a mission statement, launched a website, and produced a fundraising piece entitled, *100 Jobs and You*, that challenged prospective employers to create 100 part-time jobs for our future ELITE graduates by April 30, 2007 and generated an initial $25,000 donation from Caterpillar. Tony and Sherry created a colorful logo and commissioned an art student from Bradley University to produce it. The recognizable logo depicting one figure helping another up the stairway of success is symbolic of the nature of the program and represents it to this day.

The Elite Youth Program is dedicated to identifying motivated, trustworthy, economically disadvantaged high school youth who want to work—and providing them with a job—but only after they've earned it.

Elite Youth Program Mission Statement

Mayor Jim Ardis announces the creation of ELITE during a press conference in 2007.

Having the endorsement of Congressman Ray La-Hood and Mayor Ardis was important. In early January 2007, I personally visited each and explained the ELITE concept. Both offered their unequivocal support and hailed the program as part of a realistic and viable solution to a significant problem. Initially, I was concerned that the ELITE program might dilute the effect of the mayor's summer jobs initiative, but that was avoided when we rescheduled our news conference announcing the start of ELITE, and partnered with the City of Peoria and the mayor in a public declaration of his

ELITE making a difference.

Mayor's Careers for Youth 07' program.

Four men have served as Mayor of Peoria since I returned to Peoria after retiring from the military in 1995, and each one supported my CHOICES program and other efforts to help kids and address issues in the community. Each struggled with how to curb crime and how to make the city safer and more attractive to business. Each had his own ideas how to implement their plans, but all agreed that it began with education, opportunity, and employment.

Jim Maloof was in office when I returned and was nearing the end of a successful 12-year run that concluded in 1997. He was a good guy and loved CHOICES. "Bud" Grieves followed and had the same supportive mindset. He only served one term and was followed

by Dave Ransburg, who had less personality than the previous two mayors but more intellect than anyone I ever met in political office. He supported CHOICES scholarships through his corporation in a quiet, non-political way, but was defeated by Ardis in the 2005 mayoral election.

Although I had supported Ransburg in the election, Jim Ardis and I became great friends. I had campaigned against him because I thought he was too young and lacked understanding about our city, but he immediately reached out and offered to help without asking me to do anything political for him, which earned my respect. It was apparent early on that we shared a commitment toward bettering the lives of kids. I believe that everything he does is for the greater good of the community, and that he is willing to cross lines and shake hands with people like me who have contrasting styles. Mayor Ardis recalled the early days of ELITE:

"I knew Carl as a city council member, but I really got to know him after being elected mayor. He came to me to discuss the ELITE concept, which I knew was a winner, especially with him as the driving force. His military and corrections background provided him a lot of self-discipline, and how to provide discipline when needed. So many of his Elite kids need a little bit of that in varying doses. Many of them are just aching to have someone care about them, to love them, and to tell them that, 'I care about you and I love you,' and 'I want you to be successful.' He's the father figure that a lot don't have. He's a great role model and an outstanding motivator. Carl teaches them the skills they'll need to get a good education and a good job so they can be successful and productive to the community. And he's a natural leader. Because he leads by exam-

Opposite: ELITE kids having fun at the lock-in. Above: Hugh Sizemore and Sherry Cannon conduct a mock job interview with an ELITE candidate.

ple, he doesn't have a problem getting other people to help his missions. You can't put a price tag on how many kids he's saved from prison (or worse). You can quantify and attribute the success of his kids to Carl and his programs."

I also approached interim District 150 Superintendent Ken Hinton and explained the program and

the curriculum. I asked permission for our vetted training teams, composed of a site manager, team leader, and team members, to go into the schools and to arrange for a block of school time to provide instruction. Hinton gave his full support clearing the way.

In the first year, the ELITE Youth Program drew approximately 30 students each from three of the four Peoria public high schools (Manual, Peoria Central and Woodruff) and from Peoria alternative schools. School counselors initiated the process by identifying socially and economically disadvantaged students who they believed were good candidates for the program. I did assemblies at each school introducing the concept and the rules required, and ELITE staff then visited the schools and interviewed the students.

But we did not accept everyone. If a student lied, displayed an attitude, or wanted something for nothing, we denied them. We wanted only those students who were ready to earn the chance at employment. Candidates were then screened and selected. Once accepted, the students signed a covenant with staff

Photo captions: (Opposite page top) ELITE candidates get certified in CPR. Bottom: The first ELITE lock-in. Top: an ELITE graduate holds his "Certificate Of The Most High Achievement."

promising to remain in school, to maintain 90 percent or greater attendance, to act and perform appropriately in school, not participate in any illegal activity, and to give outstanding effort. Any violation of the covenant was grounds for dismissal from the program and from their job.

FIRST CLASS

On February 12, 2007, 90 candidates attended three different assemblies and began an intensive 10-week job skills training course based on developing and reinforcing character not upon financial need. We kicked off the program with a Zero Week assembly for all candidates where we set expectations and emphasized rules and conduct. Thereafter, training teams went into the schools for one or two hours each week and taught a variety of skills and presented practical, necessary information to help students become better citizens, better employees, and better people.

The teams gave instruction in several core areas including job market preparation, job application process, interviewing, job survival, financial literacy I, financial literacy II, job termination, dressing for success & appearance, and career opportunities. The curriculum also required that all students get certified in first aid and CPR, which was earned on a Saturday.

Halfway through the curriculum, I hosted a mandatory overnight lock-in for all students and staff at the RiverPlex. The event presented a wonderful opportunity for students to intermingle in a healthy social environment. We opened the pool and the basketball courts and had pizza and snacks delivered. That first lock-in occurred the same year that the school district was going to close Woodruff High School and move its students to Peoria High, so I made the schedule to combine the kids to offset gang issues that were prevalent at the time and to create positive relationships between the two high schools. When the schools combined that next year, we had students who were part of the same concept. Some said that this familiarization among students helped prevent potential gang issues and that the ELITE kids were difference makers. Nothing could have made me prouder.

GRADUATION

One week before graduation, park district vans picked up all potential graduates from the RiverPlex and shuttled them to the JC Penney store in Northwoods Mall to be outfitted for the inaugural ELITE Job Fair and for graduation. Like with CHOICES, each graduate received dress slacks and a dress shirt. Males also selected a tie and ladies a scarf of their choice. A few days later, female graduates received a free hair appointment at a local salon.

On May 16, 2007, 56 graduates of the inaugural ELITE Youth Program assembled in the RiverPlex and attended a job fair consisting of employers that had pledged jobs to a program job bank. Two hours later, Mayor Ardis, Superintendent Hinton, Bonnie Noble, and others presented the graduates with Certificates of Achievement. Three television stations and one newspaper covered the event. It was a proud moment for everyone. One that has been renewed every year since then and validated the concept of ELITE.

Some of the ELITE volunteers for the first class, 2007. Back L-R: Joe McCormick, Al Thompson, Cheryll Boswell, Lance Zedric, Tony Jenkins, Rev. Alphonso Lyons. Front L-R: Me, Mary Arnold, Sherry Cannon, Sandy Klabunde, Hugh Sizemore, Rose Daniels, Carrie Wahlfeld-Bottrell, Kathryn Timmes, Shaleese Pie, Jamie Powers, and DeMario Boone. Photo by Ching Zedric

CHAPTER 17
Best of Times

The only thing better than watching 56 high school students receive a certificate of achievement from the first ELITE Youth Program graduation was watching my daughter, Summer, receive a college diploma from Bradley University a few days later. Earning a bachelor's degree had not been easy, nor should it have been, and as she walked across the stage at the Peoria Civic Center to have it conferred, my heart was filled with joy. Our little girl had achieved what her parents had not, and as I reflected on how quickly time had passed, I thought of the proud parents of the ELITE students at their recent graduation and allowed myself a tiny smile. For their families and mine, it was a summer of hope.

ELITE

The inaugural year of the ELITE Youth Program was a smashing success, and everyone was happy. The concept of ELITE, implemented by an outstanding and diverse corps of volunteers and vigorously supported by civic leaders and local employers, had made an impression. More important, it had made a difference in the lives of the students it served. The following are just a few of the many comments we received from graduates.

"The ELITE program really turned my life around. It taught me to be a more well-mannered student and person. It also improved my communication skills and taught me how to approach people. This program has not only equipped me for now, it equipped me for the future. It's equipped me for life."

—K. Hill

"This program has helped me in an extreme way. I have a good summer job at Northwoods Mall. I sincerely thank the ELITE Program!"

—Anonymous

"The ELITE Program has helped me grow as a person. Before ELITE I had trouble speaking in front of big groups. I didn't know what to do in an interview or how to fill out an application. Now, I can confidently speak in front of people, and my interview skills have greatly improved. I never could have done any of those things without the ELITE Program." —S. Lopez

MORE CHOICES

Good news travels fast, and it did not take long for the community to recognize the value of the ELITE Youth Program. One week after graduation, WEEK-TV, the Peoria NBC affiliate, contacted me and requested 13 ELITE and CHOICES youth to appear in two celebrity television commercials entitled, *Do The Right Thing,* that were part of a county-wide anti-bullying campaign spearheaded by Peoria Police Chief Steven Settingsgaard and Peoria County Sheriff Mike McCoy, who appeared in the commercials with the kids. The spots were funded by a grant from the Illinois Sheriffs' Association and appeared beginning in August 2007.

Steven Settingsgaard and Mike McCoy.

Settingsgaard became police chief in 2005 and was hired out of Milwaukee. He was a religious man and serious about law enforcement. When he came to Peoria, he posted the names of convicted prostitutes and their johns, which embarrassed a lot of people, but that's who he was. He was about community policing and was open to innovative approaches with youth to control behavior. We had an excellent relationship, and he was a true friend to the program, as was Sheriff McCoy, who had assumed office when Chuck Schofield died in 2003. Sheriff McCoy supported CHOICES and ELITE for several years and took part in many graduations, vigils, and other programs.

With the first ELITE graduation behind me and summer programming around the corner, I refocused on CHOICES, which had expanded consistently for a decade, surpassing all expectations for a homegrown, volunteer-based outreach program. The addition of ELITE further enhanced the reputation of CHOICES and increased demand for both programs, which meant more time, energy, and resources were needed—neither of which I had, but to see the hope they generated in the community, I vowed to find a way.

WE ARE MARSHALL

Hope is wherever one finds it, and I had to look no further than Jack Lengyel to find mine. In 1971, he became head football coach of Marshall University after most of the team had died in a plane crash after returning from a game in November 1970. Left with only a few returning players that either had been injured or were on disciplinary suspension, he rebuilt the team and won two games in his first year. The story of Lengyel and his team was the subject of the hit movie, *We Are Marshall*, and Lengyel was portrayed by actor Matthew McConaughey.

In July 2007, he visited the RiverPlex and spoke to some 100 CHOICES kids and others about overcoming adversity and not giving up.

"One of the greatest lessons of athletics is when you're face down, to get up on your feet and move toward success," he said. "The only one who can stop you is yourself."

He was speaking to me. Every word hit home and held meaning. Despite Jack's amazing story and the publicity surrounding the movie, I was inspired by his humility, strengthened by his faith, and impressed that he knew just what I needed to hear.

Jack Lengyel, me, and Brent Wheeler.

HEROES ALL

Earlier in the summer, Red Cross CEO, Anne Fox, had invited me to attend the Central Illinois American Red Cross Heartland Heroes Dinner at the Hotel Pere Marquette. It was a formal black tie dinner unlike anything I was accustomed to, and I thought it odd that the first course began with a teaspoon of ice chips with which to freshen my palette. I soon learned why when Caterpillar CEO, Jim Owens, surprised me and presented me with the *Heartland Heroes Citizenship Award* for my work with CHOICES and ELITE.

Full Cannon

I was offered the opportunity to make some remarks, which usually is not a problem, but I was caught
off guard. For one of the few times in my life, I was
tongue-tied. It was an honor to be recognized by an
international organization like the Red Cross and to be
counted among some of the most selfless and generous people in our community, but I wish I had known
ahead of time.

A month later on July 22, the leaders of the Northwoods Church in Peoria asked me to participate in
three weekend sermons over two days as part of their
Real Heroes theme. They asked me to center my spiritual message to their congregation of more than 4000
people on how I moved kids, but also on how I moved
adults and offered them hope in human ways. This
time I had a lot to say.

*Sharing the stage with Batman and Spider-Man at North-
woods Church. Opposite: With former First Lady Laura Bush.*

Jesus Christ is my Lord and Savior and is greater than all others who have ever lived. I then look to national heroes Abraham Lincoln, Frederick Douglass, Franklin Roosevelt, and Barrack Obama as the greatest Americans because they reached out to the least of us and inspired us to rise. Closer to home, I

am inspired by former Peorians, Gen. John Shalikashvili, and Gen. Wayne Downing. Both enjoyed brilliant military careers and proved that anything was possible regardless of where a person came from.

Shalikashvili was born in Poland to a Russian émigré and a Polish mother and emigrated to Peoria in 1952, where he later graduated from Peoria High School and Bradley University. He served as the first foreign-born Chairman of the Joint Chiefs of Staff and was awarded the Presidential Medal of Freedom by President Clinton. And did I mention that we graduated from the same high school?

Downing was born in Peoria, and his dad was killed in action in Europe during World War II. After graduating from high school, he attended the U.S. Military Academy at West Point and went on to lead the U.S. Special Operations Command in charge of all our na-

Gen. Wayne A. Downing
U.S. Army photo.

Gen. John M.D. Shalikashvili
U.S. Army photo.

tion's elite forces. After 9/11, President George W. Bush called Downing out of retirement, and he served for a year as the first U.S. Deputy National Security Advisor for Combating Terrorism.

He had died in Peoria just four days before I spoke at Northwoods Church, and he was heavy on mind. I had always wanted to meet him, but I didn't reach out in time, and I promised myself that if I ever again lived in the same hometown as one of my heroes, I would stop by and say hello. On October 10, 2008, the Peoria Airport was renamed the *General Wayne A. Downing Peoria International Airport* in his honor.

By any definition, both men were heroes, and I admired them. As a former soldier, I have a soft spot in my heart for anyone who serves or who has served in the armed forces whether in peacetime or war—as a Navy SEAL or cook, as draftee or volunteer. And that includes law enforcement and first responders.

Those who answer the call to duty and put themselves in harm's way deserve to be called heroes, although most are uncomfortable with the label. I witnessed this in 1992 while in charge of security for the VIP area at Ft. Leavenworth when then Chairmen of the Joint Chiefs of Staff, Colin Powell, dedicated the Buffalo Soldiers monument honoring the all-black 9th and 10th Cavalry Regiments that were formed during the Indian Wars and served in the Spanish American War and in World War II. I was honored to meet Gen. Powell and two dozen surviving veterans of the segregated units. They carried a quiet pride for having "been there and done that" and exemplified the best qualities in all of us.

One does not need to wear a uniform to be a hero. I find heroism everywhere. I find it in everyday dads with beer guts and sore backs who work double shifts at a factory to give their families something extra at

Group shot of "Buffalo Soldiers" taken at the dedication of the Buffalo Soldier statue. Most of the men in this photo served in segregated units during World War II.

Christmas. I find it in exhausted single mothers who toil as CNAs or wait tables with aching feet and who go home late and still help their children with homework. I find it in the knowing smile and loving touch of an aging grandparent. And I find it in unsung heroes everywhere who get up, go to work, and do what they are supposed to do without fanfare, recognition, or reward. That's heroism.

My unsung heroes are also the principals, teachers, school workers, and volunteers who help kids. Those who go above and beyond what is asked or expected. My heroes are the CHOICES kids from Missouri, Ohio, and Illinois who dare to be different and who stand up against the popular wrong in favor of the unpopular right. Those who meet the unguarded moment of vulnerability with moral courage and do what is right and best. These are my heroes, and I take great satisfaction in telling the world about their courage and rec-

ognizing them each year at the ELITE Awards program.

ELITE DRUM LINE

The CHOICES Drum Line had been an integral part of my outreach efforts since 2004 and had helped create momentum going into the next school year. A week

after the 2007 CHOICES Awards Program, I created the ELITE Pulses of Hope Drum Line composed of a group of young men from the Roosevelt Middle School Band who had nothing to do during the summer months. Original members Jonathan Grimes, Timothy Tatum, Chase Krones, Austin Armstrong, Jeff Adams, and Justin were outstanding performers and fine representatives of the ELITE program. As popularity and demand increased, the park district sponsored the drum line and it became part of the outreach program and our calling card at all non-season events.

Participation was open to any high school student and required them to meet the same academic, behavioral, and attendance criteria as any ELITE student. Musically, the standards were hard and high, and the kids did not come in raw. Most had musical training and were members of their school bands, and when I wanted to find new talent, the drum line members recruited

other kids and even created several original cadences.

The drum line was popular and gave us instant credibility with kids. When they heard those drums, they wanted to be part of ELITE and everything that went with it, and the parents loved it, too. The positivity it generated shifted the community mindset, and the drum line was asked to perform everywhere. The kids

Top: CHOICES kids and their parents march through Peoria. Bottom and Top Opposite: The Drum Line performs for the crowd at the Awards Program. Opposite Bottom: Releasing balloons of hope. Photos by Ching Zedric.

were true professionals and took their performances seriously. They smiled, played to the crowd, and served as ambassadors of excellence.

A month later, I pulled out all the stops for the 2007 CHOICES Awards program. On August 9, the drum line led CHOICES award recipients and their parents carrying signs of hope on a joyous procession from the Hotel Pere Marquette down the middle of Main Street to the RiverPlex.

Once at the RiverPlex, parents and community

Above: ELITE graduates enjoy their moment. Opposite page: Shaleese Pie leads the ELITE choir.

leaders were seated in the arena, and then the drum line led the students to their seats. The kids would be waving at their parents, and once the last row of kids arrived, the drum line stopped playing. The Peoria Police Color Guard then entered up the center aisle and posted the colors on the stage for the playing of the National Anthem. After the color guard left and a pastor gave the invocation, the drum line followed them out to the steady beat of drums.

Unlike solemn high school graduations, I wanted CHOICES and ELITE ceremonies to show how excited our community should be about those who many people said were most likely to fail, but who were selected by their schools and teachers for turning it around. It was a celebration of success, and I wanted everyone to hear it.

CHOICES/ELITE CHOIR
The CHOICES/ELITE choir has created more good

will and brought more immediate joy to people than any of my programs. Composed of children from Pekin, Bartonville, and surrounding schools, I formed the choir while working at the prison in the late 1990s to demonstrate how children from different cultures and backgrounds can work together to create something beautiful.

Several outstanding volunteers have led the choir at different times, but Shaleese Pie, the Superintendent of Human Resources at the Peoria Park District, has been the creative and guiding force for over 15 years. She has done a masterful job assembling kids from the many schools that ELITE serves and has continually raised the bar to produce a beloved fixture in the community. Under her direction, the choir has performed at all CHOICES/ELITE awards ceremonies, but even more important, each year during the holidays, it visits nursing homes, schools, and other venues and helps bring the Christmas spirit to many.

HOPE RENEWED

Whenever I get down and begin feeling sorry for

myself, I recall the powerful story of Immaculee Ilibagiza, the bestselling author of *Left To Tell: Discovering God Amidst the Rwandan Holocaust.*

In early October 2007, two dear friends, Penny Scherer, and her daughter, Jill Vicary, approached me

about possibly hosting a special event in the RiverPlex Arena. Penny related that she had recently returned from Chicago where she had heard the most inspirational and spiritual account of forgiveness of her lifetime, and since she was a senior citizen, my interest was piqued.

Penny's eyes welled with tears as she explained that she was so moved by Immaculee's message that she wanted to bring her to Peoria to share it with as many young people as she could. I, too, was moved and offered use of the RiverPlex Arena for free. Penny wanted the most culturally diverse group of students as possible, so I also volunteered to reach out to area high schools to help get them on board.

On the day of the program, students from public

and private schools from nine different communities packed into the arena. Initially, I was concerned with the close environment, the blend of kids, and that this was not my typical controlled presentation, but my concerns melted away when Immaculee arrived and the Holy Spirit took over.

With no rancor or hatred, she told of how her family had been brutally murdered during the genocide in Rwanda in 1994, and how a brave pastor had hidden her and seven others in a tiny concealed bathroom for 91 days while machete-wielding death squads searched for her in the house and in her village. She went on to say how she had found her faith through prayer during her ordeal and came to forgive those who had murdered her family.

Her story was a testament to hope, one that reminded me of the many blessings I enjoyed and reaffirmed my belief in the power of love. I had much to do.

Immaculee Ilibagiza shares her message of hope at the RiverPlex. Photos by Ching Zedric.

Full Cannon

CHAPTER 18
Fertile Ground

Things were happening fast. The resounding success of the ELITE Youth Program in its first year guaranteed another. More schools wanted in, scores of volunteers lined up to help, and employers were eager to offer part-time jobs to graduates. But we had to be picky.

In early 2008, Jerry, Lew, and I took a road trip to deliver a Phase I CHOICES program to a school in Joliet, Illinois. After the program, we stopped to eat lunch at a Burger King, and the service was horrible. The manager didn't care where we came from or what we were doing, and he was dismissive and rude. The unprofessional way everyone treated us made me consider how poor leadership and a caustic work environment could destroy the positivity and high expectations that we established for our youth with ELITE. We needed employers and managers to double down on soft skills, to consistently lead by example, and to develop our young people.

After that experience, I decided that we would not place ELITE kids in businesses without first vetting them. We wanted employers to grow kids into who they needed to be while reinforcing what ELITE taught. If they didn't do that, we didn't want them. Every business had to be ELITE-certified before we allowed them access to our kids. When looking for potential employers, I wanted people who could grow character.

Terry Clark and Bud Jenkins were such people. Terry owns several *McDonald's* franchises and has been employing and growing ELITE kids and adults for years. He has been so generous and was a champion for the Peoria Ronald McDonald House built in late 2019. Likewise, Bud has employed hundreds at his many *Taco Bell* restaurants and has been a loyal and valued supporter of the program. Both created an amazing work environment that maintained the standards set by ELITE.

SUPER MARKET

In early 2009, the local newspaper published an article announcing that a new *HyVee* supermarket would be built in Peoria and would open the next summer. I called the reporter, and he gave me the name of Cathy Krieger, a corporate human resources supervisor, whom I called and asked about hiring ELITE students for entry-level part-time openings. I shared the ELITE concept with her, which she embraced, and later introduced to the corporate management team at its headquarters in Iowa.

In mid-July 2010, after about a month of training, ELITE supported the grand opening of the first *HyVee* in Peoria with over 150 new ELITE part and full-time staff, which accounted for 25 percent of the store's total work force. Most came from the nine high schools and adult Re-Entry programs that ELITE was facilitating at that time, and many other new hires were former

Cathy Krieger from Hyvee presents certificates to ELITE graduates.

ELITE students. So many ELITE kids worked at *HyVee* that it became known as "ELITE Land," which was the ultimate compliment to us and to *HyVee.*

In its inaugural year in Peoria, the store also financially sponsored the ELITE Pulses of Hope Drum Line to travel to Europe in June 2011 to represent Peoria and to perform at the 35th anniversary of the International City Festival in Friedrichshafen, Germany. All told, the drum line performed in five countries wowing crowds and building a level of self-esteem that disadvantage kids rarely experience. Without that opportunity to work and to shine, some might not be alive today.

But the drum line wasn't finished. In 2013, it earned national acclaim when it was invited to attend the National All American City Competition in Denver, Colorado, sponsored by the National Civic League.

Led by a dozen members of the Peoria Area Cham-

The ELITE Drum Line performs in Germany.

ber of Commerce, myself, and the 10-person drum line, Peoria was a unanimous selection as an *All American City for 2013*, in part due to the excitement and joy that the drum line generated showcasing the spirit of its city, which touted the revitalization of the downtown area, healthcare delivery, and youth educational success as its salient achievements. It was the city's fourth award and first since 1989. As a bonus, Ethan Mosier, a drum line member, was also the recipient of the *National Civic League Youth of the Year Award.*

As a rule, we taught every ELITE kid how to sweat, and we wanted to put them in entry level jobs where they had to work hard every day. We instilled the mentality that they went to work to sweat—not just to have fun and to draw a paycheck. We impressed upon them that potential employers worked hard building their businesses and that we were being hired to enhance businesses not to ruin them.

Not all businesses provided jobs—nor did we ask them to. Some supplied other resources. The owners of *Running Central* in Peoria, the largest independent running store in Illinois south of Chicago and north of St. Louis, has supported my outreach efforts since 2001.

Greg White, the original owner, followed by Adam White (no relation), donated hundreds of pairs of new shoes after our kids successfully completed character-based programs. Since 2006, Adam has also held fund-raisers like the *Mainstreet Mile* (the fastest mile in the nation) and others, from which we have benefited. He's been an awesome friend and has made our kids feel special.

Dave Kinnsinger and I met when the RiverPlex opened, and his inflatables company, *Fun on the Run,* has been instrumental in my outreach programs ever since. He needed a place to put up his new products, so we included them as part of our birthday party package, and I used them as part of my *Days of Hope* to motivate kids to get their grades up. He's helped me save thousands of lives.

When I was doing CHOICES, I would go into elementary schools on the south side of Peoria and present an age-based program to 2nd through 4th grade students on how to better behave. If they met the criteria, they earned a *Day of Hope* at the RiverPlex and got to go to the swimming pool and play in Dave's inflatable bubbles. It was a strategy to get a child thinking, *This is for me!* and having them return to school and telling the kids that had not received good grades how much fun they had.

Ariel and others burying "I can't" in 2007.

Participation from each school increased the next year. Later, in exchange for use of Dave's inflatables, I had ELITE High School students manage the inflatables at the *March Madness* experience and at the *Days of Hope*, which gave their teachers a well-deserved break.

Tim McShane has been a friend from Day Zero and has fed thousands of my kids. As owner of several *Little Caesars Pizza* stores, he has hired several dozens of young people from ELITE and provided a delicious and popular product, often paid for out his own pocket. His generosity allowed me to feed many hungry kids who enjoyed the added benefit of knowing they would be fed without embarrassment.

To add to the moment, we decorated tables with colorful tablecloths and balloons and placed the pizzas on them. To a deserving kid, this made a pizza feel like a steak. I wanted them to internalize what they had achieved and to be proud of themselves. A lot of kids didn't come from an environment where that was the norm. Through his generosity, Tim helped me to get the most out of ELITE, and I am forever grateful.

ROOTS OF SUCCESS

In the military, we performed how we trained, and I brought that same philosophy to CHOICES and ELITE. My expectations for myself and my staff were high, and I did everything I could to ensure that I surrounded myself with outstanding people who understood the mission and provided them with whatever they needed to accomplish it.

In the first year of ELITE, we assembled a wonderful group of volunteers that did an amazing job, but we were developing and learning as we went and needed a more systematic and standardized approach to implementing the specific components of the program in the classroom. After the success of the first year, I knew that several other schools would be interested in providing kids for the 2008 ELITE training class, so when school started in the fall of 2007, I partnered with Northwoods Community Church to help provide enough quality volunteers.

I approached Pastor Steve Schafer, and he put me in contact with volunteer extraordinaire, Sally Cloyd, who started organizing and training the trainers to be more effective. She condensed our curriculum, which was a mountain of loose papers, into a single spreadsheet that we still use today. Also, she recruited volunteers at the church, and after they were vetted, they were ready to go to work. These new volunteers joined a core group from the first ELITE class that were vital to the success of the program in the second year and beyond. They hold a special place in my heart.

Sherry Cannon is my aunt by marriage and the glue that holds me together at work. As one of the original ELITE volunteers, she is the link from the past to the present and offers objective balance, trusted counsel, and honest advice. Because she was good early on and a wonderful bridge, she streamlined ELITE in some ways that I did not like, but she made me better and made the program more cost effective to replicate.

Sherry has a huge heart, always tells the truth, and has no problem expressing views and disagreeing with me on many issues, but her loyalty is beyond reproach.

Sherry doing what she does so well. Photo by Ching Zedric.

Once a decision is made, she supports it fully. We are different people with different experiences, views, and outlooks, but because we're all about kids, our differences become our strengths, and ELITE is better for it.

Sherry is the founder of the annual *Hope Renewed Youth Conference* and has played a leading role in creating women's support groups in the Peoria area. In February 2020, she was inducted into the *Peoria Area African American Hall of Fame* for her outstanding work in the community.

I met Tony Jenkins through his wife, Taunya, the Principal of Roosevelt Middle School, when we worked assembling the CHOICES Choir. Tony came to me in late 2006 pitching a literacy program that he and another guy were taking nationwide and wanted me to invest in a curriculum that would generate resources for CHOICES. Although I didn't buy *his* literacy program, I sold him on mine!

I took to Tony because of his personality, and we

became fast friends. I hadn't known him long, but he showed his value with his big heart and passion right off the bat, and he has kept that passion since the beginning. I learned of his staying power when he told me that he was originally from Greenville, Mississippi, and that he had stopped in Peoria for a visit back in 1971, but never left. Instead, he retired from Keystone Steel and Wire Company after 32 years of service. I hope he never leaves.

Above: Tony Jenkins helps an ELITE student in class. Opposite page: Kathryn Timmes.

Kathryn Timmes was a force of nature and had dedicated her life to educating children. When she came to ELITE during its first year, she had over 50 years teaching and counseling experience in Peoria schools and was a wellspring of knowledge. Weighing barely 100 pounds, she commanded a room with quiet strength. When she spoke, everyone listened. During our ELITE staff meetings, she firmly and lovingly set me and others straight when we got out of line. What a blessing to have her help us motivate the unmotivated. For her to buy in to what we were doing was a weighty stamp of approval. She was an incredible asset in the early development of ELITE and left her mark on everyone in the program. She passed away in 2019 at age 88 having lived

a long and blessed life of purpose.

Brad Schmeider and Jim Lawson also played significant roles in the early days of CHOICES. Brad was a longtime volunteer who came to us through Northwoods Community Church. He had created a "Spiritual House" for kids as an alternative to a haunted house at Halloween. He stayed with me and did the dirty work setting up and tearing down events. He worked the streets and did everything with quality and love.

Jim was an attorney who supported us with sound legal and financial advice, but he was also a generous man who wasn't afraid of hard work. He often volunteered his time and helped with whatever needed done to support the kids. Moreover, he was a good man and became dear friends to Jerry and me.

GOING FOR GOLD

Shortly after the graduation of the second ELITE class in May 2008, the park district was named as a back-to-back finalist for the *National Park and Recreation Association National Gold Medal* recognizing it as one of the top districts in the nation. The park district had won the award in 1994 and in 2001, and although it did not win in either 2007 or 2008, it cemented its place as a top tier park district for the second consecutive year. It was no secret that CHOICES and ELITE had contributed to that success, and there were some outside of the park district that wanted them to be part of their organization.

Later in the fall, the head of United Way, Michael Steffen, and his deputy, Don Johnson, invited me lunch in downtown Peoria. We had barely sat down when Michael dropped the big question, "How would you like to do just ELITE?"

I was surprised. I was an assistant general manager at the RiverPlex and simultaneously had been doing CHOICES and ELITE, and the thought of exclusively programming kids like I was doing had not occurred to me. I returned to the RiverPlex and told Brent, who immediately drove me to see Bonnie Noble, the head of the park district, and I told her that I was considering it.

"Give me 24 hours," she said calmly. "I will see you tomorrow."

I returned the next day nervous as a cat, and Bonnie cut to the chase.

"What if we match their offer?" she asked.

Before I could respond, she followed with the big question.

"And what if you only have to do CHOICES and ELITE with no other duties? The offer comes with a vehicle and access to all park facilities. We're going to let you do something special. Think about it."

That's all I did, but it wasn't a difficult decision. Although the park district expected me to ask for more money, I had already decided to stay. I had seven years in, and I adored the people I worked with. More important, the United Way did not have the gyms, swimming pools, weight rooms, and other tangible carrots that I could use to motivate kids. And that's what mattered most. But I must admit, my new park district title, "Community Outreach & Social Equity Supervisor," sounded sweet.

Bonnie Noble (opposite page) and an ELITE student (above) are all smiles. Photos by Ching Zedric

Full Cannon

CHAPTER 19
Yes We Can!

President Barack Obama shook my hand and glanced at the logo on my shirt. "What's ELITE?" he asked smoothly.

"It's a youth outreach program, Mr. President," I replied respectfully, mindful of the cadre of stone-faced Secret Service agents flanking him.

He squeezed my hand and smiled. "Keep it up!"

"Yes, sir!" I said, as I shuffled toward the exit in a moving line of well-wishers.

I was honored that the newly-elected president had briefly spoken to me during his February 12, 2009 visit to the Caterpillar plant in East Peoria before flying to Springfield aboard *Air Force One* to celebrate the 200th anniversary of the birth of fellow Illinoisan Abraham Lincoln. He was accompanied by Secretary of Transportation Ray LaHood, Congressman Aaron Schock, and Caterpillar CEO Jim Owens, and was trying to gain support for an $800 million stimulus bill to help revive the economy from the collapse of 2008.

But I gave that no thought. I had just met the President of the United States, and the first African-American one at that, and in my mind, the popular commander-in-chief had issued a direct order that I had every intention of carrying out. Always the soldier.

Congressman Schock, a 27-year-old Republican from the 18th District in Illinois, invited me to the event and had just taken office as the youngest member of the 111th United States Congress. He broke into politics at 19, when he was elected to the local school board by write-in vote. At that time, he was the youngest school board member serving in Illinois, and I had invited him to a CHOICES program at Loucks Middle School in Peoria. At the conclusion of the program, he wrote me a check and said that if I ever needed anything to let him know. He continued to support CHOICES, and a few years later, I supported him when he ran for state representative and was elected as the youngest legislator in the state at age 23.

Many in the black community were unhappy that I supported a young Republican candidate, but party affiliation did not concern me. I openly backed those trying to help me help kids. After Schock got elected to Congress, I did not approach him professionally, but that summer my family and I rented a conversion van and took a family vacation to Washington, DC. While there, we stopped at the capitol to say hello, and he did a quick meet and greet at his office and made us feel at home.

Later that week, we stopped at the Department of Transportation building and visited Republican Ray La-Hood, who had preceded Schock as the 18th District congressman. Ray was so respected at home and in Congress that President Obama reached across the aisle and asked him to serve in his cabinet when he had announced his retirement from Congress a year earlier.

When Melinda, Danielle, Summer, Logan, my nephew, Tyler Harmon, and I entered the building, the woman at the front desk looked surprised. It's not every day that a family of six stops by to see the Secretary of Transportation.

"We're here to see the Secretary," I said.

"Which one?" she responded curtly.

"Secretary LaHood."

Her eyes got big. "Uh, please stand by," she muttered, as she went to another phone. Moments later, a man appeared and greeted us.

"I apologize for the delay. Would you please come with me?"

He led us to a private elevator and took us to Ray's office. Everyone treated us like kings on the way up, and when we arrived at the reception area, Ray came

out to greet us and a photographer started snapping photos. It was a paparazzi moment. Ray then took us into his office, which overlooked the new Washington Nationals baseball diamond, and showed us the amazing view of home plate and the surrounding area. He entertained us for over an hour and made us feel like old friends.

My 7-year-old nephew was well-versed on President Lincoln and shared his admiration for the president with Ray, a former schoolteacher, and they spent several minutes bouncing facts back and forth much

Above & Opposite: Inauguration of President Barack Obama.
Photos by Danielle Cannon.

to Ray's delight. It was an unforgettable moment in my family's life, and a testament to a remarkable public servant and to an even better man.

Meeting our local congressman and a member of the president's cabinet in their offices in the nation's capital was a thrill for everyone, although Danielle was less impressed, because six months earlier she had attended President Obama's historic inauguration courtesy of Aaron Schock, who had given us blue Congressional tickets to the event.

We had dropped Danielle off in Cincinnati, and she attended the inauguration with my mom, my sister, Alicia, her husband, Edward, and her cousins, Melissa and Jasper. I was in Peoria when a local reporter called and asked how I felt about the moment. I told him that my daughter was there, so he asked if he could call her directly.

"The *Journal Star* called me while I was in line waiting to get in," said Danielle. "We went through security and there we so many people that my aunt held me around my waist so we wouldn't get separated. There was a lot of pushing, and it was so packed that I climbed a tree to watch Obama get sworn in, while my uncle climbed on a port-a-potti and watched from it. We all laughed, but it was memorable. My dad had given me his camera, and I took a few photos and sent them to the newspaper, which they published. It was cool witnessing history."

ELITE RE-ENTRY

I inadvertently lied when I told President Obama that I would keep ELITE up. I went one step further. Armed with a new title, more time, and the full backing of the park district exclusively to run my outreach programs, I went back to prison (not as an inmate) and created the ELITE Adult Re-Entry Program.

I was invited to the Illinois River Correctional Center in Canton, Illinois to give a presentation on Frederick Douglass to the inmates for Black History Month, and I brought Sally Cloyd, a volunteer working with the High School ELITE program, and five others. My goal was to share an empowering message with the inmates and to expose my ELITE volunteers to a prison environ-

Demonstrating a device for applying and removing slave shackles at a local high school.

ment that reinforced what happens to some of the disadvantaged youth that we fail to reach.

Speaking to middle school students about Illiteracy—the chains of modern slavery.

The former slave and famous abolitionist Frederick Douglass once said, 'Knowledge makes a man unfit to be a slave,'" I noted in my opening remarks to the inmates. He also said, "Once you learn to read you will be forever free."

"Chains weren't the only thing that bound a man and made him a slave," I added. "It was also illiteracy. If a slave could read, he could find north on a map, and if he could find north, he might escape. A master didn't want an educated man or woman holding the keys to freedom, he wanted a powerless, ignorant slave to pick cotton in the fields. That was the slavery then. But today, if you refuse to read and to write and to make good choices in a civilized world, you have made yourself a slave in a prison environment. You have shackled yourselves."

I gave the inmates something real to consider, and their expressions and body language spoke volumes.

The warden approached me after the presentation and said that several inmates requested some quiet time to talk with me, and I quickly agreed. They said that they did not want to repeat the same mistakes that got them locked up and that they needed jobs when they got out.

"Hold on," I interrupted. "Let me bring some of my

Talking with inmates at Illinois River Correctional Center. L-R: Ching Zedric, Mary Arnold, Tony Jenkins, Rick Cloyd, and Sally Cloyd.

friends over, and you explain to them what you need."

Sally listened to the inmates and was moved to tears.

"How do we help these guys?" she asked on the way out of the prison. "What can we do?"

"We already have the answer," I said, shooting from the hip.

Sally stopped. "What is it?"

"ELITE," I said. "We teach ex-inmates the same soft skills and character skills that we teach to disadvantaged high school kids. We can give someone who needs a third chance an opportunity. They can use the old con method and fail again or prove over time like ELITE kids that they can do it."

Sally and her husband, Rick, went all in and developed a modified 10-week curriculum based on the ELITE model. I called Doug Huermann, the local chief of probation in the federal probation system and explained the plan. He was so intrigued that he invited

Al Thompson (left) with Sally and Rick Cloyd at an ELITE training session at the Peoria County Jail.

me to a meeting with all his federal probation officers, and I explained the program. Doug then directed the probation officers to line up inmates to attend.

BEST LAID PLANS

In early summer 2009, over 70 nervous ex-inmates reported to the RiverPlex for Zero Week of the inaugural class of the ELITE Adult Re-Entry Program. Chief Settingsgaard and Sheriff McCoy were there, along with Mayor Ardis and the Hon. Joe Billy McDade, Chief Judge of the United States District Court for the Central District of Illinois, and my staff.

The re-entry men who attended that first meeting must have thought they we're in the who's who of law enforcement and that this was serious business. I gave them the chance to walk out. The rules were designed to cull the herd and to remove the weak links. I explained this early on to protect those who were finally ready to abide by society's rules. Each week we addressed topics to progressively move the candidates forward to employability.

Initially, the annual program was 10 weeks, but we

Pastor Craig Williams addresses a new class of ELITE Adult Re-Entry candidates.

expanded it to 14 weeks and increased it to twice a year. Candidates meet for two hours each week. A typical program includes, but is not limited to, the following:

Zero Week – Registration. *Put The Rules Up Front— Are You Ready?* Candidates are given a forceful, straight-forward overview of the program that firmly establishes rules of conduct, expectations, and eligibil-

PHRASES FOR SUCCESS

PLEASE

THANK YOU

YOU'RE WELCOME

YES MA'AM

NO MA'AM

YES SIR

NO SIR

EXCUSE ME

I'M SORRY

HELP ME

I HAVE

I WILL

I CAN BE...

ELITE

--CARL CANNON

ity requirements. They are given one week to decide if they want to enter the program. Many are denied, and some elect not to enter. From the start, those who opt in must learn simple *Phrases for Success.*

The phrases may appear elementary and part of basic courtesy learned as a child, but some youth and adults view calling someone "sir" or "ma'am" as subjugating or demeaning themselves, but I require children and adults to learn them as part of all ELITE programs to build a language of mutual respect. If the adults could not recite the phrases one-on-one with a staff after four weeks in the Re-Entry program, they were removed. If a candidate's peers knew them, it told me that the failing candidate was not ready to start life anew.

Week 1 – Commitment. *Put Up Or Shut Up—The New Cool.* Collect and copy required information, review testimonial guidelines and worksheets, and have students re-read and review rules one-by-one to help gauge academic level and ability.

Week 2 – Addiction Truths. *Breaking The Cycle— Drugs, Alcohol, And People.* Guest speakers present topics related to addiction, books are issued, and pretests collected. Candidates are informed that they will be required to take a mandatory drug test in two months, and if beforehand, they self-disclose drug use or request help battling an addiction, they are provided professional services and allowed to remain in the program. However, they must test clean to graduate.

Week 3 – Conflict Resolution. *Hold That Thought — It Takes Two!* Collect completed testimonials and distribute others. Give presentations on conflict resolution and customer service skills. Emphasis is placed on candidates identifying emotional triggers, recognizing physical and emotional queues, and removing themselves from potential confrontations.

Week 4 – Anger Management. *Turning The Other Cheek.* Guest speakers present on anger management techniques, self-control, and coping strategies centered on Cognitive Behavioral Therapy (CBT).

Week 5 – Job Applications (CBT). *When Does The Interview Start?* A human resource speaker instructs candidates on the application process, and candidates complete a full practice application using proper spelling, punctuation, and grammar.

Week 6 – Elevator Speech. *The 30 Second Sell.* Human resource professionals give a class on developing a resume and share interview tips. Candidates practice writing a resume and a 30-second "Elevator Speech," an introduction containing relevant information that a candidate can provide to a potential employer in a two-floor elevator ride.

Week 7 – Resumes. *Sum It Up.* Resumes are typed. Candidates practice *Phrases for Success* and role play how to leave a business message.

Week 8 – Self-Sabotage (CBT). *People And Things That Trip You Up.* A CBT guest speaker presents on how people self-sabotage, and candidates practice giving an Elevator Speech.

Week 9 – Mock Interview. *Practice Makes Perfect.* Human resource professionals conduct mock interviews to prepare candidates for real job interviews.

Week 10 – Success/Mindset (CBT). *Sweat Game And Setting The Standard. Phrases for Success* practiced. Presentations given on job acquisition, retention, advancement, and on "Why people get fired."

Week 11 – Forklift Training. *Getting Certified.* Candidates receive a seven-hour training course ending with forklift operator certification.

Week 12 – Factory Math (CBT). *Practical Workplace Math.* Candidates learn weights and measures and practical job-related mathematics and formulas.

Week 13 – Final Certification (CBT). *Putting It All Together.* Candidates are evaluated individually and role play employment and social scenarios.

Week 14 - Graduation. *The Cherry On Top.* Candidates receive tailored business attire and haircuts.

ELITE Re-Entry candidates at the graduation ceremony at the federal courthouse.

Judge Joe Billy McDade congratulates an ELITE Re-Entry graduate.

They graduate either with the ELITE High School award recipients in their spring ceremony or in a separate ceremony in the fall at the federal courthouse, where a federal judge presents them with a medallion.

Beginning with the first class, specially trained Re-Entry candidates were required to perform "ELITE style" community service at major Peoria area social, athletic, and civic events. This included providing a visible security presence at large indoor and outdoor venues, to include the *Illinois High School Association March Madness Basketball Tournament*, *Heritage Days*, *Steamboat Days*, the July 4th fireworks on the Peoria Riverfront, and the *Heart of Illinois Fair*.

A year before the inception of Adult Re-Entry, youth crime and mob violence were prevalent at the venues and threatened public safety and enjoyment. Many parents avoided bringing children to events where open cursing, intimidation, wearing of gang colors, drug use, and other criminal activity occurred. Citizens did not want nor deserve to be exposed to such behavior and increasingly the city and its reputation suffered.

Enter ELITE. Prior to deploying to events, Re-Entry candidates received special training in conflict resolution, anger management, mediation, radio communication skills, and in ELITE style customer service, which focused on respect and non-confrontation. At events, Re-Entry candidates are under my guidance and that of my professional ELITE staff and have an established chain of command. Each participant is assigned to pa-

ELITE CERTIFIED EVENT

ATTENDING YOUTH MUST AGREE TO A SET OF GUIDELINES:

I HAVE NOT AND WILL NOT CONSUME ALCOHOL OR DRUGS PRIOR TO OR DURING AN EVENT

I WILL NOT COMMIT ANY ILLEGAL ACT OR POSSESS ANY ILLEGAL OBJECTS

I WILL RESPECT THE APPROPRIATE DRESS CODE FOR THE EVENT

I WILL SPEAK TO AND TREAT ALL ATTENDEES WITH RESPECT

I WILL CONDUCT MYSELF AS A LADY OR GENTLEMAN AT ALL TIMES

I WILL REPORT INAPPROPRIATE BEHAVIOR TO A CHAPERONE OR OFFICER

I WILL MAKE AN EFFORT TO PARTICIPATE AND TO HAVE A GOOD TIME

trol a specific area of the venue and rotates in and out of leadership roles within that area. This allows the participants to experience subordinate and management level responsibilities.

At the end of each shift or workday, each participant receives a written evaluation on observed strengths and weaknesses by their professional ELITE chain of command. The community service component and the evaluation process are designed to improve skills, build character and self-esteem, and to instill a sense of pride while working together as a team. More important, it gives those who have taken from society the chance to give back and to be redeemed.

That first year, no one knew that the small army of mostly men were Re-Entry people and ex-inmates. Being there supporting the community when no one ex-

pected them to be gave them a level of credibility that I could not. We wore bright safety yellow t-shirts with "ELITE" on the front and "Game Changer" on the back. Our presence said to lawbreakers young, old, male, and female, "Not here!"

I wanted boots on the ground "walking the talk." I wanted men and women who had "been there and done that" and who saw the same behavior in others that had led to their own dysfunction and incarceration. Our yellow shirts said to a perpetrator, "Pull your pants up, keep your language north, we're not listening to anything south, and keep your attitude clean because we're not putting up with it."

If someone wasn't willing to follow the rules, they

did not get in. Our shirt was a promise to everyone else that we would keep them safe. If someone got in and broke the rules, we asked them to leave, and if they refused, we contacted police and they removed them.

A Peoria Police officer and an ELITE Re-Entry candidate showing mutual respect.

If they pushed back against police, our guys became witnesses for the police. If an ex-con asked someone to leave because they were doing something wrong, it was wrong.

Because of our "fools looking for fools," we did not have a single incident for nine years. Every time a kid approached a public event from a block away and saw our shirts, they were already pulling up their pants.

Prior to 2009, police arrested dozens of people at those summer events, but a year after we arrived, they went to zero and stayed there until 2018 when a young man sneaked through the gate at *March Madness*. The Re-Entry team brought him to the front, and he cursed all of us out, so we called the police, and he cursed them out, too. Then they arrested him.

His dad called later, and I told him what happened. He said that his son's reputation is different than that, but I said, "That's how he acted. Sometimes behavior shifts outside Mom and Dad."

Forty-five days later, his dad brought him to my office, but in the interim, the young man had graduated from Peoria High, got a part-time job, and had enrolled in junior college. The little boy we had confronted was acting like a responsible young adult and had done everything he could do to redeem himself.

When the state's attorney called, I informed him that I would not pursue charges against the boy. He was upset at my decision, but I was not going to bury the kid when he had a loving parent in his life, God in his heart, and the courage to do the right thing. I'm proud of the young man, and I will not apologize for giving an earlier consequence that led to a lesser consequence that resulted in him gaining wisdom and grace.

Prior to the graduation of the Re-Entry class that confronted the young man at *March Madness*, I informed the graduates of his apology and subsequent

Above and Opposite page: ELITE Re-Entry staff at work in Peoria. ELITE photo.

success. They were visibly moved and proud of him, and they were also proud of themselves. They had intervened in the boy's self-destructive cycle of behavior and possibly saved him from going down the wrong path just as they had done. At that moment, they realized that a consequence given early is better than a consequence suffered too late—prison.

Tiffannie Ross, a Re-Entry graduate illustrates her process from prison to ELITE.

"I was incarcerated for possession of a controlled substance with intent to deliver. I was skeptical about ELITE at first because it turned from a volunteer service to a commitment thing. But from that point on, my life turned around for the better. Re-Entry has helped my life and career by providing me the opportunity to give back to the community and becoming a role model for children. I feel who better to help someone from a

path of destruction than someone that has witnessed that destruction firsthand."

Convicted felon, Bryan Harmon, shares his account of how he went from prison, found ELITE, and now is a paid staff member. His story is a testament to how the program has changed lives.

"I was convicted of burglary in 2015 and sentenced to 12 years in the Department of Corrections, which means I would serve six straight. After serving almost four years, I was transferred to a work release center in Peoria, Illinois, and one day there was an announcement that they needed volunteers to help ELITE with a marathon. I had heard very little about ELITE but wanted to get out because I was bored. Throughout that first day, I start talking with some of the ELITE kids at one of the local middle schools, and I was hooked.

I loved being able to share with these kids in the hopes of them not making the same choices I did. A couple weeks later when they said Re-Entry was starting, I literally ran to make sure I got a spot.

Re-Entry has taught me so much. The two biggest things are that I am not alone and that I have people in my corner to motivate me to greatness. It also gave me the tools that I needed to do a resume, to interview, and to keep a job. Re-Entry gave me a new start. Because of it, I was offered a job at a local middle school as an ELITE compliance officer, and for the last seven months I have worked with kids who mostly just need and want a father. It has given me a new lease on life and I just graduated from the college EMT program.

When I first met CO, I thought his rules were strict, but now my thought is that this man has the biggest heart that I know. ELITE has changed my life, and now I hope that I can use ELITE to change someone else's."

Former ELITE compliance officer, Angel Cruz, the

Angel Cruz addresses a new class of candidates.

current re-entry case manager for the Peoria County Sheriff's Office at the Peoria County Jail, applies some of the same techniques that he learned in ELITE in his work at the county level.

"A lot of the knowledge came from the ELITE Re-Entry program. I'm a strong believer and advocate that re-entry can reduce recidivism. What connected me with ELITE was Carl's passion. He let nothing get in his way of taking ELITE into the future. It was not to be recognized or publicized but to change the life of people. A man who was genuinely concerned with the people he worked for and with. From Day One, Carl was more than a friend—he was a father to me—and having a father brings safety and assurance."

VICTORY LAP

The CHOICES and ELITE Youth outreach programs were going strong, and the new Adult ELITE Re-Entry program was successful. The Re-Entry program had evolved from the need to address those who had violated the law, lost their freedom, paid their debt to society, and wanted to change their lives and contribute to society instead of taking from it. It was a logical and necessary next step after ELITE Youth and augmented what we were doing in the public schools. Currently, the ELITE Re-Entry program is one of the most successful Re-Entry programs in the country, and the graduates are among its biggest fans. Little did I know in the beginning, that it would help the city virtually eliminate mob violence at its spring and summer venues and help pave the way for more social initiatives.

At home, the highlight of the year was Danielle's

graduation from Richwoods High School. Although we lived out of district, she qualified for the school's rigorous International Baccalaureate (IB) Program, which was a competitive two-year program where students could earn college credits. Of the dozen or so IB schools in Illinois at the time, Richwoods was the only one outside of Chicago. We were so proud of her.

As Danielle received her diploma in a sweltering gymnasium, she stopped and waved at us. I blinked heavily and wiped the sweat from my face. Sandwiched between her waving and the streams of perspiration running down my face, I recalled my baby girl being born in Leavenworth. I remembered the pigtails and the ribbons, the karate lessons, and the tender moments between daughter and dad compressed in a few seconds.

Danielle was our biggest and most outgoing personality, and she had already mapped out her college plans. Life was moving at full speed and everyone had their foot on the gas. After the graduation, we mingled outside with family, friends, and other graduates. Although it was one of the hottest days of the year, a cool breeze blew in

Danielle and Melinda at Danielle's high school graduation.

and swept over me. I savored the moment and reflected on how far our family had come. Through love, faith,
and hard work, there wasn't anything we couldn't do.

Full Cannon

CHAPTER 20
Back to School

I kicked my 6th grade teacher's ass. I was a bully. I was thuggin'. I was stealin'. I was a punk. I was the kid every parent fears and everything that I warn kids about.

It was a typical day at Von Steuben School. My teacher had money in his desk, and I stole some. When he tried to raise my desk lid to look for it, I slammed his fingers in it, and then I went to town on him throwing haymakers. I got suspended, and my dad beat me like a slave. He beat me until I learned my name, and three days later, my mom took me back to school to apologize. I never swung on another teacher. In fact, they are American heroes and some of my favorite people.

TREWYN

Trewyn (Tree-win) Middle School in Peoria was a mess. It ranked last in reading and math among 27 area schools. Student attendance was poor and behavior even worse. Gang activity and underage sex were rampant and drug and alcohol use high. Respect for authority was dismal, and many teachers and students were just trying to survive each day. It was the worst of times, but there was also hope.

Peoria Public School District 150 had hired Dr.

Grenita Lathan as the new superintendent of schools in February 2010 to help change the culture and to improve performance in the public schools. A year later, she approached me about bringing ELITE into one middle school full time. It was a huge step. But why me? I was a former prison guard without a college degree. What did I know about running an inner city school?

A few years earlier, scores of local students from Central and Manual high schools had begun walking home from school in the middle of the streets and would not let traffic pass. The police responded by writing citations and fining kids. In turn, the parents protested at the police department and tensions escalated in the community.

In the midst of the protest, I reached out to Police Chief Settingsgaard and suggested that we educate the kids as to why it's dangerous to walk in the middle of the street, and thus, take away the excuse that they "didn't know" that it was illegal or that their behavior was unsafe. I teamed with police sergeants Greg Collins and Sam Hoskins, and we held an assembly on civic behavior and safety at all high schools. In exchange, I asked the City of Peoria to dismiss the tickets for those cited students who attended the assembly and behaved appropriately.

The impact was immediate. The principal of Peoria High asked me to return and to hold a motivational assembly. The number two of the district was in the audience and told the superintendent that I was somebody they needed on the team. The recommendation was bolstered by several recent events. Over the past year, the park district had again received the *National Gold Medal Award* in which ELITE had played a key role, and I had given several high profile commencement speeches and keynote addresses in the area. Also, I had just received the *Martin Luther King Jr. Lifetime Commemorative Award for Leadership* that shined light on the program. The superintendent then invited me to implement the ELITE concept into an everyday building. That was the last thing I expected, and I did not accept right away. "I don't know if this is something I can do," I told the superintendent. "I'll get back with you."

I was elated by the opportunity but conflicted on whether to take such a giant step. I anticipated, correctly, that some administrators, teachers, and parents did not fully understand the program, the approach, or the methods involved with ELITE, and I questioned if the time and place were right to implement it. I was unsure of my leadership role within the school and how ELITE would be used, so I had to define and agree to each role up front if I were to accept. Whatever the roles, they had to be significant. I would not allow ELITE to be window dressing, a sideshow, or a political volleyball.

I prayed over my decision and sought counsel from my minister, Cal Rychner, Bonnie Noble, and others. I wanted the ELITE initiative within the school to be park district supported, and when it committed, I asked Dr. Lathan if I could write the terms for my role. She agreed, and I wanted to cheer, but I held my composure. "I am very interested," I said calmly. "I want to help. When can I start?"

ELITE K-8

The earlier we can get to a kid and intervene, the better. For some kids, high school is too late. Their attitude, behavior, lure of the streets, and "stinkin' thinkin'" has developed a flawed and unchangeable belief system. So, what better time to make a difference than in primary and middle school? Thus far, the ELITE Youth Program was changing lives in seven area high schools, and the ELITE Adult Re-Entry Program was providing ex-cons with the employment skills needed to compete and thrive outside prison walls. The logical next step was to implement a program that helped ensure a safe learning environment for all students and gave young boys and girls a sense of hope to strive for something better. We gave them ELITE.

Unlike the ELITE Youth and Adult Re-Entry programs that teach soft skills to disadvantaged high schools students and ex-convicts in preparation for competitive employment, ELITE K-8 is a comprehensive program that addresses the behavior of the entire student body so teachers can teach. The strength of the concept is having *all* the staff enforcing *all* the rules *all* the time. Too often in public schools, rules differ widely among staff, and students receive mixed messages about what behavior is acceptable, but if enforcement of the rules is consistent across the board, kids adapt to the expectation.

ELITE is also a valuable tool that principals can use to recognize which teachers are enforcing the rules and to identify those needing help. As the behavior element within a school, we collect and interpret data that assists with student guidance and contributes to improved performance. In short, the program protects students and allows teachers to teach and to save lives.

After school let out in late May 2011, I went to work changing the environment at Trewyn School for the upcoming year. I wanted the returning students to be proud of their school starting on Day One and to see it as a place of community rather than a source of danger and fear.

I privately raised money and hired a company to build a facade down the main hallway to simulate a community. The school office became City Hall, and the principal was the Mayor. As head of ELITE K-8, I was the City Manager. Each office had signage that added to the feel, and each hall was named. The main hall by City Hall became Main Street, and the hall passing kindergarten and 1st grade classrooms became 1st Street. The hall with 2nd and 3rd grades was named 3rd Street, and so on for 4th and 5th grades. Sixth grade had its own hall, and the upstairs hall for the 7th and 8th grades became Respect and Responsibility Boulevard, a play on my CHOICES *Respect is a Two-way Street* catchphrase. A double yellow line ran down the middle of each hall reminding students to stay on their side of the street, and when they came to intersecting hallways, to look both ways and to yield to traffic. I believed that if we could teach kids early to respect and follow the rules of the community, we could keep more high school kids off the streets and prevent a repeat of what happened at Central and Manual.

SHUTTING IT DOWN

To enable Trewyn to transition from a middle school to a K-8 building, additional students had to come from nearby Garfield Primary School and Blaine Sumner Middle School. Both buildings were being closed to consolidate the effort by the school district to save money and to become more efficient, but the parents of many Garfield students were outraged because they did not want their children attending the worst school in the city.

Emotions boiled over at a town hall meeting when district administrators attempted to explain the consolidations. Angry parents cursed and shouted their disapproval over the closures. Lathan had invited me and suspected that we were entering a hostile environment since some claimed that a few disgruntled school administrators were stoking the parents to oppose the closings, but I was unaware of what I was walking into. It wasn't until I spoke that the room settled down and a civil dialogue was established. Not that I was special, but over the years I had built a level of credibility and a reputation within the community and with administrators that warranted giving the new initiatives a chance.

THE PRINCIPAL

I had met Renee Andrews several times over the years when she was a teacher, assistant principal, and principal at one of our primary schools. The district administration selected her to be the new principal of Trewyn, which would more than double its student population with the consolidation. It was important that we had a principal we could work with. One who did not cave to pressure from superiors, supported the teachers, and demonstrated leadership in all situations. The principal position is the most important in the building and sets the standard for everyone else.

I believed that Renee was the perfect administrator for this effort. She was young, smart, and comfortable playing the heavy. As part of the teacher-hiring process, Dr. Lathan and Ms. Andrews allowed me to participate in the new teacher interviews. I wanted to ensure that we were getting educators who understood what they were walking into and that were willing and capable of teaching in that environment.

I sat in on Renee's first teacher interview, and it was evident that she was the right person for the position. This was her element, and I was confident that she would do an outstanding job and that she was going to be a great partner. This freed me to do what I do best.

TEACHER MEETING

At the end of the current school year, I asked for a meeting with the Trewyn teachers to present an overview of what they could expect from ELITE in the upcoming school year. Part of the agreement with the district included an extra financial stipend for teachers that remained and allowed those leaving the option to transfer to one of three district schools of their choosing. I told the teachers that if they did not believe that the students being invited back could change, this school was not for them, and that they should choose another. Unfortunately, most did. However, we got to start with a fresh group of teachers and the teacher's union and most district administrators supported us.

ELITE STAFF

The ELITE program is only as strong as its staff, and each candidate undergoes a criminal background check and is vetted prior to being hired. They then receive ongoing professional development (PD) and additional training in the ELITE Train the Trainer concept, where experienced professionals within the community share relevant knowledge from a related field. Most have experience in education, social work, or in law enforcement, and all are serious professionals dedicated to protecting kids. The majority are men, which is an advantage when serving a fatherless community in need of positive male role models. To a school composed of mostly female teachers, it may sound loud at times, but we communicate at the appropriate level to catch the attention of that group or individual within it. We use the "dad voice" and go up the ladder when needed, and students respond well to it.

But some of the toughest teachers and staff I have had were females. Everyone can correct a behavior, and we count on that, but sometimes a strong female presence is what kids need or want, especially the girls. As most people know, a "mom voice" also can motivate and bring serious heat.

Despite our best intentions, not everyone is a fan of tough love. A social worker once complained about me using "CO" as a negative influencer, but when I walk into a building and yell, "What's my name?" the kids eat it up. Some people do not understand that in our community it's a term of endearment based on love and respect. Too many people want to coddle our youth, but firm consistency is important. And the ELITE staff has a lot of that.

BROTHER BILL

My older brother is my hero, and I needed him to help run ELITE. He came to me as part of my prayer. Growing up, he was a good kid, but whenever I did something wrong, our dad thought that he was involved, too, and since Bill was my protective older brother, he took a lot of beatings for me that he did not deserve.

We lived eight blocks from school, and I would run home, break into a neighbor's house and rip them off, return home and eat a peanut butter & jelly sandwich, and race back to school. All I did with the stolen money was buy candy and give it to friends, but when one of the neighbors finally discovered that I had been stealing from him, he called the police and they questioned me. Unfortunately, my dad was one of the officers.

Full Cannon

Although I lied to Dad and he defended me, he also searched my room that night and found the coins in my secret hiding place in a bookshelf built into the wall. He was not happy. I had given Bill a lot of the candy, and whenever Dad saw candy wrappers lying around, he assumed that Bill had helped me, which resulted in unfair treatment. When Bill and I got grounded—which was often—Mom made us scrub walls, corners, bricks, and whatever else she could find. We were cleaning freaks and actually enjoyed the time together.

I had observed Bill working in schools in Leavenworth, Kansas. Although he was not a principal or a teacher, he could run a building. He had implemented CHOICES in the Kansas City area and had brought kids to the awards program each year. The principal of his school treated him as a number two. He was an outstanding leader and a strong presence in the building. One that I wanted in mine.

I didn't know I was going to get Bill here, but since Trewyn was expanding to a K-8 school, I requested a lead compliance officer and two supporting officers each for the primary and middle school classes. Surprisingly, the superintendent agreed. Since the population of the school was primarily black, I preferred to use black males, and that is when it made sense to call Bill, but initially, he declined my offer.

However, timing is everything, and when the principal of Bill's school left, he reconsidered and returned to Peoria to help, but I told him that he could not be a lead because he was my brother, and that he had to work his way up. Bill understood the dynamic and humbly learned the program from the ground up. Over time, his innate calm, cool demeanor, and willingness to listen and to learn earned him the respect of others, and they began to follow his lead. That first year of ELITE, behavior issues nosedived, and attendance and academics improved.

Bill Cannon

Bill has a servant's heart and loves to love. He coached the baseball and basketball teams and led the neighborhood clean-ups. He was so proactive that it freed me up to spend more time with individual students who were one bad decision away from incarceration or worse. I could save their lives and get them on the right track, but I needed time, and he gave me that.

Since Bill knew the day-to-day operation of ELITE and had my ear, we could correct problems quickly. He is the obvious number two in the program and still calls me sir at school, which models the way we want our staff and kids to act.

The program would not be where it is today without him because I would not have had the freedom to think outside the box if I did not trust who had my box. We are blessed to have each other, and our parents were proud of our relationship. Nothing but respect and love in both directions.

The first year at Trewyn was a resounding success. Students improved reading and math progression scores to #4 and #5 respectively out of 27 schools, and ELITE became the hot ticket in education. The superintendent asked me to install ELITE into a second building the next year and gave me a choice of three schools. I chose nearby Harrison Middle School, which I viewed as the next worst after Trewyn, but we were unable to agree on staffing. Unlike the ELITE Youth Program which relied solely on part-time volunteers, the ELITE K-8 program required full-time employees to provide an everyday presence in the school from 6 a.m. to when the last student and teacher left for the night, to include home visits, evening athletic contests, and more. This was a significant commitment, and neither side budged. Despite a year-long conflict with the district, ELITE remained in Trewyn and was asked to move into Harrison School the next year.

NEIGHBOR VISIT

A neighbor visit was the next step in the process. During the summer, teams of ELITE compliance officers fanned out and visited every neighbor in a three-block radius from the school and enlisted their unofficial help. We promised senior citizens in the neighborhood that the kids behave better and become better citizens. In turn, we gave each a business card and asked them to call us when they saw inappropriate behavior. The visits put a face with the school and empowered the residents by giving them a voice within their neighborhood and a small measure of ownership in making a difference in the lives of kids.

HOME VISIT

Prior to the beginning of the new school year, the school administrative team and selected teachers and ELITE staff examined the files of each returning Trewyn student and placed them in one of three categories based on previous behavior and/or grades. Like medical triage, we categorized students requiring immediate attention as being in *critical condition*, while those in *serious condition* and *stable condition* required less. Students in the *critical* or *serious* category received a summer home visit by their ELITE team.

A summer home visit was a game changer and a wonderful opportunity to recruit parents and/or guardians to help address issues affecting their child. The shock on a kid's face when he/she answered a knock at the door by ELITE staff was priceless and signaled to the student that our reach was long and that we were not going away. We sat down with parents and the student and reviewed his/her behavior and academic issues.

"We've been looking through your file," our officers would say, "and it says you've been in trouble. Is that correct? We've got to start working on this now."

There was nowhere to run. We tried to get every kid to acknowledge their behavior and to set our expectations for them for the upcoming school year. We also informed the parents that students would be required to wear a school uniform provided at no cost. The uniforms consisted of khaki or black trousers and a colored polo shirt. Each grade had its own color; kindergarten—red; 1st—royal blue; 2nd—green; 3rd—navy blue; 4th—orange; 5th—maroon; 6th—light blue;

7th—gold; and 8th—black.

The colored shirts helped parents and neighborhood residents identify students out of school, and although a resident might not know the name of a student doing something in the neighborhood, they could identify the color of shirt, which told us which grade they were in and in which direction they were headed. When the kid came to school that morning or the next, we were waiting for them to discuss the issue.

It wasn't long before kids knew that we had eyes on them all the time and began doing things the right way. This was especially true with the dress code. We zip tied belt loops every day when boys sagged their pants or did not wear a belt. We also did not allow girls to tie knots at the base of their shirts to make them form fit. When kids pushed the rules, we pushed back.

After we explained everything, parents and students signed a covenant agreeing to follow basic rules of conduct. If the student, parents, or guardians became aggressive, abusive, or would not sign the covenant, we explained alternative placement options. A family could opt out and go to another building, but that has not happened. The parents became allies, and although their kids might have said that they wanted to leave, most just wanted to be loved, and love is not telling them what they want to hear, it is telling them what they need to hear.

On one occasion, I had a 7th grader who refused to sing the school song, which violated his covenant, so I took him home in the middle of the morning for a home visit. His dad invited me in, and I explained that his son refused to honor his contract. Dad said, "Can you give me about three minutes?"

I went on the porch and waited, and few minutes later, the dad and his son joined me.

"Mr. Cannon," said the dad, "would you ask him to sing the school song?"

That boy came out of the house singing, and I never had to take him home again. I learned who the influencer was in that house.

Bad parenting contributes to the problems that children face, and while bad parenting is not exclusive to underprivileged families, financial stressors, lack of resources, and other factors compound it for them. Despite the challenges, I saw an opportunity to work with teachers in devising a plan to help offset it and to get our parents some help. This was especially important for younger students and their parents. The earlier we intervened on behalf of both, the greater chance we had at offsetting or changing bad parenting and helping the student. Not being successful could mean a tragic life, prison, or worse.

ADMIN REVIEW

Next came an administrative review. I received a list of all school rules and policies and applied ELITE concepts to them. School administrators and ELITE staff then made respective adjustments, and once agreement was reached, we took the rules to the teachers and other adult staff and together we examined each rule and made relevant changes. Once the rules were finalized and distributed, they were ready for the kids.

~

BOOT CAMP

Student Behavior Boot Camp began the first day of school and was held by grade level. Teachers and ELITE staff presented the rules to the kids and explained them in an age-appropriate way so there was no misunderstanding or any way they could claim they didn't know the rules, and since we had already triaged those students with attendance issues, behavior problems, and academic deficiencies, we were ahead of the game.

It was an ELITE surge with all hands on deck and every room was reinforced by ELITE staff and volunteers. Teachers, custodians, service workers, secretaries, and all staff were on board and enforced the rules throughout the school. Whether in class or on the bus, in the gym or on the playground, in the cafeteria or in the neighborhood, rules were rules, and the trained and ELITE-certified staff ensured compliance. The key to success was the consistent application of the program at all levels and the willingness of leadership to firmly and evenly enforce the rules.

Once the surge was complete, we bridged to the school day routine and dismissed students by grade level to their assigned areas. If we encountered inappropriate behavior or serious academic issues, we corrected them on the spot in real time. We did not let anything fester and become a bigger problem later. Some people predicted chaos but having 8th graders singing the school song (*Phrases for Success*) at the school assembly each morning proved otherwise.

JR ELITE

At the beginning of our second year in Harrison School, we implemented the JR ELITE concept that focused on rewarding the well-behaved, well-performing 7th and 8th grade kids, which was the majority of the students. The initiative allowed us to begin teaching soft skills sooner and was limited to 30 students. We vetted each student through *Phrases for Success* and through their behavior, which included a daily contact by an ELITE compliance officer.

We realized that if we constantly gave the lion's share of attention to the misbehaving and under-performing minority, we would lose some of the kids on the fence, so we then set academic and behavior criteria that gave those kids something to shoot for. We wanted to offer and reward them with more fun things than the under-performing kids received. Most kids want to belong to something, and for those who were not athletes or scholars, it was an enticing opportunity. We wanted to catch them being good—and that was fun for everyone.

THE END GAME

The ELITE K-8 program began in one public school in 2011 and is currently in five buildings, including one charter school. It is an innovative social tool that augments the traditional educational toolbox, and like any tool, it is only as effective as the person using it. We took on the toughest group of young kids imaginable and gave them unbendable rules and tough love. We acted like responsible parents and told them the truth; that if they do not trust us to do what is best for them,

Full Cannon

that if they refuse to follow simple school and community rules when they are young, they will be at risk of following simple prison rules when they are old.

CHAPTER 21
Mean Streets

DON'T SHOOT

I love Peoria, but it can be a tough place to live. In the calm predawn hours of August 11, 2009, 8-year-old Albert Billups was sleeping in his upstairs bedroom with two other children when gunfire erupted near his home. He never woke up. The boy was killed during a violent drive-by shooting when a bullet struck him in the head.

The area where he lived had become a hotbed of gang activity, and some believed that the shooting was in retaliation for the shooting of a 3-year-old boy the previous winter. By late 2012, the city had seen an increase in gang activity, drugs, and gun violence, and city leaders attempted to do something about it. I was asked to help.

Police Chief Steven Settingsgaard and Assistant U.S. Attorney, Tate Chambers, were implementing a modified version of *Don't Shoot*, an initiative based on David Kennedy's book by the same name, in which law enforcement, community leaders, gang members, and others united to curb violence.

They formed a *Don't Shoot* Governance Board led by Mayor Jim Ardis; Peoria County State's Attorney, Jerry Brady; U.S. Attorney, Jim Lewis; Peoria County

Sheriff, Mike McCoy; and me. My role was advising law enforcement and the mayor based on my work with the ELITE Adult Re-Entry Program and experience working with troubled youth in the tougher part of the city.

At the first meeting, I realized that a lot of eyes would be on this initiative and that the optics had to be right. Understandably, Settingsgaard was worried that many would see *Don't Shoot* as a "race thing"— white America versus black America, so I suggested he put a victim's face on it—to put a why to it—and to get permission from the Billups family to put little Albert's face on it, which he did. He needed to show that Albert was just an innocent child who was only trying to sleep when he was murdered in a senseless act of street violence. This approach took race out of it and allowed Peoria to understand that it wasn't a "black thing." It was a right and wrong thing.

CALL-IN

As a first step, the board identified those involved in serious criminal activity in the community. The police violent crimes unit worked with the U.S. Attorney and the State's Attorney, and together they compiled a list of "target offenders" and went after them hard. The idea was to identify those who perpetrated the most violent crimes and to send the top dogs away to prison leaving those who did not want to be sent away next on the list. Law enforcement built cases against the leaders, arrested them, and threw the full weight of the law behind prosecution.

Parole and probation officers then contacted those who could have been prosecuted and warned that if they did not cease their violent criminal activity, they would be next. The officers went down the line and followed with calls to suspected violent criminals and their gang affiliates and warned that if they did not attend that they could face potential violation of their conditions for parole or probation. All bases were covered.

The meetings took a hard approach from the standpoint of a community that had a lost a child and warned perpetrators that if they kept doing what they were doing, and we attached them to it, we would lock them up. Family members attended the call-ins and were in a separate room. Posters and mugshots of those previously arrested were prominently displayed and were an ominous warning of what would happen. This involved someone like me saying, "This is the result of what you've been doing. I will tell on you, snitch on you, and turn you in because I love my community."

In 2014, after Settingsgaard resigned and took a global security job with Caterpillar, *Don't Shoot* was augmented by the Peoria Community Against Violence (PCAV) group, which advocated an increased community role and reduced police presence, but was still governed by the board.

In 2016, under Angel Cruz, the *Don't Shoot* Community Outreach Coordinator, the call-ins became less punitive. After researching the effectiveness of the *Don't Shoot* initiatives in other cities similar in scope to Peoria, and from throughout the country, changes were made. The posters were eliminated, and call-In participants were offered education, job training, and social services as positive alternatives to crime. The ELITE Adult Re-Entry Program was also included in the offer, and although *Don't Shoot* is ongoing and results are mixed, everyone involved was, and is, trying to save lives.

DON'T START

I created *Don't Start* in 2014 as an initiative to "de-gang" gang members. It was supposed to be an off-shoot of *Don't Shoot*, but it did not get the participation it should have. Funded through a state grant aimed at late primary and middle school students, I brought in several outside instructors to speak on the destructiveness of gang life and tried to use after school and weekend programming, but the program did not catch on. When the state pulled the funding, I pulled the cord. Because we did not get that second year, I consider it a failure. Although the next year, the failure of *Don't Start* led to something better.

SCHOOL WITHIN A SCHOOL

In November 2015, the behavior of a dozen kids in Harrison Middle School was so disruptive that it was negatively affecting the education of other students. Violence, profanity, and gross disrespect toward staff was so frequent and severe that even experienced educators were having trouble teaching. Based on the success of the K-8 ELITE program, I was asked to bring an even more intensive version into the school to help address the behavioral issues and to help create a safe learning environment.

As with ELITE K-8, I put all teachers and staff through teacher boot camp to prepare. We trained teachers and staff on techniques for establishing a culture of respect, enforcing the rules, maintaining consistency, avoiding power struggles and conflict, following safety guidelines, and on how to use ELITE as a "force multiplier" to augment and enhance teaching.

School Within a School (SWS) is a middle school non-punitive concept that identified the worst behaved students and placed them in a self-contained classroom with a certified teacher and a paraprofessional supported by ELITE staff. Students followed a point-system, received special programming apart from the rest of

A promotional shot for School Within a School.

the student body, and remained in that class until they earned their way back into the regular school schedule. This included different bus times, staggered starting and ending times, a separate lunch period, and no extracurricular activities.

The first step in the intervention was identifying those students in critical condition and making a home visit where we informed parents that their child might be or was being pulled from regular classes because of their behavior. We explained that their child could or would be placed in SWS, and that they could earn their way back to "regular school" when they had met the criteria. At this point, most kids understood that they would have to come out of the classroom and fell in line, but those that did not, would be joining us soon.

Initially, most parents were not in favor of the move, but when their phone stopped ringing informing them that their child was in trouble at school, they became strong allies. Knowing that their jobs would not be jeopardized by having to leave work to pick up their child at school because of behavior issues took pressure off the parents, and conversely, when their child did better in school, it reduced the pressure they felt from parents.

Once the child was placed in the SWS classroom, teachers taught the curriculum and addressed individual academic needs. If behaviors occurred, ELITE staff handled them. The intensive classroom had a lower teacher-student ratio that increased individualized instruction and allowed staff to build relationships with the students. Moreover, teachers had extended opportunity to address learning delays and/or deficiencies that often contributed to the frustration and anger that a student exhibited prior to getting into trouble. This was key to success.

Educators stressed the social-emotional learning (SEL) aspects of teaching the whole child. This approach was so successful that some of the most difficult students made strong, healthy attachments with staff and worked hard to make them proud. With assistance from ELITE, the program emphasized citizenship and took students to awards ceremonies, restaurants, and even on tours to the jail and to the morgue. This added mentorship further strengthened the positive relationship with adults. For many students, it was the first time they felt valued and viewed themselves as a part of the community.

After two weeks of intensive instruction and having met the required point total, students incrementally bridged back into regular school one class at a time to ensure that they were not overwhelmed or would not regress behaviorally without support. ELITE's job was simply to do whatever we could to help teachers teach. If that meant spending extra time with a student in need, we did it. If it meant driving a disruptive kid home in the middle of the day for a home visit, we did that, too. Whatever it took. That intensive, personalized approach told each student that we did not lie to them when we promised to hold them accountable. That's love.

The following heartfelt account by Assistant Principal Lisa Kurtz, best illustrates the impact that SWS had on teachers and students.

"SWS was brought to our school at a time when the school was in crisis. Our administrative team was let go mid-year. We struggled with teacher retention and our students were the victims. I was serving as the RtI [Response to Intervention] Coordinator. I, along with the new administration and school staff, was tasked with decreasing discipline referrals and increasing academic achievement. The role I played in the SWS

classroom was to teach some, but to implement and track the data carefully in order to support interventions both behaviorally and academically.

SWS is an incredible concept that has data to support that the intervention works, but the most incredible data is not what we see on paper, but in the significant relationships and connections made during the SWS program.

We can't quantify the effects of this portion of the program, but the SWS classrooms keep kids in school. We had students from the inner city of Peoria who lived in poverty and have experienced a variety of trauma. I witnessed students who were victims of gunshot wounds (community violence), homelessness, uncontrolled anger, and displacement in foster care. Students would come to our classroom day after day to be a part of our community. They would look forward to being a part of a safe zone, and we eventually became a family. They started to tell us when they were in need of help, hungry, needing new clothes or shoes or just needed to sleep a while before doing work.

SWS teachers and me at ELITE boot camp.

im gives teachers and intervention-
r toolbox and support in places where
d support is low. I was just putting the
ELITE way into action in the classroom.
We made the program work by focusing on student needs, employing best practices in teaching, using research based interventions, and incorporating an incredibly strong social-emotional learning component to build relationships with students. SWS classrooms should be a regular intervention in all urban schools."

STREET FATHERS

After the unsolved murder of a 4-year-old and the wounding of his mother's boyfriend outside their home in May 2019, many feared that an early summer street basketball tournament would lead to more violence. No one wanted to sponsor it because of a lack of police awareness and protection. Although the *Don't Shoot* initiative generated some success, it took a lot of police off the streets and away from intelligence gathering. Emotions were high on the street and it was too dangerous. Then it hit me. We need the streets to police the streets.

I was introduced to a 25-year-old OG (old gangster) who had been shot 13 times.

"We're getting tired," he said. "Young people have nothing to do but terrorize. They need positive options."

"Are there more people who think like you?" I asked.

"Yes," he said.

"Then let's meet tomorrow and bring me two people like you; one from the East Bluff and one from the North Side."

Over the next several days, I met with more OG and then with the Chief of Park Police, Sylvester Bush; Security Chief, Ernest Sparks; and Park Board President, Robert Johnson, a progressive leader and the first African-American to hold that position in the park's 125-year history.

After a brainstorming session, we planned that I would arrange a life skills field trip to Chicago with several youth. We asked the OGs to identify 20 boys, ages 12-16, that fit the profile of being most likely to join or be in a gang. I also instructed the OGs to bring only those kids who fit the profile and who they believed were savable. They did not disappoint.

ATTITUDE CHECK

When I met the 20 kids in the lobby of the Noble Center early on a Tuesday morning, I didn't know squat. Some of the 12-year-olds were among the worst of the group. They were real gang bangers with attitude, and I feared I was going to spend the entire day snapping

Above: Loading up for the trip to Chicago. Opposite page: Street Fathers and kids outside the DuSable Museum.

off on these knuckleheads. The plan was to take the three OGs and the kids to the DuSable Museum of African American History for the day. I wanted to take them someplace where they could learn some history and see that they were not society's throwaways.

As we were boarding a *Peoria Charter* bus, the three OGs go off on the kids. "Pull up your pants!" they shouted. "Now shut your mouths and sit down!"

The kids fell in line, and it was an amazing three-hour trip. We had the kids watch the movie, *The Hate U Give*, and the OGs talked with the kids telling them, "Don't do what I did."

Because of the OGs' leadership, I did very little, and when we arrived at the museum, we toured a replica of a slave ship and a 6'5-inch mannequin dressed as a Ku Klux Klan member stood near the exit. That caught the kids' attention.

"Who's right—him or you?" asked Ernest Starks. "He used the N word because of hate. Why do you use

it? And what makes you right?"

Total silence. On the way home we gave the kids a written test on the movie they watched on the trip up. What a day!

I knew that I could not let it end there, so I took the Street Fathers concept to my boss at the park district. He saw that I was determined to implement the program and knew that he could not stop me, so he conditionally gave his blessing, reminding me that I was budgeted and that I did not have the money to fund the program.

"If you do it," he said, "you've got to raise 75 percent of the money up front."

I raised $40,000 in three days. Since I rarely asked people for money, when I did, they knew I was serious and responded accordingly. Donors love to see the fruits of their labor and are willing to support valid causes, especially if they help kids.

CAMP

I created an 8-week summer camp that ran three days per week. The Street Fathers (OGs) were hired by my department at the park district and got certified in *Phrases for Success* and to drive park district vans. Some had never turned in a timesheet or earned a paycheck, and the opportunity was as big for them as it was for the kids.

Upon arrival at the camp, we laid down the rules and warned that anyone violating them would be kicked out. No one could get arrested. Cussing was not allowed, and everyone must be on time all the time.

For the kids, each day simulated a school day and began at 6:45 a.m. Street Fathers picked up the kids and delivered them to the Noble Center classroom by 7:10, where they were fed a hot breakfast. At 7:30, they began a full day of life skills classes.

On Mondays, they learned life skills, received anti-gang and anti-bullying messages, and were certified in *Phrases for Success*. Wednesdays were service days, and the kids gave back to the community by picking up garbage, cleaning up yards, and doing other service projects. On Fridays, we allowed them to be kids again, and we programmed a day of play for those who earned it. On Sundays, the Street Fathers received professional development. I assigned roles for the upcoming week and taught them skills that they passed on to the kids.

Although the park district had legitimate concerns about the program, I'm proud that we made it through the summer without incident and that we helped prepare a raw group of boys for the upcoming school year.

SCHOOL FATHERS

Once the school year began, each Street Father was assigned a student caseload and given access to them at school. To remain in the program, kids had to attend school, not get suspended or expelled, and be advancing in their grades. Everything was measured and recorded, but the strength of the program was that

Street Fathers and kids.

when 2:30 p.m. came and the school day was over, the Street Fathers went home to the same neighborhood as the kids and could direct them in real time after school and on the weekends.

The Street Fathers felt a paternal connection to the kids because they and most of students did not have fathers. In turn, I put an ELITE Re-Entry man in front of each Street Father completing the circle of having old OGs supporting young OGs who supported the kids. No one is no one better equipped to reach kids than someone who has been there, done that, and wants to help. I saw this initiative as an opportunity to reach the bottom 10 percent of society by using those on the bottom, and the relationship the Street Fathers developed with kids was critical to success. They were able to approach some kids that many had written off and made them feel like they had value. The Street Fathers are not perfect, but they are learning, growing, changing, and making a difference in kids' lives.

In the fall of 2019, 14 of the initial 20 students completed the first Street Fathers class. The graduation was held at the federal courthouse in the courtroom of Judge Joe Billy McDade, who wiped his eyes during the emotional ceremony because he knew that these kids had a fighting chance and fewer excuses not to be successful. He had sentenced hundreds of adults with similar childhood profiles, but he believed that these were the right kids. We later learned that some of these kids had come to us as strong-arm robbers, car thieves, and drug dealers. But that day, they were just kids filled with hope.

Judge McDade (center), Pastor Craig Williams (right), and me at a Street Fathers graduation.

Full Cannon

CHAPTER 22
Three Wise Monkeys

SEE NO EVIL

The annual Park District Employee Christmas Potluck is one of my favorite events of the year. In mid-December 2013, I had just sat down to enjoy a heaping plate of fried chicken, mashed potatoes and gravy, green bean casserole, and a hot buttered roll when a line of people, including my family and the state director of the FBI, filed in from another room and informed me that FBI Director, James Comey, would present me with the *FBI Director's Community Leadership Award* in Washington, DC in the spring. It was the best Christmas gift I could receive.

A month earlier, U.S. Attorney General Eric Holder, had visited Peoria, and I gave him a presentation on the ELITE Youth Program. I was supposed to get five minutes, but I got 25 minutes, because once I got started, he wanted to know more and kept asking questions. I took him through the *Respect Pledge*, and he went through it with FBI agents, U.S. attorneys, and others. It was powerful, and he enjoyed it, too. Based on that presentation and my work with *Don't Shoot*, the FBI from Illinois put me in for the award.

The trip to Washington, DC in April 2014, was a family affair. I took Melinda, Dad, and my grandson,

Logan, and the cherry blossoms were in full bloom. We were escorted from our hotel to FBI headquarters in the J. Edgar Hoover Building on Pennsylvania Avenue. I was separated and wound up in a courtyard with other recipients when Director Comey's limo pulled up, and he got out and began congratulating us. Then we were ushered into an auditorium and seated in the order we would receive our respective awards.

Comey knew a lot about the ELITE program apart from what I had told him, and I was impressed that he cared enough to learn about our concept. At the reception, I introduced him to Logan, and Logan told him that he was going to be an FBI agent one day, and Comey gave him his card. I seized the opportunity. "If your calendar permits," I began, "would you please come to Peoria and be our speaker at an ELITE graduation?"

Comey turned to his number two. "Write that down. I will commit."

He was true to his word, but it took three years. On May 19, 2016, Director Comey delivered our ELITE keynote address at Riverside Community Church, and his speech was brilliant. He spoke without notes about character and values, and everyone there recognized that having a speaker of his stature was a big deal, especially when events in Washington required his immediate attention.

"I was speaking to the president in Washington, and I told him about you and the ELITE program," Comey told me at a private reception. "I offered to cancel, but the president said, 'That's more important. I'll see you when you get back.'"

Less than a year later, Comey was fired by the new-

FBI Director James Comey and me.   *FBI Photo.*

ly-elected chief executive, President Donald Trump. Despite whatever people think about Comey and how he handled the Hilary Clinton email situation during the 2016 presidential election campaign, or his views about Trump's alleged involvement in the Russia investigation, I found him to be an honorable man based on his past federal service, how he treated me, and through the words of wisdom he shared with my ELITE students that night.

HEAR NO EVIL

Caterpillar, Inc., had supported my CHOICES, ELITE, and other outreach efforts for a decade and was my most cherished benefactor. Without its support, some of my programs would not have survived and others would not have grown as quickly.

As a hometown *Fortune 100 Company*, it was among the world leaders in business, and I was honored that they had supported me through thick and thin. I had forged relationships with CAT CEOs Glen Barton, Jim Owens, and Doug Oberhelman, and was blessed to count foundation managers Henry Holling and Will Ball as personal friends.

To a man, they had the best interest of the kids at heart and believed in what I was doing and in the way I was doing it.

"I want you to rule the world," said Henry Holling. "Whatever you need, just ask."

Being a black man from the projects, hearing that from Caterpillar was a dream come true. But that dream became a nightmare when a highly-placed rogue employee, whom I'll refer to as "Jane Doe," ruined that relationship and tried to destroy a lifetime of work. I never heard it coming.

Two months after my meeting with Attorney General Holder, Jane recommended that I become a 501(c3) not-for-profit corporation and offered to help set it up.

She said, "Now that you're talking to the likes of U.S. Attorney General Holder, it takes our relationship to a whole new level. CAT believes that additional scrutiny is coming and we cannot risk supporting an operation that cannot withstand its own financial audit."

At the time, I simply believed that Doe was exercising due diligence and clearing the way for larger donations from CAT, and although a retired CAT manager had created my bookkeeping and data collection platforms, I complied with her wishes.

Prior to forming the corporation, donations were

made to the Park District Foundation, and they distributed the funds to ELITE as needed. When CHOICES dissolved and blended into ELITE, we wrote to the IRS stating that ELITE would work under the park district. The IRS gave its blessing, but Doe now wanted me to assemble a large board of directors and to hire an executive director and a director of development. This was financial suicide.

ELITE's status with Peoria Public Schools for the next year had been in limbo due to its budget issues and with the turmoil surrounding the embattled superintendent, but she resigned in June and the interim superintendent and school board president immediately renewed ELITE's contract. Throughout the fall of 2015, the park district was also struggling and was forced to cut programs and close facilities. During this time, local and national charitable organizations approached me about merging ELITE into their programs, which I did not for fear of losing operational control and autonomy.

On June 21, 2016, I informed Emily Cahill, the incoming Executive Director of the Peoria Park District, that I was shutting down the CAT-generated ELITE 501c3, and requested that all funds again be handled by the park district. This led to a meeting between a CAT representative and Cahill. Doe then joined by phone and implied that I was "out of control" and that I had money "in all kinds of places."

The next day, Emily called me into her office for a closed door meeting and shared the content of her conversation. Doe informed Emily that CAT was withdrawing all future support and that she had advised other donors not to contribute to my operation. Furthermore,

I was denied access to Caterpillar executives, and Doe warned that if I did not cease and desist in contacting them, she would report me to her.

I was shocked. Not only had Doe implied that I was guilty of malfeasance or worse, she had done so to my new boss. It was Emily's first day on her new job and maybe my last. My integrity and career were at stake, and I asked the park district to investigate. They reviewed all ELITE not-for-profit financial records and validated all Peoria Park District youth outreach accounts, and after extensive review, debunked all notions of impropriety. But the damage had been done to my program and to my reputation.

SPEAK NO EVIL

On January 1, 2017, Caterpillar moved its corporate offices to Deerfield, Illinois, thus ending a professional relationship with CHOICES and ELITE that touched thousands of kids across the country. It was the darkest time since I returned to Peoria after retiring from the military, and I did not tell anyone, including my wife, how much stress this caused. It affected me personally and at work.

But the situation with CAT paled in comparison to the tragedy our family faced when my sister, Elizabeth (Cannon) Morrow, was hospitalized and died unexpectedly from unknown causes a few days later at age 54. She was supposed to be released on my birthday, but her husband called me at 5 a.m., saying that she had passed. The whole family was grief-stricken at the loss of our beloved "Liz."

Fittingly, her funeral service was sweet and festive

reflecting her beautiful spirit. The family struggled to understand why God had taken such a kind, devout soul that we loved deeply, but we believe that he had his reasons and that he wanted her by his side sooner rather than later.

Elizabeth (far right) with her husband, Albert, and her daughter, Jessica.

Shortly after Liz died, Dad was diagnosed with cancer, and my faith was again tested. But I believe that God never places more bricks on one's shoulders than they can bear. I prayed hard, and after about a month, I doubled down and worked even harder for my family and for the children and young people of my community that I serve. It is my ordained mission to do this.

From the hurtful experience with CAT and through the pain of personal loss, I learned that working from the ground up is better than falling from the top down, and that everything I had done was for the right reasons. For ten years, CAT had been my financial champion, and I harbor no animosity or ill will toward it or its people. To the contrary, I am forever grateful for the friendship and generosity of the many people there who shared the fruits of one of America's great companies. Although I could not have foreseen it at the time, the end of our relationship opened the way to broader opportunities and more ways to make a difference.

Elizabeth (2nd from left) with Mom (center) and my sisters, Ramona Harmon (far left), Alicia Williams (next to Mom), and Anita Ingram.

CHAPTER 23
Mr. Chairman

BOARD STIFF

I am not a big meeting guy. I would rather be boots on the ground marching than butt in the chair swiveling, but at a certain point, a boardroom is where the direction of an organization is decided and its future is hammered out. I have served on nine boards and currently chair two, which is all I want.

After I returned to Peoria, I joined a lot of boards out of ego. Coming from being an enlisted soldier and a prison guard without a college degree, being invited to serve alongside the movers and shakers of my community was heady stuff. It was a brave new world, and although it was sophisticated and noble, it could be bloody.

In April 2017, I was elected the top vote-getter in an 8-person race for one of three seats on the Illinois Central College Board of Trustees. Three years later, I am the chairman. I decided to run because I had already established programs for economically disadvantaged youth in the K-12 world, but I needed to build a bridge out of that world into higher education. For many disadvantaged youth, vocational education is the bridge that creates opportunity, leads to jobs, and gives hope for a brighter future.

Unlike many kids from economically advantaged homes who have a strong culture of education and the means and familial support to pursue it, disadvantaged kids often lack career awareness and support. Most advantaged kids know what to do and how to do it regarding college, but a gaping divide exists between them and disadvantaged kids. If a disadvantaged kid does not get into a career field, they often get stumped. I wanted to increase career awareness and create immediate opportunity.

In 2007, Mayor Jim Ardis created *Peoria Promise*, an innovative approach to funding community education based on a model established in Kalamazoo, Michigan that provided direct ICC scholarships to graduates of Peoria public high schools. After a few years, the foundation-based program stopped giving direct scholarships and began reimbursing students after each semester they had successfully completed, which made financial sense and preserved resources.

But many disadvantaged students could not afford the initial outlay of money for classes or books, and inner city enrollment suffered. Furthermore, many urban students coming out of Peoria schools had to take remedial classes to address academic shortcomings, and by the time they took regular courses, the money had run out. *Peoria Promise* is still going strong after 13 years and will be shining part of the mayor's legacy. But more could be done.

Before I decided to run for the ICC Board, I called the college and asked for the zip codes representing the lowest enrollment within the college's district that served students in parts of 10 counties. The lowest zip

codes were from the poorer parts of the community, and although the disparity was disturbing, I saw it as an opportunity to make a difference at the next level by increasing enrollment and by addressing the needs of potential students from underrepresented areas.

After joining the board, I discovered the need was deeper than I first thought. At the most basic level, many applicants from poorer zip codes did not know how to fill out a financial aid form or were unaware of the many avenues available for aid. Parents were in the same boat making it even harder to break the cycle and to move forward. It was overwhelming for many and reinforced my belief that many adults need to better educate kids about financial matters, especially given the availability and open access to resources and financial education in today's age of technology.

But all the resources in the world mean nothing if a kid isn't interested or motivated, and that's where every adult needs to take responsibility. We must not leave kids to their own devices. They don't know what they don't know, and it is our responsibility to put down our phones, and theirs, and to talk to them. Find out what motivates them. Discover what they like and ask them about their dreams. And if they do not have any dreams, present them with opportunities to find them, and help them understand that they will not enjoy everything they do along the way. Make them work and sweat and feel good about themselves when the have finished. Teach them that the best rewards are not immediate nor are they always tangible, and that none of them are obtained without effort, hard work, and even harder thought. Success takes effort, and wherever a person lands after giving effort, that's where they're supposed to be. The best way to motivate the previously unmotivated is to give them something they can be excited about, and once they get excited, they become motivated. Selling a product is easy if the buyer wants or needs it, but not so much if they do not.

As chair of a college board, part of my responsibility is motivating others to develop new products and learning how to modify and sell old ones. One of my goals is to push for a diverse curriculum that is more appealing to urban and rural students and motivates them to pursue further education. Another goal is to see cost effective satellite courses developed in disadvantaged parts of the city. This entails meeting kids where they are academically and financially and inching them forward. My mission is to speed up certification allowing students to enter the competitive work market sooner. I want to make it more accessible to those who are not taking advantage of it. If it doesn't work, what chance does anyone have? The skilled among us are dying and we are going to need that labor force. It's my philosophy that if we can't make it work at a junior college, it won't work anywhere.

The sign at ICC says it all.   *ELITE photo.*

People are hungry for something that will work, and I was losing people in my ELITE Adult Re-Entry Program because they did not have a General Educational Diploma (GED). I had to find a way candidates could eat and lose the excuses while earning it. And sitting on the ICC Board led to a solution. Midway through Adult Re-Entry, candidates are enrolled into full-time, self-paced GED classes and earn a state-funded, hourly stipend while working toward a GED. Once they obtain a GED, they become eligible for competitive pre-apprentice programs at the college and are given aptitude tests to determine which apprenticeship they are best suited for. Upon being accepted into an approved program, students who have completed ELITE Adult Re-Entry are on their own for employment.

For many, the relationship between the student and the ELITE family continues when graduates volunteer to help guide a child who might be going in the wrong direction, and in doing so, give back and pay it forward. Nowhere else in the country is this being done.

HOUSING DIVIDED

Since I grew up in the housing projects, sitting on the Peoria Housing Authority Board of Commissioners since 2003, and serving as its chairperson since 2018, has been a privilege. In assuming my role, I never forgot that we were good people and that everyone in my family held their head high. Whatever we had, we didn't feel poor. I understood that economic hardship could be brutal and that most residents that lived in Section 8 public housing were there for the right reasons. They want to move in, move up, and eventually move into something better, and my mission was to help them do that, but much of the battle has been helping residents overcome the stigma of living in the projects and in making them safe.

Part of the issue was that we were flailing and needed help, so we reached out to the Springfield Housing Authority Board of Commissioners and asked for their support and a temporary partnership with their executive director, Ms. Jackie Newman. When they came in the results were immediate. Our HUD scores began trending upward in all major categories generating a surge in confidence and providing momentum for the PHA staff, which allowed us to focus on improving living conditions and ensuring the safety of residents. This included reducing crime, providing maintenance of property and living units, and supporting the creation of a summer school program for middle students in Taft Homes to ensure that kids living there received a quality education.

School is a lifeline for many poor. For some, it is the only refuge from dysfunction, violence, and despair, but the benefits of school are often negated by the allure of quick money and drugs, and by those offering both.

For the past two years, I have worked to rid the projects of those who do not belong there. In 2010, the PHA committed to tearing down Taft Homes, the site of much gang violence and crime, and evicting those residents who violated housing agreements by allowing non-approved people into their homes. Meanwhile, compliant residents were relocated to other parts of town and the location of the former project will be commercially developed.

However, community backlash was swift. Homeowners feared that allowing low-income Section 8 housing in their neighborhoods would lower property values and lead to a repeat of what happened in Taft. Their argument is valid.

In the meantime, we continue to advocate for the disadvantaged. True service occurs in the daily fulfillment of duty, and I derive more satisfaction ensuring that an elderly woman's rent doesn't rise or that the locks on all the doors work, than it does in evicting someone. Even more, helping someone to their feet while they are down and creating an opportunity for them to take the next step toward living in an apartment or owning a home warms my heart.

The administration of government in any form at any level is difficult, and only those brave souls who have the best interests of those they serve will be satisfied with the process and enjoy being rewarded with

Taft Homes. We lived in Apt. #88 on the left.

more work. I'm in a position now to help fill that board with members who care about people, ask the tough questions, and do the work. It is a young and energetic board, and because of that energy, I will step away soon, but not without finishing some of the hard work I have begun.

In late July 2020, the PHA received a $45 million

tax credit from the State of Illinois to begin work on the Taft Homes project. At the same time, I have made significant progress toward bringing major supermarket chains to the geographically underrepresented areas throughout Peoria considered as food deserts. We hope to obtain a commitment from these chains when we break ground for the new affordable housing that includes town homes, duplexes, and mixed income dwellings.

While I believe I have earned the respect of the residents in public housing and in the community as a whole, some in the black community still call me an "Uncle Tom," and complain that I have not done enough for those who look like me, and although I don't take the insults personally, I challenge them to walk a mile in my shoes. I challenge them to walk the Taft. To walk the Harrison. And to walk in the communities that I have walked in. They are us.

A NEW SHERIFF IN TOWN

Shortly after my election to the ICC Board of Trustees, I seriously considered running for the position of Peoria County Sheriff, then occupied by interim sheriff Brian Asbell, who took over for Sheriff Mike McCoy when he accepted a job as chief of police in a nearby town. I assembled an inner circle of family, friends, and supporters whom I had worked with and trusted. I even held a meeting when I was hospitalized for a couple days with kidney stones, but buoyed by my election to the ICC Board and solid resume in law enforcement, I thought I had a puncher's chance to win and prepared for a tough campaign against an opponent I respected but knew little about.

Before Asbell became sheriff, I arranged to bring students who were part of my School Within a School (SWS) program at Manual High School, and those who were rising to the top in a negative way, to the Peoria County Jail for a *Straight Talk* program. As the deputy sheriff and super-

Sheriff Brian Asbell

intendent of the jail, Asbell was my point of contact. He always asked about the profile of the kids so that he could arrange to bring in the appropriate inmates that could do the most good for kids and for whom the program would be the most therapeutic. He made it a reward for the inmates and taught them how to present to the students. I never knew the inmates, but I trusted his judgment. He loved the prevention aspect of what we did, and although I did not know him well, he was always accommodating.

Throughout the summer of 2018, I readied for the November election. Although the local Republican Party backed Asbell, and the Democratic Party supported Brian Fengel, the chief of police from nearby Bartonville, I sought and received the endorsement of several organizations without having publicly declared my intention to run. In mid-September with the deadline approaching, Asbell wanted to meet, so I invited him to attend a JR ELITE morning assembly at Manual Academy. To his credit, he accepted my invitation—and more.

When he arrived, I welcomed him and introduced him to a few people. He soon peeled away from me and started talking to students, teachers, and counselors. I watched him go from person-to-person. An hour later, he said, "I wanted to hear from others what you do. Sheriff or not, if you need anything from me, all you have to do is ask."

Twelve days later, Asbell invited me to lunch, and when I sat with him, I thought, *Why the hell am I running? This guy is the real deal!*

He was telling me everything that he had already done, and it made me rethink my position. He was a military veteran, experienced, smart, and a good leader, and I agreed with his thoughts on where changes needed to occur. I looked at where I was mentally, and I just decided then and there to back him.

In November, he was elected and made the jail even safer. Since that first encounter, he has become a friend and a staunch supporter of my ELITE programs and other initiatives that help keep kids out of jail. Not only was he the best person for the job and for the community, his excellence allowed for me to stay in my own lane and to follow the course I was meant to follow. God is good—all the time.

Full Cannon

CHAPTER 24
God Moves

It takes money to sustain four outreach programs. Some comes from the state. Some is donated. The rest is earned. It is rarely enough. In early summer 2019, the ELITE outreach programs needed help, and although we are excellent stewards of our resources, summer months normally are lean. Grants often come with stipulations, but I will not accept a grant that changes what ELITE does or alters how it does it.

On any given day, I receive 25-50 phone calls and scores of texts and emails. Many are requests for personal presentations, speaking engagements, and the like. Others are desperate pleas from parents asking me to intervene with their children and to help set them on the right path. A lot of emails are spam, but on an early Monday in June, one caught my eye.

It was from what I assumed was a not-for-profit company from New York that was producing a documentary on unique community-based programs. They asked if I was interested in allowing them to share the story of ELITE if it was selected, and I responded.

Following an initial Skype interview, the producer requested another with some of the ELITE Street Fathers, and a few days later, Sarah, the lead producer, selected a date to come to Peoria to scout the city, but she had already been in town and had spoken to the mayor, the school superintendent, and others on the condition that she would pull the plug on the program if anyone told me that she had been there.

When Sherry and I met her on a Sunday, we thought we had a good chance to be selected for the program. A few days later, Sarah informed us that we had been chosen and supplied dates they wanted to film. She said there would be two or three cameras and a couple producers and directors, but I still hadn't a clue.

On the first day of filming, I gave a CHOICES presentation to the 7th grade at Lincoln Middle School. I was nervous, but it went well. After the program, Mike Rowe introduced himself, but I didn't recognize him. He had done a lot of television work and was the star of *Dirty Jobs*, a popular show that appeared on the *Discovery Channel* from 2005-2012. His face and voice were familiar, but I could not place him.

"Hi, I'm Mike," he said. "Can we sit and talk?"

For an hour, he questioned me about the ELITE concept and how it worked. It was enjoyable because the Lincoln School principal, a few teachers, and some of the ELITE staff got to participate. Afterward, the technical guys mounted a camera in my vehicle, and we visited the Peoria County Jail where Sheriff Asbell explained how the county and ELITE work together. Mike talked to inmates, including one who said and did all the right things, so much that I invited him to the next ELITE Re-Entry class. Two weeks later, he was murdered.

Then Mike, the cameraman, and I went into a cell and the door was closed behind us. It made me think of my days at the Disciplinary Barracks at Fort Leavenworth. I soberly offered why my role now with ELITE is so important to the disadvantaged, and I think everyone involved felt the loneliness and seriousness of those few minutes behind bars.

When we left the jail, Sarah asked me to open my hand, and when I did, she put $40 into it. "I want you to go somewhere, sit down, eat, and rest," she said in a motherly tone. "You have to do this. You've got a lot to do."

"I don't need the money," I countered meekly.

"Take it."

A good soldier follows orders, and I recognized it as such. I trudged off to Haddad's Restaurant in West Peoria for lunch but was panicky when I discovered that Sherry had my phone. I asked the staff if I could use their house phone, and they all laughed when I called Tony Jenkins looking for Sherry. He lied saying that he hadn't seen her, but she was there. Everyone knew what was going on except me.

The next stop was Harrison Homes where the ELITE Street Fathers met me. I told them to be themselves and to save some lives. Two camera crews converged on us and a drone appeared overhead bringing the residents out of their apartments in the middle of the day. Then the Street Fathers told a couple kids to, "get the hell out of here and go back to school!"

Something didn't feel right. Then Sarah said, "I'm going to the Noble Center to re-interview some of your past students. A van is going to follow, and I'm going to tell you the path to get there. Get in."

I thought it odd, but I was exhausted by that time

and willing to do whatever she wanted just to be done. The camera crew followed us to the Noble Center, but when we arrived, two *Peoria Charter* buses were parked nose-to-nose in front of the building blocking the driveway and obscuring the area in front of the building, and I wondered what was going on. Sarah told me to turn to the lower dock area, a remote gravel section away from the main parking lot where few people park, and I saw my boss, Emily, sitting on a nearby picnic bench.

"How's it going?" she asked. "I get to sit in on your Re-Entry interview."

I thought it odd that Emily was sitting there, but I shrugged it off and went inside to find several ELITE alumni telling their stories to Mike Rowe. He's got one camera, and I'm thinking, *How neat is this—these folks sharing their stories.*

Sarah whispers in Mike's ear, and he says, "Carl can we finish this in 10 minutes? I need to take a photo of you outside before we lose light. "

We get to the front door of the Noble Center and the buses are still blocking the view to the field in front of the center. I'm irritated, tired, and wondering why the buses are even there, and then they separate.

A loud roar erupts. About 400 members of the community stood in the grass waving signs and cheering. I did a double-take because I still didn't realize what was happening. I was even more confused that so many people from my past were there. People from when we started CHOICES, my family, the mayor, my minister, members of the chamber of commerce, and others. Rarely in my life have I been speechless, but this blew me away. I was so overwhelmed that I couldn't utter a word, but Melinda took the mic and thanked the world for me. Like so many times in my life, she was there when I needed her most. My rock.

Before I could catch my breath, someone brought up three large checks. Mayor Ardis presented me with one from the City of Peoria for $24,000, and Sarah Field, the Vice President for Criminal Justice Reform for the Stand Together Foundation from Washington, DC followed with a check for $50,000. Then Mike Rowe stepped up and gave me a check for $50,000 from his show, *Returning the Favor*.

Mike Rowe holds a check from the Stand Together Foundation. ELITE photo.

I had never heard of the show, and I still wasn't sure who Mike was until I got home that night. Never had I imagined that I would appear on such a show or have my program the center of such attention. It was humbling and made me want to drop to my knees and give all the praise to God. *That's it,* I thought. *This is the reason they did all this.*

Sarah approached me. "I need for you to go home and to get some rest. We have more footage to shoot tomorrow."

What else could she possibly want? I thought. We started early the next morning at Lincoln School filming the School Within A School (SWS) in action. They took each kid out individually and interviewed them. A few months earlier, these kids could not have appeared in front of a camera, but they stepped up and shined, and honestly told how the program had helped them.

We left Lincoln and I followed a van with the back open while a cameraman filmed me driving back to the Noble Center. When we arrived, my ELITE Street Father kids were waiting, and with their Street Fathers facilitating, each one shared what the program had done for them.

When I thought I was finally done, the producers sat me down and re-interviewed me for four hours. We did not finish until after 8 p.m., and I was wiped out. The producers returned to Los Angeles, and then their post producer started contacting us. There was more work to do.

Fast forward to January 20, 2020 to the *Returning the Favor* Watch Party. We were scheduled to be the 4th episode of the 2nd season, but the producers wanted to air my piece in conjunction with MLK Day, and that's how we set up the watch party. I will be forever grateful to Mike Rowe and his fine group. They were exceptionally professional and cared about what we were doing.

The money I received that day is saving lives. I am using it to hire more team members for all ELITE programs. With that money, we can generate more resources by hiring people to write grants and to make a difference. I wish Mom and Dad could have been here to see it, but I know they had a heavenly view.

COVID-19

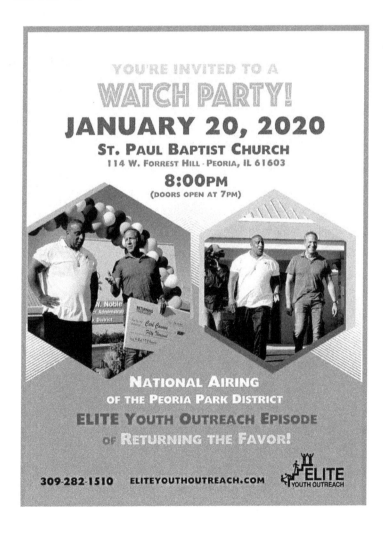

Full Cannon

The deadliest human virus in a century descended upon the world out of nowhere and struck like a sledge-hammer. It affected every country in the world in one way or another. Hundreds of thousands of people died and billions felt the economic impact of an enemy they could neither see nor control. In a few short months, the virus reminded us of our mortal vulnerability. Health-

A masked ELITE worker delivers food during the Covid-19 pandemic.

care resources were stretched to the breaking point, a booming economy was brought to its knees, and social distancing, sheltering in place, and remote learning became catchphrases of a new normal. Assuredly, we will conquer the virus, but at what cost?

Kids are among the most affected, and a crucial challenge is educating students during a pandemic where face-to-face contact in the traditional classroom is impossible. For many children, school is a daily refuge from a dysfunctional home life and a lifeline to normalcy, but when that lifeline is cut and the kid is exposed to dysfunction without reprieve, they become even more vulnerable. Building and maintaining relationships with at-risk and disadvantaged kids are significant obstacles during times of isolation.

Part of the success of ELITE has been the daily contact between students and staff. A pat on the back, a high-five, a fist-bump, and a hug are likely to be casualties. Sadly, many kids, especially those without fathers or those who experience violence or other issues at home, crave appropriate physical attention from adults. To deprive kids of that aspect of the relationship will be difficult for everyone, especially those kids who are too young to fully understand the health implications. All they know is that the people who used to hug them good morning, now stay six feet away.

Social-distancing is a medical necessity but detracts from emotional health. The added stress of isolation within a dysfunctional household and lack of exposure to positive influences can cause a child to lose perspective and turn their thinking inward, and in many cases, revert to negative feelings and behavior.

ELITE staff delivering lunch to students during the coronavirus pandemic. Spring 2020.

For schools with ample resources, technology is part of the answer to the question of how do we educate students remotely? Some schools furnish every student with *Chromebooks* so remote learning is possible and functional, given that teachers are trained, but in poorer districts, a disparity exists. Not every student has reliable technology or internet access at home to utilize it appropriately. Teachers also need help obtaining technology and/or hotspot access.

However, during the first week of April, my brother, Bill, and eight ELITE staff clad in protective masks and gloves and trained in social distancing protocol, delivered 310 *Chromebooks* in half a day to the homes of students of Glen Oak, Sterling, and Lincoln middle schools so teachers could teach and students might learn.

We knew the streets, where to go, and who to contact. Having knowledge of the families and their respective situations was huge. It was an opportunity to enhance the relationships that we had worked so hard to build and a chance to use technology to meet the kids in their lane. It was an on-sight virtual hug, which is vital to teaching student self-correction when they return to school.

Technology without effective guidance can also have a negative effect. If unmonitored, students can be exposed to inappropriate material that influences attitudes and behavior. With each passing day in isolation, we lose the chance to excite kids for the day when they return to school. Nothing can replace boots on the ground, a real side hug, or a teacher kneeling next to a student's desk offering help.

Lack of food is among the most devastating effects of the pandemic and directly threatens the disadvantaged. With over 70 percent of the families with children in the Peoria Public Schools below the poverty line, many students receive free or reduced breakfasts and lunches at school, but with schools closed during the pandemic, families incurred added financial pressure despite efforts by the schools to provide food relief. In a country of abundance, we must always ensure that our citizens are fed. Without food, learning is near impossible, and without education, hope dies. And where there is no hope, we must strengthen our faith and find it.

HITTING HOME

My own personal struggle with COVID-19 began on February 8, 2020, when Sherry, Melinda, and I flew to Washington DC to meet with representatives from the Bill & Melinda Gates Foundation, the Stand Together

Foundation, and the National Caring Foundation to explain the evolution of the ELITE concept, to share plans for the future, and to acquire funding to support further growth. Each foundation was receptive and encouraged me to formally pursue funding, which I was confident that we would receive.

At that time, concerns about the coronavirus were beginning to surface, but we didn't think much about it. Sherry only stayed in DC a few days, and Melinda and I returned on Valentine's Day. Two weeks later, I started feeling bad in a hurry. On March 6, I was so ill that I intentionally missed ELITE High School boot camp at ICC, and I had to call in to talk to the kids over the phone. It was downhill from there.

That morning, I went to the doctor and he tested me for the flu, but the results came back negative. He prescribed a Z-pack anyway, and I gutted it out for the next week, but increasingly had difficulty breathing. Moreover, I was coughing heavily and had lost my appetite and sense of taste and smell.

I normally avoid doctors, but on the morning of March 13, I returned to mine with a high fever and suffering from dehydration, but he sent me home. My condition worsened throughout the day, and finally, my brother took me to the ER at 6 p.m., and I was admitted to the hospital.

It was the sickest I have ever been, and it would have been okay to die. I then understood why people want to die when they do not feel well. I thought of Mom and how ready she was to go after suffering through chemotherapy. I could not sleep, was coughing uncontrollably, and was feeling even worse because visitors were not allowed. I had lost eight pounds the week before being admitted and another 20 pounds in the five days I was hospitalized. I was diagnosed with double pneumonia and put on oxygen. I was a day away from going on a ventilator, and that was not what I wanted to do, so I got better in a hurry. I begged the doctor to discharge me and convinced him that I felt fine. I lied.

On March 17, I was discharged from the hospital and arrived home about 4 p.m., to find Melinda exhausted and running a fever. I rushed her to the ER, and she was diagnosed with bronchitis and sent home. But on July 20, she was tested for the coronavirus and confirmed to have the antibodies.

My three-year-old granddaughter, Melanie, was also diagnosed with pneumonia around the same time and spent several days in the hospital, as did Sherry,

Sherry and I survived COVID-19 in 2020!

who after being released, asked for a COVID-19 test and tested positive for the antibody. That's when I knew I had contracted the virus. I then requested a blood test and also tested positive. I fired my doctor.

IMPERFECT STORM

I barely had time to get my feet on the ground when the death of George Floyd sparked worldwide protest calling for the end of systemic institutional racism. It also re-ignited the Black Lives Matter (BLM) movement and launched a social initiative to address police brutality and unfair treatment of minorities.

As I watched the event on television, I knew the police were killing him. I kept waiting for the officer to remove his knee from Floyd's neck, but even while Floyd pleaded with police and the paramedic checked his pulse, one officer kept his knee on his neck. The others remained on his body. There was no other way to describe it. It was murder.

Cops can go on a power trip. I know, I have been there and done that. Most are good, but like people in every occupation or station in life, a few are bad. Sometimes, good people do bad things, and that is everyone at some point in their lives. In my experience in law enforcement, race is not the salient issue. Most of the people who trained me did not look like me, but they trained me to do the job the right way because it was the right way to do the job. No other reason.

Make no mistake, being a police officer is not easy, and I support real police and legitimate police work. I believe the role of the police is to ensure public safety not to determine innocence or guilt. That is the function of the court—repeat—not the police or the private citizen. However, an increasing lack of respect for lawful authority within our society, coupled with the revelation of systemic abuses of power within law enforcement, have produced a volatile mix.

The lack of respect for authority is increasingly evident in schools where children imitate and mirror the attitudes of society. But ELITE has been at the forefront of the effort to reverse that trend by role modeling and establishing a climate of mutual respect, racial tolerance, and social inclusion. In programming at every level, ELITE has tried to be part of the solution—not part of the problem—by implementing non-judgmental policies promoting racial, gender, and cultural awareness.

I never imagined that the George Floyd incident would spill over like it did, but since much of the country was home watching television while sheltering in place, it witnessed the horror within hours of it happening. And the reaction was swift.

Millions of protesters took to the streets and demanded justice for the killing. While most demonstrations were emotionally charged yet peaceful, some devolved into chaos and led to violent clashes with police. While I strongly support the right to protest and agree that social injustice, police brutality, and all forms of racism should be eliminated, I also believe that a legal process must be followed. Past or present injustice is not a collective moral license to violate the rights of others or to commit violent acts in the name of a cause. Nor does anger or social outrage legitimize attacks on police, justify looting, or validate destruction of public,

*Logan and I show our support at the
Black Lives Matter rally in Peoria.*

private, or government property.

In response to rising tensions, destruction of property, and widespread looting within our community after the Floyd incident, I was asked to participate in a televised press conference with the local president of the NAACP and with other local activists to help quell the selfish criminal activity of the minority. My message was simple:

"You're mad at the police. I get it, but don't allow the actions of four bad policemen cause you to destroy your own neighborhood! Don't tear down *Walmart*! What did they ever do to you—and where else are you going to shop?"

I even implored the entire ELITE community to take charge and to lead by example. Afterward, criminal vandalism and looting reduced dramatically, and I like to believe that many of those responsible were wanting and needing to hear a voice of reason and to be reminded by someone they trusted that they weren't making a difference by destroying, and that the best way they could bring about change was through positive action.

A week later, Melinda, Logan, and I attended a peaceful Black Lives Matter rally in downtown Peoria. It was inspiring to see so many young people of different races, cultures, and identities unite in a common cause rooted in basic human values, and it was doubly meaningful to have Logan at my side and to mutually carry a generational torch lighting the way to a better tomorrow.

I believe that George Floyd's death, though brutal and tragic, is serving the greater purpose of effecting social change for generations. It has forced us to start an uncomfortable but needed dialogue with the goal of implementing real change at all levels of society, particularly within law enforcement and in schools, where inclusion and social equity take root.

George Floyd did not know his God-given purpose in life, but I believe that God uses the least and most unlikely of us to effect the most profound change, and George Floyd offers us that example. I now believe that a glowing new chapter of American history is being written—one where a great nation, through turmoil, experiences a transitional period and faces the painful, ugly truths of its past and emerges better than before.

We're still protesting, but for the most part we're not rioting and looting. We're still hurting, but we're beginning to talk and to heal. America is also shifting, growing, and shedding the old rigid skin of provincialism in pursuit of a new one, and although the process has been painful at times, it is necessary and right. To that point, the State of Mississippi, a vanguard of the old South, removed the Confederate symbol from its state flag. It is a testament to the people of that state and to their willingness to change. It may take a while, but once we see a better way, we have the ability to change. That's the greatness of America.

George Floyd's dying refrain, *"I CAN'T BREATHE!"* is a chilling reminder that when we veer from moral true north, it is time to course correct and to refind our way even if the path is difficult and wrought with danger. It is also an opportunity to celebrate the power of hope; to respectfully view one common man's death as a progressive instrument of irrevocable change. And that is a refreshing breath that we can all take.

GRACE ALIVE

Amidst one of the most challenging and turbulent years in my adult life, Pastor Bryan Chapell of Grace Presbyterian Church in Peoria honored me with the opportunity to appear as his guest on *Grace Alive*, the ministry's long-running television show, to share how my personal relationship with God has sustained me and been a guiding force in my life.

Taped during the state's sheltering at home period, there were only a dozen people in the church, but the spirit of God filled the room. I listened to Pastor Chapell's inspirational and impassioned message which I interpreted as a calling for all of us to be "lions for God," brave and ferocious in our faith.

This struck a resounding chord considering the ongoing COVID-19 pandemic, the George Floyd incident, and growing intransigence within the country. I considered the millions of Americans showing the moral courage and conviction to stand up and to be heard; to fight for what they believed in and for what was right.

My thoughts then turned to a personal incident that occurred in Peoria several years ago while I was working at the prison in which I encountered one of God's lions in a most unsuspected place.

Danielle and I had gone shopping at a Cub Foods store and were standing in a checkout aisle behind an elderly white lady placing our groceries on the belt waiting to check out, when the young male cashier barked, "Sir, sir, link cards are taken in aisle 12! Go to aisle 12!"

Pastor Bryan Chapell and me filming Grace Alive.

Full Cannon

He pointed to a crude, handwritten sign. The lady in front of us looked up from writing her check in disbelief.

Because I was black, he assumed that I was on government food assistance. I was outraged and wanted to go full Cannon on him reverting to my days as a crusty drill sergeant encountering basic training recruits for the first time. More than that, I wanted to snap off on him as a man who had been embarrassed, belittled, and marginalized in front of his little girl, but I realized that as a father that I had to lead by example. In a few seconds, I crammed 10 years of thought into how to respond.

"Young man," I began in my deepest bass, barely containing my anger, "you have three issues right now. One, you assume that I cannot read the sign. Two, you assume that I am a link customer, and three, you assume that you are going to be allowed to serve me. Go get your boss!"

He sheepishly scurried away and a female manager returned. I explained what had happened and how I felt. The manager satisfied me that the young man's attitude was not representative of the store, and as she checked us out, I glanced to my right and noticed the elderly lady still standing at the end of our aisle. She had remained there while I paid for my groceries to ensure that the boss said and did the right things and that I had received justice. That tiny old lady had roared like a lion.

We all walked out of the store together. That was 20 years ago, and I will never forget her.

As I concluded the story on camera, I called for the church and the community to echo that same moral courage and I challenged them that whenever they see something to say something and then to do something. It is the same message that I convey to the youth and men I counsel in our ELITE programs.

Full Cannon

CHAPTER 25
Hope

"What is your dream?" Jehan Gordon-Booth, the Deputy Majority Leader in the Illinois House of Representatives, asked me flatly in early spring 2019.

"I've seen what you have done; I believe in what you are doing; I want to help. And I want you to dream big!"

So I did. A short time later, we met again and I submitted a $20 million concept for the construction of a state-of-the-art ELITE Community Recreation & Development Center in Peoria that I envisioned as the hub of ELITE programming and administration, professional staff development, and hands-on client instruction. When I revealed my dream, Jehan didn't blink. In fact, she smiled and pressed for more information.

Consisting of a combination of new construction and renovation of an existing building, the center will feature numerous classrooms, an auditorium, a communications studio, multi-use training facilities for musical, visual, computer and media arts, indoor and outdoor athletic facilities, and more. It would also serve as a model that leaders from other communities could visit and learn how to replicate and tailor the ELITE concept under another name in their own communities with the same or a better outcome.

Later that year, she doubled down in Springfield and advocated for timely money to grow ELITE as a violence prevention strategy, as she had witnessed the positive effect it was having upon young people and in reintegrating adult offenders back into society.

In March 2020, at a time when state resources were thin because of COVID-19, ELITE received a staggering $744,000 line-item grant for violence prevention from the State of Illinois, one of only seven grants awarded to help urban communities fight violence, which is predominantly black-on-black. Of the seven grants, only three were outside of Chicago and East St. Louis. Jehan's leadership and her determined fight to stop terrorism within the black community using a preventative approach was instrumental in securing the funds, and I am thankful that she seeks forward-thinking solutions to a generational problem rooted in poverty and a lack of opportunity.

The grant came at a perfect time for a proven concept. ELITE is the only program in the nation that touches all the bases from juvenile to adult. The Adult Re-Entry Program targets young adults who have redeemed themselves and who have earned another chance to contribute to society. Through successful completion of the High School ELITE Program, thousands of teenagers have acquired meaningful jobs leading to viable careers, and through the Street Fathers, JR ELITE and ELITE K-8 programs, we continue to mentor and to enhance and grow character building concepts in young adults and youth of all ages to lay the groundwork for the future of our entire community and others.

My dream was coming true—but sooner than I

ELITE COMMUNITY RECREATION & DEVELOPMENT CENTER

Architect rendering of the ELITE Community Recreation & Development Center.

expected. Enter San Diego-based entrepreneur and philanthropist, Kim Blickenstaff—a native of nearby Spring Bay, whose dynamic vision for a thriving, robust ELITE community center exceeds even mine and that of Jehan. Resources doubled, plans tripled, and time-tables advanced. Hope is everywhere, and the future is bright.

Rep. Jehan Gordon-Booth, me, and Illinois Governor J.B. Pritzker in Peoria during the COVID-19 pandemic.

UNFINISHED BUSINESS

I am a man of faith, and I believe that love moves mountains, and that without it, life is meaningless, and we are nothing. Love for God, family, country, and fellow man.

I also value leadership in all things. Whether one leads from the front, middle, or from the rear to complete a small task or to accomplish a grand mission, it is important to lead by example—to be a role model—to do the right thing when no one is watching—to be that person who others look to for answers, inspiration, or hope—or perhaps to reach out with a helping hand or a kind word.

It is said that the only constant is change, and that is why I believe we must continually adapt, modify, and improve our methods and ourselves to be effective and to make a difference in the lives of those we love and those we do not. The world will not stop for us; therefore, we must keep changing to meet it, and that is especially true in working with young people who need help.

They have an inexhaustible amount of energy, understand ever-changing technology, seem to have no attention span, and are in constant peril in a dangerous world. Helping to protect and to provide for them is our responsibility, and teaching and instilling in them an understanding of right and wrong centered around a solid belief system is our mission, just like it was for the generations before us, and as it will be for generations to follow.

So, let's get started.

Full Cannon

Epilogue

Fifteen years ago I wanted to write a book, but I wasn't ready. I hadn't accomplished enough or failed enough. I hadn't experienced enough loss, and I lacked seasoning and understanding. The time just wasn't right, but that has all changed since then.

My life has passed in the blink of an eye. It has been a blur, and I have lived it so fast and forward that I rarely took time to stop and more fully appreciate the singular moments and loving people that have comprised it. Writing this book has helped me do that. It has been an exercise in self-examination and a restorative process that has brought me closer to my family and to my faith. It is God inspired.

I hope that my story exemplifies what a person can accomplish and become regardless of background, race, or station, because they are all meaningless in God's eyes. I believe it is important to do good with one's life and to share one's talents, abilities, and gifts in service to others or in pursuit of noble and just causes. It is a hallmark of a life well-lived.

As I write this last page, I hear my young granddaughters, Melanie, Laila, and Ava playing nearby, and the familiar smell of Melinda's pot roast cooking wafts into the room. My little Sheltie, Maci, enters with tail wagging, and I smile and consider how blessed I am to have a loving family, a nice home, more friends than I deserve, and hope for the future.

I glance at a faded brown folder on my desk. It is dated almost 30 years ago and contains a tragic story of a soldier whose name I never knew, who took his own life in Cell 138. I slowly open the folder containing the official death report and narratives from those who tried to save him. I begin to read. My words of three decades past, long since forgotten, resurface in growing clarity in my mind. I mumble them in a barely audible voice mindful of my granddaughters outside the door.

I sigh and push the report aside. I reach to the far edge of my desk and retrieve a college math book. It is the last class I have to complete to earn my bachelor's degree in law enforcement. I scan the problems and consider a plan of action. Math has always been difficult for me, but as with everything in my life, I know that I will be successful if I keep the faith, work hard, take no shortcuts, and always go all in—full Cannon. It's what I do best.

What's my name!

Melinda and me enjoying our grandchildren.

Full Cannon

The Authors

Carl Cannon still lives in the Peoria area and continues to help kids. For information about the ELITE programs or to schedule a speaking engagement, visit his website at www.eliteyouthoutreach.com.

Carl Cannon and Lance Zedric - 2019

Lance Zedric has authored 11 books and is a critically acclaimed historian and lecturer specializing in military special operations. He has taught special education for 23 years and is a former U.S. Army intelligence analyst. He lives in Peoria with his wife, Ching, and daughter, Ariel. When not writing or teaching, he helps Carl help kids. Visit his website at www.lance-books.com.

Visit

www.Eliteyouthoutreach.com

to

Make a Difference

CPSIA information can be obtained
at www.ICGtesting.com
Printed in the USA
BVHW051818220223
659018BV00024B/395